T0329123

The Strategies of China's Firms

ELSEVIER

Asian Studies Series

Series Editor: Professor Chris Rowley,
Cass Business School, City University, London, UK
Institute of Hallyu Convergence Research, Korea University, Korea
Griffith Business School, Griffith University, Australia
(email: c.rowley@city.ac.uk)

Elsevier is pleased to publish this major Series of books entitled Asian Studies: Contemporary Issues and Trends. The Series Editor is Professor Chris Rowley of Cass Business School, City University, London, UK and Department of International Business and Asian Studies, Griffith University, Australia.

Asia has clearly undergone some major transformations in recent years and books in the Series examine this transformation from a number of perspectives: economic, management, social, political and cultural. We seek authors from a broad range of areas and disciplinary interests covering, for example, business/management, political science, social science, history, sociology, gender studies, ethnography, economics and international relations, etc.

Importantly, the Series examines both current developments and possible future trends. The Series is aimed at an international market of academics and professionals working in the area. The books have been specially commissioned from leading authors. The objective is to provide the reader with an authoritative view of current thinking.

New authors: we would be delighted to hear from you if you have an idea for a book. We are interested in both shorter, practically orientated publications (45,000 + words) and longer, theoretical monographs (75,000−100,000 words). Our books can be single, joint or multi-author volumes. If you have an idea for a book, please contact the publishers or Professor Chris Rowley, the Series Editor.

Dr Glyn Jones
Email: g.jones.2@elsevier.com

Professor Chris Rowley
Email: c.rowley@city.ac.uk

Elsevier Asian Studies Series

The Strategies of China's Firms

Resolving Dilemmas

Edited by

Hailan Yang, Stephen L. Morgan, Ying Wang

AMSTERDAM • BOSTON • CAMBRIDGE • HEIDELBERG
LONDON • NEW YORK • OXFORD • PARIS • SAN DIEGO
SAN FRANCISCO • SINGAPORE • SYDNEY • TOKYO
Chandos Publishing is an imprint of Elsevier

CHANDOS
PUBLISHING

Chandos Publishing is an imprint of Elsevier
225 Wyman Street, Waltham, MA 02451, USA
Langford Lane, Kidlington, OX5 1GB, UK

Notices
Knowledge and best practice in this field are constantly changing. As new research and experience broaden our understanding, changes in research methods, professional practices, or medical treatment may become necessary.

Practitioners and researchers must always rely on their own experience and knowledge in evaluating and using any information, methods, compounds, or experiments described herein. In using such information or methods they should be mindful of their own safety and the safety of others, including parties for whom they have a professional responsibility.

To the fullest extent of the law, neither the Publisher nor the authors, contributors, or editors, assume any liability for any injury and/or damage to persons or property as a matter of products liability, negligence or otherwise, or from any use or operation of any methods, products, instructions, or ideas contained in the material herein.

ISBN: 978-0-08-100274-2

British Library Cataloguing in Publication Data
A catalogue record for this book is available from the British Library

Library of Congress Control Number: 2015935582

For information on all Chandos Publishing
visit our website at http://store.elsevier.com/

www.elsevier.com • www.bookaid.org

Contents

List of contributors

P. Bai Xi'an University of Architecture and Technology, Xi'an, China

M. Chen King's College London, London, UK

Q. Cheng Xi'an Jiaotong University, Xi'an, China

R. Gao Xi'an Jiaotong University, Xi'an, China

F. Henderson Victoria University, Melbourne, VIC, Australia

M. Jiang Xi'an University of Architecture and Technology, Xi'an, China

B. Liu Shandong Jianzhu University, Jinan, China

T. Liu Beijing University of Technology, Beijing, China

S.L. Morgan University of Nottingham, Ningbo, China

J. Shen Shenzhen University, Shenzhen City, Guangdong Province, China

Q. Shi Beijing University of Technology, Beijing, China

S. Tong University of Maryland, College Park, MD, USA

E. Wang Xi'an University of Architecture and Technology, Xi'an, China

Y. Wang Xi'an University of Architecture and Technology, Xi'an, China

Y. Wu Jiangnan University, Wuxi, China

H. Yang Shandong Jianzhu University, Jinan, China

L. Yang Xi'an Jiaotong University, Xi'an, China

S. Yang Beijing University of Technology, Beijing, China

J. Zhu Jiangnan University, Wuxi, China

Y. Zhu Xi'an University of Architecture and Technology, Xi'an, China

Preface

Over the past 35 years, China has slowly shifted away from state socialism toward market capitalism. Due in large part to the reforms underpinning this economic transition, the Chinese economy has grown to be the world's second largest, after that of the United States. Many foreign companies continue to see the world's second-largest economy as one of the most attractive markets now and in the future. Although economic reform opened up new opportunities for firms in the wake of this transition, there have been unprecedented challenges in the economic environment nationally and globally.

In terms of domestic factors, economic reform has achieved great success. In the absence of political reform and a high degree of state intervention in the economy, political connections have become more important for acquiring state-controlled resources and for gaining state authorization of business activities that have allowed firms to take advantage of these opportunities. In addition, firms in China face such challenges as a weak demand at home, increasing labor costs, rising raw materials costs, tighter land supply, an appreciation of RMB, and the increasing costs of environmental protection.

With regard to international factors, one outcome of the accelerated process of globalization is that the economic fortunes of one country are intertwined with the global environment. The financial crisis in the United States, debt crisis in Europe, and slow economic growth in Japan resulted in anemic global demand, which has adversely affected China's firms, especially manufacturers.

Facing the dilemmas at home and abroad as they have developed, China's firms need to rethink and readjust their strategies. The in-depth investigation of China's firms will not only enhance their competitive position but will also provide a developmental pattern on how to adapt to the dynamic environment of their counterparts in a transition period. While many scholars and business managers feel excited about the further growth of China's firms and their increasing influence among international counterparts, some are concerned.

The book aims to investigate and provide answers to the following questions:

- What are the primary drivers of the growth of China's firms?
- Can Chinese firms sustain their growth?
- Can other countries emulate the Chinese business model?
- What are the long-term effects of the growth of China's firms on the global economy?

Addressing these questions will deepen our understanding of how firms in China try to survive or even prosper facing constraints and opportunities. A transition economy leads to China's unique structure and system. This fundamental difference is the key to many challenges when doing business in China. This is important because businesspeople and scholars from free-market economies have failed to look at China differently. Instead, they try to put China into the free-market economy mold. As such, our book combines Western theories of management and the practices of China's firms for testing enterprise reform; the result is different from what might be suggested by mainstream management literature.

This book, with contributions from internationally respected researchers, analyzes a variety of topics from different perspectives. It describes and examines the methods of development by China's state-controlled firms; the experiences, administrative environment and industrial administration of the firms; and the changing nature and behavior of China's firms.

Suitable for today's scholars, teachers, and students in the field of business management, the book will also appeal to marketing and commercial managers and policy makers in meeting business challenges in the Asia-Pacific region, the United States, and Europe. It is also suitable for classroom use for undergraduate or graduate courses. This book serves as a reference for understanding and teaching about the next economic superpower. If people want in-depth knowledge of the firms in China, the book is an avenue to understanding the political–economic context, experiences, administrative environment and industrial administration of the firms; thereby helping readers to understand how the various parts of an event are linked.

The book opens with an introductory chapter by H. Yang and S.L. Morgan, *Development of China's state-controlled firms, the case of the consumer electronics sector*. It identifies the specific characteristics of China's state-controlled firms, which operate in a transition society undergoing social and economic transformation. In addition, a company transformation relies on the joint effort of the government and enterprises. Given the vast differences between the pace of economic and political reforms, this article takes into account the interplay between economic and political institutions during the China's economic transition.

Chapter 2, *The impact of the ownership structure of business groups on the listed affiliated firms*, by H. Yang and B. Liu, explores the link between the state-owned shares in the business groups and the performance of the listed affiliated firms in China. Based on a sample of 80 business groups in Shandong Province, China, the study shows that improving the management style and providing more decision-making power, rather than simply pursuing diversification of property rights, is an efficient way to enhance the performance of state-owned business groups.

In Chapter 3, *Labor litigation in China*, Professor J. Shen exams the characteristics and process of China's labor litigation and its role in settling labor disputes. The study indicates that although labor litigation has become one of the most important mechanisms for settling widespread labor disputes, it has a number of limitations in its current state.

In Chapter 4, *The overseas location strategies of Chinese transnational corporations*, M. Chen explains the general location strategies of transnational companies and analyzes their overseas risks and investment motives. Mengyao compares the nature and economic environment of Western and Chinese companies in her analysis of the overseas office-location strategies of Chinese transnational corporations.

Next, in Chapter 5, *Research on the relationship among large shareholders and its economic consequences of listed companies in China*, T. Liu, S. Yang, and Q. Shi state that the relationship among large shareholders would increase the social capital of shareholders' network of the listed companies. Their study forges a new path to exploring the impacts of social relationships (*guanxi*) in Chinese society on the organization of the listed company in China.

Real estate development is a pillar industry in China, and property developers have achieved huge growth in recent years due to soaring housing prices. Chapters 6 and 7 by Y. Wang and her coauthors focus on the development of real estate companies in China. The first paper focuses on the intent to survey the operational efficiency of 33 developers from 2004 to 2011 based on DEA analysis. The second sets up an assessment model to analyze the core competitiveness of real estate developers based on supply chain theory.

Chapters 8 and 9 by L. Yang and her coauthors explore the e-market in China. As Internet technology grows rapidly, consumers like to share their opinions on the products, the brands, and the businesses on the web. Their first study focuses on the influences on consumers' purchase decision with respect to the content of electronic word of mouth (eWOM) and the interaction between the suppliers and users of the information. Methodology of questionnaire is implemented to carry on the empirical study. In their second study, they review and analyze the double eleven online shopping festival in China. Their studies are meaningful in a practical sense for consumers' rational decision making, companies' business strategy, and retailers who are constantly looking for new ways to increase market share and gain competitive advantage.

The collection concludes nicely with *The transformation of the Chinese photovoltaic industry under globalization—The revelations from the bankruptcy reorganization of Suntech* by J. Zhu, Y. Wu, and F. Henderson. The authors made great efforts to collect the data and exchange points of view during their research process. They explain Suntech's stages of strategic development and conclude that the company's early success was due to accurate positioning, international perspective, technical innovation, brand building, and maintaining an unprecedented scale and speed at the beginning of its development. Their study provides lessons and experiences for the development of state-owned companies in China.

A very special word of thanks goes to four reviewers whose valuable comments and suggestions greatly improved our book. Our gratitude also goes to the Management Revue Publisher for providing us with the copyright permission to republish the article *Development of China's state-controlled firms, the case of the consumer electronics sector*. We also thank the staff members of Elsevier Limited for their efforts explaining the guidelines and requirements and patiently answering our questions.

About the editors

Hailan Yang teaches at the Business School of Shandong Jianzhu University in China. She received her PhD in International Business from the Management and Marketing Department of Melbourne University. She also has a BA in International Economics from Shandong Finance University and an MA in Political Economics from Shandong University of China. Her research focuses on the impact of cultural, social, and economic changes on China's companies. During the past 10 years, she has been involved in many projects, including research on diversification of China's companies and the reform of Chinese state-owned enterprises. Based on her research experiences in China, the UK, and Australia, she has not only gained a deep insight into Chinese companies but also into the differences and similarities between enterprises in China and Western companies. She acted as a trainer for Global Business Strategies in Melbourne from 2005 to 2007, where she provided regional briefings and business orientation and negotiating workshops on China for clients doing business in China. She specialized in providing Australian company executives with a deeper insight into Chinese companies and their internal mechanisms. She also developed a new workshop titled "The State of Corporate Governance in China."

Stephen L. Morgan is Dean of the Faculty of Social Science at the University of Nottingham Ningbo, China, and Professor of Chinese Economic History in the School of Contemporary Chinese Studies (SCCS) at the University of Nottingham, UK. He joined the SCCS at Nottingham in September 2007 after 13 years at the University of Melbourne where he was a lecturer and senior lecturer in Asian economic history. He has more than 30 years of experience studying and writing about China. In an earlier life, he was a journalist with, among others, the Standard Newspapers in Melbourne, a China-based contributor to the *South China Morning Post*, the chief correspondent of the *Hong Kong Standard*, as well as the assistant political and business editor of the *Far Eastern Economic Review*. His primary research interest lies in the fields of the economic and business history of China from the eighteenth to the twentieth centuries, while he mostly teaches in graduate and undergraduate programs in international business and strategic management.

Ying Wang engages in teaching and research in the area of real estate and urban economics as Associate Professor at Xi'an University of Architecture and Technology's School of Management and Head of Business Administration Department. She completed her PhD in Economics at Xi'an Jiaotong University in 2008, and received her bachelor's degree in real estate management in 1997 and her master's degree in management in 2000 from the Xi'an University of Architecture and Technology. She worked at City University of Hong Kong in 2003 and King's College London in

2014 as a visiting academic. Her research interests include urban development issues and the theory and methodology of real estate investment. Since 2000, she completed a series of governmental decision supportive project, involving Xi'an urbanization quality assessment, dynamic regulation scheme on urban land supply, as well as evaluation on tourism land intensive use. Besides, she has acted as a consultant of real estate companies conducting many investment appraisal reports for real estate development projects. Recently she focuses more on international comparison on urban regeneration, especially on Green neighborhood construction and evaluations.

Contributing authors

Bowen Liu is an undergraduate student majoring in Business Administration at the Business School of Shandong Jianzhu University in China. His professional interests include enterprise strategic management, business communications, and family-owned firms. He has published two articles in leading Chinese journals and is involved in a research project funded by the ShanDong Science and Technology Department.

Jie Shen currently is Professor of Human Resource Management (HRM) at the Shenzhen University. Previously, he was Professor of HRM at Curtin University (received market loading), and Associate Professor of HRM at the University of South Australia and Monash University. He currently holds a number of visiting professorship positions, including ones at Shanghai Jiaotong University, Southwest Jiaotong University, Jiangxi University of Finance and Economics, Shanghai University, Fujian Normal University, and Northwest Agriculture and Forest University. His main research interests are HRM, industrial relations (IR), and organizational behavior. He currently serves on the editorial boards of the *International Journal of Human Resource Management*, the *Journal of Organisational Transformation and Social Change* and *International HR Issues* (now known as *Evidence-based HRM: A Global Forum for Empirical Scholarship*).

Mengyao Chen is a PhD student at King's College London. She received her MSc degree in International Financial and Political Relations, which contained several courses related to globalization and global cities, from Loughborough University. This subsequently sparked her interest in and passion for urban geography. Therefore, she did her master's dissertation on the topic of *The rise of Shanghai as a global city in the contemporary globalizing world*. After learning more about the importance of transnational corporations (TNCs) in the global economy, she started to be interested in why TNCs are located where they are in global cities, especially in China. As a result, for her PhD, she researched the location strategies for the regional headquarters of some TNCs in mainland Chinese global cities, namely Beijing and Shanghai.

Tingli Liu is an associate professor at the Beijing University of Technology, China. She earned a master's degree in Management Science and Engineering from Xi'an University of Architecture and Technology, and she received her PhD in Business Management from Renmin University of China. She worked at Beijing Union University before joining the Beijing University of Technology in 2009. Her professional interests focus on corporate governance and earnings quality. She has published more than 40 academic articles and 3 academic books.

Songling Yang is Head of the Finance Department at the Beijing University of Technology. He earned his PhD from Renmin University of China in 2002. Now, he is the PhD tutor at the School of Economics and Management at the Beijing University of Technology. His professional interests include shareholder relationships, performance evaluation, and capital control. He has presented widely and published numerous articles as well as two academic books.

Qianqian Shi is a postgraduate student studying for her master's degree in Business Administration at the Beijing University of Technology, China. She received her Bachelor of Administration degree in Engineering Management from Qingdao Technological University of China. Her professional interests include shareholder relationships and earnings quality. She has published three academic articles, and in 2014 she developed software called Shareholder Relationship Analysis software.

Yanfei Zhu is studying for her master's degree in Construction Economics and Management at the Xi'an University of Architecture and Technology. She is researching real estate investment management, especially housing price rigidity based on tacit collusion between real estate companies. In 2012, she received her bachelor's degree in Engineering Management from the Henan University of Technology.

Miao Jiang completed his undergraduate study in engineering management at the Anhui Architecture & Industry Institute in 2010 and received his Associate Constructor certificate in 2011. He then worked as a construction engineer at Nanjing Newtown Wanlong Real Estate Company Ltd., where he was responsible for site construction supervision. In 2012 and 2013, he interned at Chinese Construction Steel Structure Company as an associate technician and at Tianzheng Property Appraisal Consulting Firm as an associate surveyor. He received his master's degree in Construction Economics and Management from the Xi'an University of Architecture and Technology in 2013.

Pengying Bai is studying for her master's degree in Land Resources Management at the Xi'an University of Architecture and Technology. Her interests are strategy management in real estate companies and land use sustainability appraisal on Chinese towns and villages. She received her bachelor's degree in English from Xi'an Eurasia University in 2011.

Ertao Wang completed his undergraduate degree in engineering management at Nanyang Industrial Institute in 2010. He received his Associate Constructor certificate in 2011 and worked as a construction engineer at Xi'an Gemdale Real Estate Company, where he was in charge of the overall quality of and schedules for construction projects. He received his master's degree in Industrial Engineering under Construction

Economics and Management from the Xi'an University of Architecture and Technology, and he published a paper titled "Research on Core Competitiveness of Real Estate Enterprise Based on Factor Analysis and Clustering Analysis" in *Applied Mechanics and Materials* in 2013.

Linyan Yang is a professor at the School of Management, Xi'an Jiaotong University. She received her MS and PhD degrees in economics from Xi'an Jiaotong University as well. She was a visiting scholar at the University of Alberta (Canada), Gunma University (Japan), and the University of Maryland (USA). She has hosted and was involved in two provincial research projects, and she was also the major participant in several projects under the National Science Foundation of China and the National Social Science Foundation of China. Her papers have been published in *Systems Engineering, Forecasting, Modern Economic Science, Science of Science and Management of S. & T.*, and others. When she is not working, she likes to play tennis, read books, and travel around the world.

Qi Cheng received his bachelor's and master's degrees in Industrial Engineering from Xi'an Jiaotong University. He currently works in a Chinese commercial bank.

Shimeng Tong graduated from the University of Maryland with a bachelor's degree in finance in 2013. He presented a paper at the 10th EBES (Eurasia Business and Economics Society) Conference in Istanbul, Turkey. He currently works for a hedge fund company in Manhattan and the China Foreign Exchange Trade System in Shanghai. His professional interests include advertising, mass communication, and marketing.

Rui Gao (Ray Rui Gao) is a postgraduate student at the Hong Kong University of Science and Technology, pursuing his master's degree in accounting. Previously, he received his bachelor's degree in business administration from Xi'an Jiaotong University. His research interests include corporate governance, financial information, and accounting information systems.

Yuanyuan Wu is an associate professor at the Business School of Jiangnan University in China. She received both her master's degree and PhD in historical geography from Fudan University. She was a visiting scholar at King's College London from 2014 to 2015. Her professional interests include cultural tourism, heritage marketing, and business history. She has published more than 30 articles as well as 2 academic books.

Jinwei Zhu is a professor and Deputy Dean at the Business School of Jiangnan University in China. He received his master's degree in economics from Fudan University and his Doctor of Commerce and Management degree from Hitotsubashi University in Japan. His professional interests include multinational company management, cross-culture management, and entrepreneurship. He has published 40 articles and 3 academic books.

Fiona Henderson is a senior lecturer in Academic Language and Learning (ALL) & Coordinator of Academic Support and Development at Victoria University in Australia. She was a co-researcher and author of VU's national grant *Improving Language and Learning Support for Offshore Students* in 2005. She received a Carrick Citation in 2007, a Victoria University College Award in 2011, and a Victoria University Award in 2012. She was a senior team member for the highly successful Academic Literacy Project (funded by a VU Teaching and Learning Grant), which was the pilot project for the national project *Investigating the efficacy of culturally specific academic literacy resources for Chinese students*, for which she was the chief investigator. She has led VU's eight annual Teaching and Learning conferences with Chinese partner institutions in China. Her PhD research investigated employability skills from the perspective of Chinese employers. He was also Chief Investigator for an OLT project on Academic Integrity. Her primary research interest is the academic success of international students. Her involvement in the development of the resources for the Collaborating for Success website and English-for-Uni website are indicative of this pursuit.

Development of China's state-controlled firms: The case of the consumer electronics sector

1

H. Yang[a], S.L. Morgan[b]
[a]Shandong Jianzhu University, Jinan, China; [b]University of Nottingham, Ningbo, China

1.1 Introduction

China's state-owned enterprises (SOEs) have experienced radical transformation during the transition from a planned economy to a market-oriented economy over the past three decades. At the end of 2009, 1604 large enterprises had become listed firms on the Chinese stock exchanges of Shanghai or Shenzhen (Shanghai Stock Exchange, 2009; Shenzhen Stock Exchange, 2009). More than 70% of the listed firms are state-controlled firms in which the state is the largest shareholder (China Securities Daily, 2009). Although the state owns a majority of the stake, many of the state-controlled firms have been given some market or market-like incentives (World Bank Group, 2001). Such newly acquired autonomy and flexibility have motivated the state-controlled firms to build resources and capabilities to compete.

Development of business strategy and appropriate form of ownership structure are two of the major internal means to achieve the competitive advantage of the firms (Child & Pleister, 2003; Filatotchev & Toms, 2003). Past empirical studies have largely neglected the link between institutions, business strategy, ownership, and firm performance in a transition economy such as China. Changes in these elements may influence the degree of strategic fit between the choices of firms and their external environment. An examination of the interaction between various internal and external elements helps enrich our understanding of the processes that influence the growth of the state-controlled firms in China during the transition period.

Our focus on only one industrial sector—the consumer electronics (CE) sector—enables us to minimize the influence of industry and technology on the management attitudes and organizational behavior of the firms. Different industrial sectors will display different characteristics regarding the adoption of market orientation since they operate under different conditions and with varying degrees of government regulations (Deng & Dart, 1999). The focus on one industry avoids conflicting conclusions based on the aggregate discussion of various industries.

This study integrates exploitation–exploration framework with the institution theory to propose a dynamic strategic fit of the firms in a transition environment. The formation of a firm's strategies is dependent on the environment in which the firm operates. The matching of strategy and environment can obtain better performance—a poor match can hurt performance (Miller, 1988). Business strategy is a necessary but not sufficient condition for performance. Performance is also influenced by the

ownership of the firms (Filatotchev & Toms, 2003). The appropriate ownership structure is seen as the means to better enable the managers to first strategically exploit
the internal resources of the firm, and second to position the firm to better explore
external resources, thus improving the performance of the firm (Jefferson & Su,
2006; Thomsen & Pedersen, 2000).

Here, the following questions are asked: How does the exploitation and exploration
construct apply in China's state-controlled firms in the CE sector? How do the state-
controlled firms in China evolve their ownership structure? This chapter sets out to
investigate the development of China's state-controlled firms using case studies of
firms in the CE sector; we focus on the evolution of firm business strategy and ownership structure, two aspects of a firm's internal organization crucial for competitive
advantage. The study is organized as follows: First, the institutional situation in the
Chinese CE sector is provided. Second, the different ways of firms have developed
are described, followed by a description of the exploitation and exploration learning
strategy in transition economies. The fourth part deals with the efficiency of the state
ownership. Next, the research design is explained. The sixth part focuses on findings
on strategy and ownership evolution of the case study firms and includes a discussion.
The chapter concludes with a summary of theoretical implications and future research.

1.2   The institutional situation in the Chinese CEs sector

The CE sector in China has been one of the fastest-growing industrial sectors during
the past three decades. It has experienced many changes in production, market
composition, firm behavior, ownership structure, and level of government intervention (Jiang, 2001). For this reason, the sector is broadly representative of the
manufacturing sectors at large in the process of economic transition.

The development of China's firms in the CE sector has evolved through two broad
stages with a turning point in 1993 when China's State Council issued its *Decisions on
Some Problems in the Establishment of a Socialist Market Economic System*. Since
the start of economic reforms in 1978, the government has sought to improve the management and performance of SOEs (www.China.org.cn, 07/11/2003). During the first
stage, the reform aimed to grant SOEs more autonomy by allowing SOE managers
increased authority over the allocation of their profits and decisions about production
(Naughton, 1995; Peng, 2004). Shanghai and Shenzhen stock exchanges opened in
1990 and 1991, respectively. At this stage, however, the state-owned distribution organizations were highly rigid and inefficient for manufacturers. For the CE sector, this
meant that the sales of products were centralized, and companies did not have their
own distribution outlets. Consequently, the firms were unable to respond to changing
customer needs promptly and flexibly (Simon, 1992). The increasing misfit between
the distribution system and consumer demand led some firms in the CE sector to adopt
corresponding business strategies to rectify the problems in the economic system.

The year 1993 was a watershed for the conversion of China's SOEs because
central government initiatives spurred on a more supportive economic and social

environment that provided incentives for firms to engage in technological learning (Xie & Wu, 2003). Both central and local governments became less directly involved in commercial activities and further deregulation of production and circulation of products. The control rights over state-controlled firms were gradually devolved from the central government to local government. The decentralization of economic authority triggered increased competition. Accordingly, the manufacturers had more freedom and willingness to innovate according to market liberalization, competitive pressure, and consumer demand (Jefferson & Su, 2006; Song & Yao, 2003). In addition, the government allowed international firms easier access to the Chinese market. The entry of new firms—not only foreign-invested but ostensibly private-owned firms—intensified competition in the CE sector (Jiang, 2001). Although the government was deeply involved in bailing out large, failing state firms, such cases were more the exception than the norm. Increasingly, only in extraordinary circumstances do state firms obtain such support from the government (Jiang, 2001). Increased market competition, globalization, and technological innovation have reshaped the competitive landscape of the state-controlled firms (Tan, 2005).

1.3   Different ways of development of firms

The development of business strategy and the appropriate ownership structure are major internal means to achieve the competitive advantage of the firms (Child & Pleister, 2003; Filatotchev & Toms, 2003). According to debates on the development of the firms, two schools of argument have come into being: the ownership school and the management school (Qu, 2003). The "ownership school" argues that the form of ownership—and especially its reform—is the key to the development of the firms. State ownership is held to be intrinsically less effective than private ownership mostly because politicians force state-controlled firms to pursue political goals or other social objectives rather than profit maximization. Therefore, the key to reform is to diversify state ownership in order to eliminate government control of the firms. Not so the view of the "management school," which emphasizes the need to improve the management of the firms, such as the development of a market-oriented strategy without the shackles of state demands (Liu & Garino, 2001). This school of thought does not believe there is anything intrinsically inefficient about state ownership itself. Ownership of the firm is an irrelevant concept if a firm is regarded as a Williamsonian nexus of contracts (Fama, 1980). State-controlled firms are not different from those listed firms in market economies that have wide spread public ownership, and a firm's performance depends on its management culture and the clarity of goals and objectives (Chang & Singh, 1997; Wortzel & Wortzel, 1989). Therefore, according to management school, the solution for the inefficiency of the state-controlled firms is to grant the firms more managerial autonomy and adopt more commercially oriented business strategies (Liu & Garino, 2001), which would positively influence future performance. In this chapter, we investigate the ways or processes of development of state-controlled firms by discussing business strategy and ownership, respectively, and how these influence their performance.

1.4   Exploitation and exploration learning strategy in transition economies

Strategy is commonly understood as the means by which a firm adapts its internal organization, goals, and resources to the demands of the external market environment in ways that enable it to compete effectively with rivals (Baron, 1995). A firm's specific strategy selection is based on the careful evaluation of its unique resource portfolios (Barney, 1991). All firms face common organizational challenges: they begin with an initial complement of resources and capabilities at their founding and over time, as products and markets change, have to acquire the additional resources and capabilities to remain competitive and survive. Two distinct ways of developing the resource and capability base of the firm are exploitation and exploration strategies (March, 1991). Surviving in a transition economy often requires that firms pursue a dual strategy that attempts to balance the need to leverage their current competencies and resources, which is a strategy of exploitation, while preparing to acquire resources anticipated for the future through a strategy of exploration and experimentation (Wiseman, Dykes, Weidlich, & Franco-Santos, 2006). Both activities consume scarce resources, which require organizations to set explicit decision-making policies for allocating the resources available for resource renewal (March, 1991).

Exploitation is a strategic renewal process aimed at leveraging existing firm-specific assets by improving them or by improving their use. It includes matters such as refinement, choice, selection, efficiency, implementation, and focused attention (Crossan, Lane, & White, 1999; Hitt, Lee, & Yucel, 2002; Holmqvist, 2004; Levinthal & March, 1993; March, 1991). Exploration, by way of contrast, is a strategic renewal process that seeks to acquire new firm-specific assets (March, 1991). It entails activities such as search, variation, risk-taking, discovery, innovation, and research and development. Based on these two definitions, exploitation is a requirement for implementing an advantage-seeking growth strategy, while exploration is needed for succeeding in opportunity-seeking growth (Caldart & Ricart, 2007). Meyer (2007, p. 1500) highlighted the challenge for firms of using such strategies in transition economies: "Exploitation learning refers to the pursuit and acquisition of knowledge, which is new for the companies in a transition economy, but already in existence in the West. Exploration learning is the creation of new knowledge to develop strategic flexibility, leading to sustainable competitive advantage." According to Masini, Zollo, and Wassenhove (2004), turbulent environments require continuous adaptation. The choice between exploitation and exploration is important in a dynamic transition environment: better matching of a firm's strategy and the environment make for better performance, and vice versa (Miller, 1988).

Exploitation and exploration strategies are complementary, despite the acknowledged tension between the two. Although exploration primarily involves the acquisition of new knowledge from external sources, it may involve the novel combination of existing technologies and know-how within the firm. Levinthal and March (1993, p. 105) observed firms must engage in both strategies: "An organization that engages exclusively in exploitation will ordinarily suffer from obsolescence. The basic problem confronting an organization is to engage in sufficient exploitation to ensure its current viability and, at the same time, to devote enough energy to exploration to ensure its future viability." Striving for a balanced focus would appear desirable for businesses operating in complex environments such as a transition economy.

1.5 The efficiency of the state ownership

Business strategy is a necessary but not sufficient condition for firm performance. The structure of ownership also influences performance. It affects the motivations of managers in making decisions that have cost and benefit implications (Fee, Hadlock, & Thomas, 2006).

The ownership structure that has emerged in many Chinese-listed companies is unique. Large corporations that were wholly state-owned have been partially privatized during the transition, resulting in a mixed ownership structure with varying proportions of equity retained by the government, either directly or indirectly (Lu & Yao, 2006; Megginson, 2005; Megginson & Netter, 2001). Besides the straightforward government direct control, where the state exercises control via its ownership of the controlling nonlisted parent company, ownership vested in related state entities enables indirect control. The government uses a control chain, including state solely owned companies, state-controlled nonlisted companies, state-controlled publicly listed companies, and state-owned academic institutions to control listed firms (Liu & Sun, 2003). Control is further exercised through the state's prerogative to appoint the senior management and the chair of the board of directors and supervisory board. The main feature of the structure of listed Chinese firms is the dominance of state, which ultimately controls these companies.

Searching for uniform superiority of either private or public enterprise is an objective that has eluded past research (Kwoka, 2005). One key debate is whether state ownership is generally associated with inferior performance (e.g., Bai, Liu, Lu, Song, & Zhang, 2004; Gunasekarage, Hess, & Hu, 2007; Qi, Wu, & Zhang, 2000; Sun & Tong, 2003; Wei, Xie, & Zhang, 2005). There are three main reasons for believing that state ownership impairs performance. The first one has to do with the nonprofit-maximizing behavior of state ownership. Governments are interested in realizing political and social concerns such as maintaining employment (Shleifer & Vishny, 1994). The better the financial shape of the firm, the easier for the state to pursue these goals external to the firm. This may adversely impact firm performance (Li, Sun, & Zou, 2009). The second reason is that state ownership is considered to possess significant agency costs. The *de facto* absence of owners in the firms increases managerial discretion in a potentially adverse way because the monitoring of managers is more difficult in state-controlled firms (Agrawal & Knoeber, 1996; Jensen, 1986; Jensen & Meckling, 1976). Unlike the Anglo-American model of dispersed shareholding ownership, where shareholders exercise control through election of directors and annual meetings, the mechanism to discipline managers is wanting if not absent. Thus, state ownership is incompatible with the managerial structure of modern firms in terms of ownership efficiency. Thirdly, state-controlled firms do appear to face especially soft budget constraints; that is, they are propped up with government support for political or social reasons. Such firms can lose money in larger quantities and over longer periods of time without exiting the industry than private firms (Ballou, 2005). The soft budget constraints distort incentives for firms, inducing inefficient allocation of resources and market-irrational economic behavior.

On the other hand, there is considerable evidence that the long-standing debate over the relationship between ownership and performance may require some rethinking (Kwoka, 2005; Tian & Estrin, 2008; Wang, 2005; Whitley & Czaban, 1998). Most of the studies providing evidence for the relation existing between ownership and performance rely on the assumption of exogeneity, which means that ownership is external or outside the nature of the firm (Goergen, 1998). The relationship between ownership structure and firm performance is insignificant when controlling for endogeneity of ownership structure (Demsetz & Lehn, 1985; Demsetz & Villalonga, 2001). The endogeneity problem arises when ownership is chosen as a function of performance or as a function of unobserved variables that also affect performance. In other words, ownership has been justified in terms of a series of factors within the firm itself, inherent to the area of industry or sector in which it operates (Leech & Leahy, 1991). Research on ownership endogeneity concludes that ownership is not due to value maximizing behavior, but rather determined by the circumstances or factors of the firm such as its contracting environment, size, the inherent riskiness of the assets or its performance (Demsetz & Lehn, 1985). The state-controlled firms in many countries are less competitive not because they are owned by the state, but because of the lack of explicit goals and objectives and state demands that can compromise the pursuit of efficiency and profitability (Heracleous, 2001). It is unreasonable to suppose that ownership *per se* has an impact on profit maximization (Demsetz, 1983).

1.6   Research design: Case study, performance measurement, and data analysis

This study is based on longitudinal and cross-sectional case studies (Yin, 2009). It spans the period from the initiation of economic reforms in 1978 to 2007. There were two steps in the collection of information for this study. First, the secondary sources of information such as company reports and published information in both the Chinese media and Western media were reviewed. Based on these data, a list of questions was developed, focusing on strategies and ownership. Second, 26 semi-structured interviews were conducted with senior managers and board members in the case companies, government officials, and professionals in order to achieve triangulation. The profile of the interviewees is outlined in Table 1.1.

The interviews were conducted during the years 2006–2008. The first round of interviews was conducted during five months between March and August 2006. The second round of interviews was conducted from April to July 2008. The 20 interviewees of the case companies were senior executives, board members including

Table 1.1 **The list of interviewees from organizations**

Organizations	Interviewee no.	Interviewee role	Years with co.	Years in current post	Date of interview
S1	1	Non-executive director	15	8	04/2007
	2	Senior manager	12	11	04/2007
	3	Non-executive director	23	8	04/2007
	4	Executive director	11	5	04/2007
	5	Senior manager	18	8	04/2007
	6	Senior manager	12	11	04/2007
	7	Independent director	N/A	6	04/2007
	8	Senior manager	18	10	04/2007, 05/2008
	9	Senior manager	25	5	04/2007, 05/2008
	10	Non-executive director	9	9	05/2008
	11	Executive director	28	4	04/2007, 05/2008
	12	Senior manager	16	10	05/2008
S2	13	Independent director	N/A	7	05/2007
	14	Non-executive director	27	13	05/2007
	15	Executive director	30	5	05/2007
	16	Senior manager	30	4	05/2007
	17	Non-executive director	25	4	05/2007, 06/2008
	18	Senior manager	15	5	06/2008
	19	Senior manager	23	5	05/2007, 06/2008
	20	Board secretary Executive director	18	4	05/2007, 06/2008
Other	21	Deputy director in Policy and Regulation Office	3	3	07/2007
	22	Senior consultant in Securities Co.	14	14	07/2007
	23	Senior consultant in consulting firm	15	15	05/2007

Continued

Table 1.1 **Continued**

Organizations	Interviewee no.	Interviewee role	Years with co.	Years in current post	Date of interview
	24	Vice president in Electronics Bureau	10	34	07/2007
	25	Assistant to general manager in Asset Management Co.	5	5	04/2007
	26	Senior manager in Securities Co.	12	12	04/2007

executive directors, non-executive directors, and independent directors. In addition to the company informants, six noncompany persons were also interviewed. The six people were from the local government, an asset management company, a securities company, and a consulting company.

The adoption of different types of business strategies and ownership structure of the cases was conducted in different phases. Therefore, the questions related to the earlier period were normally answered by the interviewees who worked in the company for a long time, covering the different stages of the development of the firm. The selection of informants was aimed at collecting data from those who were in a good position to be informed about the firm's business strategies and ownership structure. Each interview was conducted in Mandarin and, on average, took around 2 h.

Two cases were analyzed in some depth. The cases in the study were purposive, rather than random. The two firms were selected since they represented *prima facie* two extremes transformation of state-controlled firms. The names of the cases are represented by S1 and S2, whose main business is televisions. They used to be stand-alone factories wholly owned, managed, and operated by various levels of government. After undergoing corporatization, they proposed an initial public offering to be listed on Shanghai Stock Exchange in 1997 and 1996, respectively. S1 was established by the government in 1969 and is a dominant player in the Chinese market for the CE sector. In the face of the fierce competition in the market, S1 seemed to be changing rapidly toward the market-oriented reform. Founded in 1936, S2 has experienced success and crisis during the recent past. As the earliest electronics enterprise in China, S2 used to be a large and leading SOE in the CE sector. However, the transition toward a market economy has brought huge institutional change in China. S2 demonstrated a slow pace of change toward the increasingly competitive market, which made it uncompetitive with other domestic firms.

The analysis of S1 and S2 is divided into two stages, with 1993 as a watershed. Since S1 and S2 were not listed until 1997 and 1996, respectively, they were referred to as SOEs before listing and state-controlled firms after listing.

1.6.1 *Measuring performance of the firms*

Two variables of performance of firms are examined in this study—market share and the growth rate of annual sales. In developed nations, accounting profit and stock returns are two major indicators of a company's financial performance. However, new strategies and competitive realities demand new measurement systems (Eccles, 1991). There is a shift from treating financial measures as the foundation for performance measures to placing these nonfinancial measures such as quality and market share on an equal footing with financial performance measures (Stainer & Heap, 1996). Other authors (Johnson & Kaplan, 1987; Kaplan & Norton, 1992) lay out arguments against judging performance based solely on financial criteria.

Jiang (2001) points out that not all the major changes in the Chinese economic development can be accounted for from the perspective of the economic system. For instance, falling profitability may result from the emergence of competition from the nonstate enterprises, which is a desirable effect of economic reform (Jefferson & Rawski, 1994; Naughton, 1995). Competition has caused government-monopolized profits to drop. A drop in the profitability of the manufacturing industry is an inevitable stage in reform. But this does not mean that reform has failed to improve efficiency (Jiang, 2001). Moreover, managers have both the incentive and discretion to manipulate the financial account. For example, the profit figures have been inflated or fabricated by the management to support the stock price (Feinerman, 2007). Firms have also shown a loss in order to obtain a subsidy from the government. In order to avoid the misleading conclusions based on potentially unreliable financial data in the Chinese context, this study assesses the performance of the firms that is measured by the market share and growth rate of sales of the companies.

Market share refers to the percentage of the overall volume of business in a given market that is controlled by one company in relation to its competitors. The important factor in computing relative market share is not the exact number associated with the sales volume. The position relative to the competition is more important (Cook, 1995). It is easier to measure than some other common objectives, such as maximizing profits. Ambler and Wang (2002) compare the performance measures employed in China and the UK and find that more Chinese respondents than UK considered market share as an important marketing metric. The focus on market share results from the transition to the era of hyper competition in China. Facing the increasing intensified competition, market share became more concentrated during the1990s (Schlevogt, 2000). The idea that firms in China may improve their production efficiency is driven by increasing market share of their products (Brandt & Zhu, 2005).

However, a company may be tempted to set too low a price to achieve higher market share. To remedy the weakness of market share, the second competitive position indicator chosen is the growth rate of the annual sales. Information on a firm's relative market share should be correlated with the growth rate of the firms. If both the company's competitive position and growth rate are strong, then the company occupies a fortunate position and is known as a "star" (Urban & Star, 1991).

1.6.2   Data analysis

Cross-case analysis is used to detect similarities and compare differences among cases. At an early stage, the analysis focused on within-case analysis. The overall idea is to become intimately familiar with each case as a stand-alone entity. This process allows the unique patterns of each case to emerge before investigators generalize patterns across cases (Eisenhardt, 1989). The interviewees' descriptions were carefully perused to develop a broad picture of the firms, their main activities, and their economic and administrative environment. Next, following prescriptions for grounded theory building (Locke, 2001), a search was made for common categories across cases (Ravasi & Zattoni, 2006). Selecting categories and then looking for within-group similarities coupled with inter-group differences are keys to good cross-case analysis (Eisenhardt, 1989). The third step was to conduct cross-case analysis based on within-case analysis. This step aimed to look at within group similarities and inter-group differences. In a further round of comparative analysis, combining within-case analysis with cross-case comparison, the chapter explains differences in the observed patterns across business strategies and ownership structure.

1.7   Findings: Business strategies, ownership structure, and performance of the case firms

1.7.1   Exploitation and exploration strategies of case firms

The development of the firms in the area of business strategies has experienced two major stages, from 1978 to 1993 and from 1993 to 2007 (Table 1.2). Change in the business and institutional environmental required the firms to obtain new resources and capabilities. During the reform period, the strategies of the managers and their complement of resources and capabilities have changed dynamically. S1 has made great strides in terms of adapting to the market, thus making it possible to raise productivity and efficiency. S2, however, has been slow or unable to adapt to the evolving market conditions, and its competitive position has slipped.

1.7.1.1   Stage 1: 1978–1992

The exploration strategy of S1 during this period was mainly centered on sales and distribution, which grew rapidly as managers became more attuned to the workings of the market. Market knowledge and a high degree of operational flexibility can be achieved through business networks (Interview 5). The distribution routes owned by firms would achieve two positive outcomes. First, unlike state-run distribution activities, the distribution channels owned by the firms themselves were consumer focused by necessity and encouraged firms to generate improvements in quality, pay greater attention to consumer needs, undertake better warranties and repair services, make greater efforts at sales promotion, and develop new product varieties to meet market needs. Second, the strong commitment to understanding and working with this distribution system helped prevent problems that arose in different regions and symbolized a commitment to the Chinese market (Interviews 3 and 5).

Table 1.2 **Stages of firms' pursuit of business strategies**

	S1	S2
Stage 1 (1978–1992)		
Institutional factors	Government support for the SOEs was declining; increasing competition in domestic and broad market	Government support for the SOEs was declining; increasing competition in domestic and broad market
Business strategies	*Exploitation*: acquire knowledge through alliances from buying patents and licensing to establishing joint ventures *Exploration*: create distribution network	Heavily dependent on government; no positive learning strategies
Stage 2 (1993–2007)		
Institutional factors	Government has begun to further relinquish control over the state controlled firms Increased market competition, globalization, and technological innovation	Government has begun to further relinquish control over the state-controlled firms Increased market competition, globalization, and technological innovation
Business strategies	*Exploitation*: further expanded distribution network; international partners and "buying in" *Exploration*: technical centers; locate research centers in advanced counties; R&D on quality enhancement	Heavily dependent on government; no positive learning strategies

During this stage, S1 began to build its market knowledge through interaction with customers and the creation of extensive distribution networks. S1 was one of the earliest firms in the sector to build a nationwide system of provincial sales offices. Senior management from S1 believed that during the early stage of development, creating a distribution network to acquire market knowledge was more practical than developing advanced technology independently, as the latter required heavy investment and faced high risk (Interviews 8, 9, and 11). As one senior manager from S1 (Interview 11) claimed:

> *Contrary to the developed market where firms must rely on research and development and strong products to be competitive, in China the technology inherent in the products was similar. We began to build up our understanding of Chinese consumers and their purchasing habits through creating our own distribution network. Thus the advantage of the distribution channels explained to some extent the good performance of some firms.*

The sales network of S1 reduced its distribution costs and enabled it to compete better on price. Until the early 1990s, S1 was a relatively unknown firm. In 1992, the second year following the establishment of its own distribution channels, the output of its main business, color TV sets, exceeded 1.4 million sets, ranking the firm fourth among TV producers in China (Interview 3). This boosted S1's image in the market.

With high technological turbulence and tight budget constraints, staying ahead of competitors technologically was not an easy task. At this stage, S1 broadened its R&D activities in order to support its marketing activities. Since the huge cost and high risks involved in the development of new products were extreme in the early phase, the firms that had limited resources were unable to afford extensive exploration (Interview 8). A firm's ability to obtain knowledge faster than its competitors was a key component of its competitive advantage in the first stage. Consequently, cooperation with multinational corporations (MNCs) was often identified as a proper strategy to acquire technology.

These collaborations with MNCs enabled S1 to acquire the technology quickly and reduced the stigma of lagging technology being attached to its brands by Chinese consumers. As early as 1984, S1 had entered into collaboration with Matsushita to acquire color TV technology. Subsequently, other agreements for collaboration were signed between S1 and foreign companies (Interview 11). Although buying technology from foreign firms was a common practice, S1 bought only advanced technologies from Western countries. Senior managers of S1 considered that this would be more effective when competing with local firms and in catching up with MNCs. When facing the choice of buying technology from a Hong Kong firm for US$1.5 million or from Matsushita for US$3 million in 1992, S1 chose to buy from Matsushita, which had more advanced technologies (Gao, Zhang, & Liu, 2007).

Unlike S1, S2 was less eager to cooperate with firms from advanced countries to obtain technology and paid less attention to distribution channels (Interviews 15 and 29). The company had a substantial aviation and defense electronics business producing for state-owned clients in addition to consumer lines. S2's managers lacked incentive mechanisms to reorient their operations toward consumer needs. As a consequence of its privileged government supplier role, managers were more inclined to resort to government support when faced with sales and profit decline rather than develop an effective business strategy (Interview 24).

1.7.1.2   Stage 2: 1993–2007

During the second stage, senior managers from S1 believed that independent distribution channels remained crucial for them. They expanded their distribution network, which has given them increasingly broader geographical coverage compared with other domestic producers. By the end of 2006, S1 had 200 branches and more than 10,000 sales and service outlets throughout China, covering all provinces and major cities (*Asia Port Daily News*, 04/01/2007).

Expansion of S1's distribution network and sales and service activities supported decision making in its marketing and product design activities. S1 incorporated feedback and experience of users that it obtained from its distribution channels and marketing departments into product design and innovation efforts in its business-level R&D centers (Interviews 1 and 8). The management of S1 further identified technology and innovation as the focus of its new strategic development at this stage, essential for growth in the CE sector, which is characterized by rapid changes in product features, functions, and performance. However, S1 found it difficult to leverage its technologic knowledge without controlling key complementary assets (Interview 2). Overreliance on a "buying in" strategy had not allowed it to develop what the literature would consider a stable and efficient manufacturing process (Katz, 1997; Miller, 1990). As an interviewee from S1 (Interview 6) explained:

> *The technology suppliers from Western countries are not always usually willing to disseminate core technology to us. The firm can only acquire some medium or low-level technology in this way.*

S1 had accumulated and upgraded its resources and capabilities in the first stage, which in turn enhanced its innovative activities and investments at the second stage (Interview 2). From the mid-1990s, S1 had embarked on establishing an internal R&D capability in addition to the import of technology.

Since overproduction of the CE products has forced market prices down, to the detriment of producers, S1 felt that it could demand a price premium that was good for profits. Rather than being content to play in the conventional business segment, it sought the higher margins of new technology and a leap forward in CE through technology (Interview 23). Its first attempt was to lay a solid foundation for the manufacturing of high-tech products. S1 invested in manufacturing capabilities and establishing large-scale manufacturing plants. S1's Technical Park had more than 1500 staff, 11 professional institutes, 5 sub-developing centers, and a postdoctoral R&D working station by the end 2007. In the early 2000s, the company also began to locate its research facilities in Japan and the United States, where the world's cutting-edge technology was being developed. S1's strategy was to build an international brand name in the toughest developed markets from which it could gradually expand other markets. S1 became a leader in its respective area (Interview 12).

However, S2's managers still resorted to government support and help when S1 was continually increasing investment in R&D and innovation. The extent of the relationship networks with the government that S2 managed to build up over time was one of its most striking features. The dependence of S2 on the government made it unresponsive to market changes. The comments of an S2 interviewee (Interview 20) were illustrative:

> *You cannot imagine the intricacy of relationship web of [S2] in the government. It will be unbelievable if [S2], one of the earliest and ever most famous SOEs, is closed down.*

In 1996, S2 was the premier competitive domestic color TV manufacturer in China. S2 lost over one-third of its market share in China in 1998. By early 2007, S1 took over S2's position as a leading TV maker in terms of market share (Interview 21). S2's survival was no longer possible without government support. S2 was one of the largest companies in the province and one of the earliest national brands in China, and the government was thus reluctant to close it despite its continuing losses. The state pledged that every attempt would be made to assist S2 to overcome its financial plight (Yu, 2005), which in turn weakened the incentive of the managers to adopt positive learning strategies to achieve economic benefits.

1.7.2   The evolution of ownership structure of case firms

Until the early 1980s, S1 and S2 were stand-alone factories wholly owned, managed, and operated by various levels of government. Above the factory was a complex array of government agencies that administered every aspect of the factory. Both control and ownership were vested wholly in the state. In effect, they were not companies in a Western sense, but rather a set of administrative production and distribution units subject to the direction of the Chinese State (Groves, Hong, McMillan, & Naughton, 1994; Jefferson & Rawski, 1994). The employees and managers had few incentives to maximize profit or efficiency under such conditions (Chow, 2002). Managers, therefore, did not have autonomy over production decisions and wage determination.

With the deregulation of government policy in the CE sector, central government decentralized its control rights over the state-controlled firms to local governments. In the context of the Chinese transitional economy, political promotion of the local leaders is closely related to the economic performance of the region (Walder, 2003). Local governments have incentives to provide more autonomy to firms, provided they are profitable. This has seen the decentralization of the control rights to managers that allow them to implement market-based decisions that improve competitive capability of the firms. The competitive firms in turn help the local governments to fulfill their economic goal. During the years following S1's initial listing in 1997, the largest shareholder of S1 was the local government in the area in which it was located; at one time it accounted for 70% of total shares (S1 Annual Report, 1998). These state shares were not publicly traded in China; another 10% was held by related state parties. Only about 20% of issued shares belonged to individual shares; these could be traded freely on the market. Compared with 1997, the ownership structure of S1 had changed greatly and the ownership concentration reduced.

The concentration of state ownership in S1 was reduced from 74.07% in 1997 to 48.4% in 2007 (S1 Annual Report, 2008); that still means only about half the issued nominal stock of shares were traded on the market. One of the independent directors of S1 (Interview 7) elaborates as follows:

> *[S1] is a new form of state-controlled firm. Its operational mechanism including acquisition of the resources and the assessment of the employees is market-based. Even if [S1] is state-controlled, its owners and CEO are driven by performance incentives and objectives, such as profit maximization or market share maximization.*

With the decentralization of the ownership from the central to the local government, the local government is able to make a residual claim, while more decision-making power has been delegated to them as well (Fan, Wong, & Zhang, 2005). Local government has placed more attention on the economic development of the firms. Decentralization provided incentives to the managers of the firms. Managers interviewed from S1 said that under local government ownership, the government would be dependent on the performance of local firms for economic benefits (Interviews 5, 6, and 18). The dependence of local government on the performance of S1 gave the firm more bargaining power, which in turn provided incentives to the managers. The managers of S1 have gained great autonomy despite the ultimate control of local government. In this situation, the S1 does not subsume its profit motive under other requirements such as employment and social welfare. Although state controlled, ownership and management were increasingly separated in practices, as seen in the increased autonomy of decision making without recourse to government approval. One of the independent directors of S1 (Interview 4) elaborates as follows:

> *The government now hardly intervenes in the business of the company. The board has much more decision-making power nowadays. Although the most important decisions require consultation with the state-authorized organizations… the local government would accept the recommendation of the board as long as it thinks they are reasonable and can improve the local economy.*

In contrast, the state ownership in S2 has remained unchanged since its first listing (S2 Annual Report, various years). Since 1998, the firm has been trapped into financial trouble but has enjoyed significant preferential treatment from the government (Interview 14). The government rescued S2 through an agreement instead of closing it down. S2's special status (aviation-defense electronics producer) and its large scale brought a higher level of direct state–party control and a corresponding higher level of state shareholding and reluctance to relax control over operations. State ownership has always remained 54.2% since it was listed in 1996. For S2, the state's need to guarantee its survival is greater than the need to guarantee returns on capital (Interviews 21 and 24).

1.7.3 The performance of the case firms

Table 1.3 indicates the domestic market share of each case, respectively. S1 had a prominent share of its domestic market segment and was ranked among the top five for market share from 1995 to 2007. S2's market share dropped from 9.7% in 1995 to 5% in 2007 (Chinese Household Electronics Report, various years).

Table 1.3 The firms' domestic market share, 1995–2007

	1995 (%)	2000 (%)	2003 (%)	2007 (%)	Ranking by product market share (2007)
S1	2.94	10.91	11.11	16.23	1
S2	9.7	3.79	3	5	N/A

Source: Chinese Household Electronics Report (various years).

S1's growth rate of main business sales was 25% in 2007, far above the average growth rate of 17.2% in the similar cases filed (S1 Annual Report, 2008). The negative growth rate of S2's main business sales of 10.44% in 2007 resulted in its inability to compete with other manufacturers (S2 Annual Report, 2008).

1.8 Discussion: State ownership and competitiveness

In terms of their competitive position, Chinese state-controlled firms are neither inevitably less competitive or more competitive than firms that have other types of ownership forms. Competitive state-controlled firms such as S1 were able to grow and continuously expand their market shares, while the less competitive firms such as S2 have found survival increasingly tough going. We can explain these differences in terms of a virtuous circle of positive feedback in response to market stimulus or a vicious circle of defensive and negative feedback that reinforced anti-market orientations associated with their administrative heritage before the advent of economic reforms. Figure 1.1 shows our model: the competitive state-controlled firms created a virtuous circle of their development while the less competitive firms became trapped in a vicious circle.

1.8.1 The virtuous circle of the development pattern of state-controlled firms with competitive position

For S1, the virtuous circle of development is associated with a more market-oriented external environment that increased the incentives for managers to develop their business. Increased incentives for the managers to pursue profit-seeking goals enabled them to become more market- and learning-oriented in their business strategies, which in turn led to the firm adopting a more competitive position and resulting in better performance. Since such competitive firms helped the government to achieve their economic goals, through employment and taxation, the role of the local government

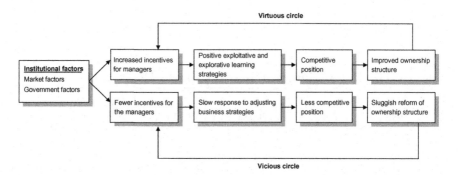

Figure 1.1 The two ways state-controlled firms of development of state-controlled firms.

in these state-controlled firms has shifted from direct administrative control of firms to an indirect role of guidance. This shift has benefited management's decision making and responsiveness to the market. It has also allowed for the ownership structure to become more diversified and property rights more clarified. This in turn further strengthened incentives for managers to focus on the competitiveness of firms in the market, thereby initiating another iteration of a virtuous cycle.

The emergence of competitive markets and decentralized government control are two striking features of transformation in the CE sector. Since the emergence of the buyer's market for products where competition is the rule, product market competition has been associated with a relatively high degree of managerial autonomy, which has provided incentives for firms to improve their production efficiency. The findings also suggest that the government has recently started to value the market-disciplining function implicit in public listing and reduced its interference in the firm that might affect performance. Central government gradually streamlined its internal economic sections and shifted the decision rights to the local government, which then shifted the rights to business enterprises.

What makes local government different in the transformation period is that their officials mainly depend on the performance of local businesses to demonstrate and valorize their own capabilities. Correspondingly, the local government was motivated to allow firms it oversaw to adopt strategies that were more independent provided there was a credible expectation that the strategies could induce faster growth of firms and higher sales than would be the case if the government had intervened in firms. Local government therefore devolved to the management of the firms the rights to devise and implement strategies so as to encourage a response to the market and maximize the value of the firm. The residual claims were thus transferred from local government to the manager. According to Walder (1995, p. 270), "governments at the lower levels are able to exercise more effective control over their assets than are governments at higher levels." This decentralization of rights promotes sufficient competition to constrain government intervention in state and nonstate firms.

The incentives derived from the environmental dynamism of this institutional transition compel the firms to be learning-oriented in their business development. If the firms were able to respond to the dimension and pace of institutional change, such newly acquired autonomy and flexibility motivated the firms to design strategies to build resources and capabilities to compete. Motivated by profit, the managers responded enthusiastically to opportunities for growth. Since the firms play increasing role in the managerial decision making during China's economic transition, the managers exercised the freedom required to design and implement the business strategies necessary to satisfy their target customers. The analysis shows that the firms became learning-oriented in order to survive the fierce competition. The changes of the business strategy over time reflected their adaptability to the changing structure and opportunities of the market. The analysis shows that in the context of the business environment discussed above, the business strategies of the firm were determined by the incentives for the managers. The firm itself was transformed through a series of learning behaviors sharpened its competitiveness.

This study holds that the better performance of a firm such as S1 would lead to dilution of state ownership. Seemingly, the better the performance of the firm, the less concentrated is the ownership of the firms. This is consistent with the idea of Kole (1996) that corporate performance could influence the ownership structure rather than being determined by ownership structure.

However, this is not a simplistic argument to infer that ownership determines firm performance in a unidirectional way; we need to take an explicit account of the mutual links between the firm performance and the ownership. Superior performance may lead to lower concentration of ownership of the firms. Since S1 provided substantial benefits to local government, it was more successful in improving its bargaining power, which provides it with leverage to resist interference from the local government. In general, the greater the firm's bargaining power, the greater its ability to reduce government interference. The growing indispensability of the firms has contributed to their influence and created a new power balance in favor of firm managers. When it comes to business decisions, the prestige and reputation of the firms usually carries weight in decision making as long as local government officials believe their strategies are sound. Accordingly, government relinquishes its majority stake in the S1 as maintaining ownership becomes increasingly counterproductive in a competitive marketplace. Decentralized ownership structure gave managers more control and more rights to claim residual income, which established appropriate incentive mechanisms related to firm performance, thereby starting another iteration of the virtuous circle.

1.8.2   The vicious circle of the development pattern of state-controlled firms with less competitive position

There were fewer incentives for S2 to adopt market-oriented strategies, and it became trapped in a vicious circle of reliance on state support, which reduced its competitiveness over time. S2 had expected the past model of business operation would still work in a fast-changing market: governmental authorities or agencies, rather than the market, would primarily determined the fate of the firm. Although the level of government intervention was reduced, S2 adapted poorly to the market and continued to seek protection from the government. Thus, its managers lacked the incentive to adopt positive learning strategies to grow the firm. S2 had weaker aspirations to exploit opportunities in the external environment and to develop production, technological and organizational capabilities, which meant it was less inclined to engage in learning-oriented strategic activities. Sticking to old strategies in changing environments may lead to poor performance and undermined the firm's competitive position (Audia, Locke, & Smith, 2000).

Although S2 was less competitive than S1, it was very large, and the government wanted to retain a majority shareholding in such a state-controlled firm to prevent it from going out of business. Interference from the government in S2 strengthened as its performance worsened, which further impaired the incentives of the managers. The firm was unable to seize the opportunity provided by the changing institutional and market environment, thereby initiating another iteration of the vicious cycle.

1.9 Conclusion: Theoretical implications and avenues for future research

1.9.1 Theoretical implications

This study is exploratory. It seeks to explore the ways of development of China's state-controlled firms in transitional China. Polarization has emerged among the state-controlled firms since the beginning of reform in China. Some have grown and continuously expanded their market shares, while the less competitive ones have found survival from the fierce competition increasingly tough.

Three contributions emerge. First, in discussing the business strategies, the study identified the processes by which firms are able to maintain dynamic strategic fit in a changing environment. Our research explicitly incorporates this dynamic perspective into the study of the fit between firms and their changing institutional environments. Second, our analysis has shown the dominant view that state-controlled firms are associated with fewer positive learning strategies should be reconsidered. State-controlled firms are not all alike. Managers of competitive state-controlled firms in general have more managerial autonomy than do managers of less competitive state-controlled firms, and act in a more entrepreneurial and market-inspired competitive spirit. Third, the evidence found in the cases in the context of China's transition economy is not a repetition of the dominant theory that the strategy configuration is directly influenced by the type of ownership an organization has (Tan, 1996, 2002). This chapter argues that the state-controlled firms are not necessarily less positive in using exploitative and explorative learning strategies than the firms with private ownership. In this light, private ownership is neither a necessary nor sufficient condition for market-oriented learning strategies. The cases studied here constitute a potent challenge to the widely held view that private ownership is an indispensable prerequisite to market-oriented learning strategies.

1.9.2 Avenues for future research

This study is not free of limitations, particularly owing to its exploratory nature. The limitation is common to any case study, that is, the reliance on a small sample. For this limitation, this part proposes the need for further research related to the following broad issues.

First, future research should consider the generalizability of the findings of this study to firms in other transition economies. In fact, in many ways, it is difficult to compare the cases of firm reform in China with those in Eastern Europe and the Soviet Union, not only because of the different approach but also because of the very different historical, economic, and cultural contexts (Buck, Filatotchev, Nolan, & Wright, 2000). To further assess its distinctiveness, the practices of China's firms in these two areas and their antecedents should be compared to samples of companies in other countries.

Second, only large firms were included in this study. However, the nature and outcomes of small- and medium-sized firms in China might produce results that differ from the findings in this study. For example, the political effects of local government organizations on firms of various sizes might be significantly different. It will therefore be important to extend the analysis to firms of different sizes in China.

China has a diverse, complex, and rapidly changing economy. This study suggests that China's experience with enterprise reform differs from what might have been suggested by mainstream management literature. We have argued that the CE sector is representative of the manufacturing industry in China's transition to a market economy. Quite a few of the front-runners in this sector are state-controlled firms. If the experiences of these firms are extrapolated to others, Chinese state-controlled firms as a whole may continue to maintain their competitiveness, despite the importance of the market for China.

References

Agrawal, A., & Knoeber, C. (1996). Firm performance and mechanisms to control agency problems between managers and shareholders. *Journal of Financial and Quantitative Analysis*, *31*, 377–397.

Ambler, T., & Wang, X. (2002). Measures of marketing success: A comparison between China and the United Kingdom. *Asia Pacific Journal of Management*, *20*, 267–281.

Audia, P., Locke, E., & Smith, K. (2000). Paradox of success: An archival and a laboratory study of strategic persistence following radical environmental change. *Academy of Management Journal*, *43*, 837–853.

Bai, C., Liu, Q., Lu, J., Song, F., & Zhang, J. (2004). Corporate governance and market valuation in China. *Journal of Comparative Economics*, *32*, 599–616.

Ballou, J. (2005). An examination of the presence of ownership effects in mixed markets. *The Journal of Law, Economics, and Organization*, *21*(1), 228–255.

Barney, J. (1991). Firm resources and sustained competitive advantage. *Journal of Management*, *17*, 99–120.

Baron, D. (1995). Integrated strategy: Market and nonmarket components. *California Management Review*, *37*(2), 47–65.

Brandt, L., & Zhu, S. C. (2005). *Technology adoption and absorption: The case of Shanghai firms*. Working paper, Department of Economics, University of Toronto.

Buck, T., Filatotchev, I., Nolan, P., & Wright, M. (2000). Different paths to economic reform in Russia and China: Causes and consequences. *Journal of World Business*, *35*(4), 379–400.

Caldart, A., & Ricart, J. (2007). Corporate strategy: An agent-based approach. *European Management Review*, *4*, 107–120.

Chang, H., & Singh, A. (1997). Can large firms be run efficiently without being bureaucratic. *Journal of International Development*, *9*(6), 865–875.

Child, J., & Pleister, H. (2003). Governance and management in China's private sector. *Management International*, *7*(3), 13–23.

China Securities Daily (2009 December 20).

Chinese Household Electronics Report (various years).

Chow, G. C. (2002). *China's economic transformation*. Malden, MA: Blackwell Publishers.

Cook, K. (1995). *AMA complete guide to strategic planning for small business*. Chicago: American Marketing Association.

Crossan, M., Lane, H., & White, R. (1999). An organizational learning framework: From institution to institution. *Academy of Management View*, *24*, 522–537.

Demsetz, H. (1983). The structure of ownership and the theory of the firm. *Journal of Law and Economics*, *XXVI*, 375–390.

Demsetz, H., & Lehn, K. (1985). The structure of corporate ownership: Causes and consequences. *The Journal of Political Economy*, *93*, 1155–1177.

Demsetz, H., & Villalonga, B. (2001). Ownership structure and corporate performance. *Journal of Corporate Finance*, *7*, 209–233.

Deng, S., & Dart, J. (1999). The market orientation of Chinese enterprises during a time of transition. *European Journal of Marketing*, *33*(5/6), 631–654.

Eccles, R. (1991). The performance measurement manifesto. *Harvard Business Review*, *69*(1), 131–137.

Eisenhardt, K. M. (1989). Building theories from case study research. *Academy of Management Review*, *14*(4), 532–550.

Fama, E. (1980). Agency problems and the theory of the firm. *Journal of Political Economy*, *88*, 299–307.

Fan, J. P. H., Wong, T. J., & Zhang, T. (2005). *The emergence of corporate pyramids in China*. Working paper, The Chinese University of Hong Kong.

Fee, C. E., Hadlock, C., & Thomas, S. (2006). Corporate equity ownership and the governance of product market relationships. *The Journal of Finance*, *LXI*(3), 1217–1251.

Feinerman, J. (2007). New hope for corporate governance in China? *The China Quarterly*, *191* (September), 590–612.

Filatotchev, I., & Toms, S. (2003). Corporate governance, strategy and survival in a declining industry: A study of UK cotton textile companies. *Journal of Management Studies*, *40*(4), 875–920.

Gao, X., Zhang, P., & Liu, X. (2007). Competing with MNEs: Developing manufacturing capabilities or innovation capabilities. *The Journal of Technology Transfer*, *32*(1), 87–107.

Goergen, M. (1998). *Corporate governance and financial performance: A study of German and UK initial public offerings*. UK: Edward Elgar Publishing Limited.

Groves, T., Hong, Y., McMillan, J., & Naughton, B. (1994). Autonomy and incentives in China's state enterprises. *The Quarterly Journal of Economics*, *109*, 183–209.

Gunasekarage, A., Hess, K., & Hu, A. (2007). The influence of the degree of state ownership and the ownership concentration on the performance of listed Chinese companies. *Research in International Business and Finance*, *21*, 379–395.

Heracleous, L. (2001). State ownership, privatization and performance in Singapore: An exploratory study from a strategic management perspective. *Asia Pacific Journal of Management*, *18*, 69–81.

Hitt, M. A., Lee, H. -U., & Yucel, E. (2002). The importance of social capital to the management of multinational enterprises: Relational networks among Asian and Western firms. *Asia Pacific Journal of Management*, *19*, 353–372.

Holmqvist, M. (2004). Experiential learning processes of exploitation and exploration within and between organizations: An empirical study of product development. *Organization Science*, *15*(1), 70–81.

Jefferson, G., & Rawski, T. G. (1994). Enterprise reform in Chinese industry. *Journal of Economic Perspective*, *8*(2), 47–70.

Jefferson, G., & Su, J. (2006). Privatisation and restructuring in China: Evidence from shareholding ownership, 1995–2001. *Journal of Comparative Economics*, *34*, 146–166.

Jensen, M. C. (1986). Agency costs of free cash flow, corporate finance and takeovers. *American Economic Review*, *76*, 323–329.

Jensen, M. C., & Meckling, W. H. (1976). Theory of the firm: Managerial behavior, agency costs and ownership structure. *Journal of Financial Economics*, *3*(4), 305–360.

Jiang, X. (Ed.). (2001). *China's industries in transition: Organizational change, efficiency gains, and growth dynamics*. Huntington, New York: Nova Science Publisher, Inc.

Johnson, H., & Kaplan, R. (1987). *Relevance lost: The rise and fall of management accounting*. Boston, MA: Harvard Business School Press.

Kaplan, R. S., & Norton, D. P. (1992). The balanced scorecard-measures that drive performance. *Harvard Business Review*, *70*(1), 71–79.

Katz, R. (1997). *The human side of managing technological innovation*. New York: Oxford University Press.

Kole, S. (1996). Managerial ownership and firm performance: Incentives and rewards? *Advances in Financial Economics*, *2*, 119–149.

Kwoka, E. J. (2005). The comparative advantage of public ownership: Evidence from U.S. electric utilities. *Canadian Journal of Economics*, *38*(2), 622–640.

Leech, D., & Leahy, J. (1991). Ownership structure, control type classifications and the performance of large British companies. *The Economic Journal*, *101*, 1418–1437.

Levinthal, D. A., & March, J. G. (1993). The myopia of learning. *Strategic Management Journal*, *14*(Winter), 95–112.

Li, T., Sun, L. X., & Zou, L. (2009). State ownership and corporate performance: A quantile regression analysis of Chinese listed companies. *China Economic Review*, *20*, 703–716.

Liu, G. S., & Garino, G. (2001). Privatization or competition. *Economics of Planning*, *34*, 37–51.

Liu, G., & Sun, P. (2003). *Identifying ultimate controlling shareholders in Chinese public corporations: An empirical survey*. Working paper, The Royal Institution of International Affairs, UK.

Locke, K. D. (2001). *Grounded theory in management research*. London: Sage.

Lu, Y., & Yao, J. (2006). Impact of state ownership and control mechanisms on the performance of group affiliated companies in China. *Asia Pacific Journal of Management*, *23*, 485–503.

March, J. G. (1991). Exploration and exploitation in organizational learning. *Organization Science*, *2*(February), 71–87.

Masini, A., Zollo, M., & Wassenhove, L. (2004). *Understanding exploration and exploitation in changing operating routines: The influence of industry and organizational traits*. Working paper, London Business School.

Megginson, W. L. (2005). *The financial economics of privatization*. Oxford: Oxford University Press.

Megginson, W. L., & Netter, J. M. (2001). From state to market: A survey of empirical studies on privatization. *Journal of Economic Literature*, *39*(2), 321–389.

Meyer, K. (2007). Exploitation and exploration learning and the development of organizational capabilities: A cross-case analysis of the Russian oil industry. *Human Relations*, *60*(10), 1493–1523.

Miller, D. (1988). Relating porter's business strategies to environment and structure: Analysis and performance implications. *Academy of Management Journal*, *31*(2), 280–308.

Miller, D. (1990). *The Icarus paradox*. New York: Harper Collins.

Naughton, B. (1995). *Growing out of the plan: Chinese economic reform, 1978–1993*. New York, NY: Cambridge University Press.

Peng, M. (2004). Outside directors and firm performance during institutional transitions. *Strategic Management Journal*, *25*(5), 453–471.

Qi, D., Wu, W., & Zhang, H. (2000). Shareholding structure and corporate performance of partially privatized firms: Evidence from listed Chinese companies. *Pacific-Basin Finance Journal*, *8*, 587–610.

Qu, Q. (2003). Corporate governance and state-owned shares in China listed companies. *Journal of Asian Economics*, *14*(5), 771–783.

Ravasi, D., & Zattoni, A. (2006). Exploring the political side of board involvement in strategy: A study of mixed-ownership institutions. *Journal of Management Studies*, *43*(8), 1671–1702.

S1 Annual Report (various years). http://www.sse.com.cn/assortment/stock/list/stockdetails/company/index.shtml?COMPANY_CODE=600060.

S2 Annual Report (various years). http://www.sse.com.cn/assortment/stock/list/stockdetails/company/index.shtml?COMPANY_CODE=600775.

Schlevogt, K.-A. (2000). Doing business in China, part I: The business environment in China—Getting to know the next century's superpower. *Thunderbird International Business Review*, *42*(1), 85–111.

Shanghai Stock Exchange. (2009). http://www.sse.com.

Shenzhen Stock Exchange. (2009). http://www.szse.cn.

Shleifer, A., & Vishny, R. (1994). Politicians and firms. *Quarterly Journal of Economics*, *109*(4), 995–1025.

Simon, D. F. (1992). Sparking the electronics industry. *The China Business Review*, *19*, 22–28.

Song, L. G., & Yao, Y. (2003). *Impacts of privatization on firm performance in China*. Working paper, China Centre for Economic Research, Peking University.

Stainer, A., & Heap, J. (1996). Attachment H: Growing importance of non-financial performance measures. *Management Services*, *40*(7), 10–12.

Sun, Q., & Tong, W. (2003). China share issue privatization: The extent of its success. *Journal of Financial Economics*, *70*, 182–222.

Tan, J. (1996). Regulatory environment and strategic orientations in a transitional economy: A study of Chinese private enterprise. *Entrepreneurship: Theory and Practice*, *21*(1), 31–47.

Tan, J. (2002). Impact of ownership type on environment strategy linkage and performance: Evidence from a transitional economy. *Journal of Management Studies*, *39*(3), 333–354.

Tan, J. (2005). Venturing in turbulent water: A historical perspective of economic reform and entrepreneurial transformation. *Journal of Business Venturing*, *20*(5), 689–704.

Thomsen, S., & Pedersen, T. (2000). Ownership structure and economic performance in the largest European companies. *Strategic Management Journal*, *21*(6), 689–705.

Tian, L., & Estrin, S. (2008). Retained state shareholding in Chinese PLCs: Does government ownership reduce corporate value? *Journal of Comparative Economics*, *36*, 74–89.

Urban, G. L., & Star, S. (1991). *Advanced marketing strategy*. Englewood Cliffs, NJ: Prentice Hall.

Walder, A. G. (1995). Local governments as industrial firms: An organizational analysis of China's transitional economy. *The American Journal of Sociology*, *101*(2), 263–301.

Walder, A. G. (2003). Elite opportunity in transitional economies. *American Sociological Review*, *68*(December), 899–916.

Wang, C. (2005). Ownership and operating performance of Chinese IPOs. *Journal of Banking and Finance*, *29*, 1835–1856.

Wei, Z., Xie, F., & Zhang, S. (2005). Ownership structure and firm value in China's privatized firms: 1991–2001. *Journal of Financial and Quantitative Analysis*, *40*, 87–108.

Whitley, R., & Czaban, L. (1998). Institutional transformation and enterprise change in an emergent capitalist economy: The case of Hungary. *Organization Studies*, *19*(2), 259–280.

Wiseman, R., Dykes, B., Weidlich, R., & Franco-Santos, M. (2006). *Pursuing a dual strategy of exploitation and exploration in Central and Eastern Europe*. Working paper, The Eli Broad Graduate School of Management, Michigan State University.

World Bank Group. (2001). Reform of China's state-owned enterprises. http://worldbank.org/html/prddr/trans.

Wortzel, H., & Wortzel, L. (1989). Privatization: Not the only answer. *World Development*, *17*(5), 633–641.

Xie, W., & Wu, G. S. (2003). Differences between learning processes in small tigers and large dragons: Learning processes of two color TV (CTV) firms within China. *Research Policy*, *32*(8), 1463–1479.

Yin, R. (2009). *Case study research: Design and methods*. London and New Delhi: Sage Publications.

Yu, K. (2005). Nanjing government helps S2 out of the plight (in Chinese). *Capital Market*, *4*, 42–43.

The relationship between the share structure of business groups and the performance of the listed affiliated firms

2

H. Yang, B. Liu
Shandong Jianzhu University, Jinan, China

2.1 Introduction

What is a business group? A business group is a set of legally independent firms that are bound by economic (such as ownership, financial, and commercial) and social (such as family, kinship, and friendship) ties (Khanna & Rivkin, 2001). Large business groups serve as the primary economic engine for the development of the national and local economies in China (Keister, 1998; Nolan, 2001). The formation of business groups is a significant strategy to reform state-owned enterprises (SOEs) in China. Most business groups were transformed from previously SOEs and are protected from competition.

As the device to achieve a rapid economic growth in China, business groups have distinctive economic and organizational structures and micro-environments embedded in China's unique political, economic, and cultural background. It is of particular interest to note that business groups in state-owned sectors are not only the "product" of policy inducement, as found in Korea's emerging economy (Chang & Hong, 2000), but also the instrument used by the Chinese government to facilitate institutional transition and ownership reform (Ma & Lu, 2005; Yiu, Bruton, & Lu, 2005). This chapter focuses on the affiliates' performance of Chinese business groups in a period of institutional change and improvement in the quality of the market institution.

Business groups emerged and developed as an important organizational form in China under economic transition. Beginning in 1987, the State Commission for Economic System Reform promulgated "Several Opinions Regarding the Establishment and Development of Business Groups" to encourage the formation of business groups in the state-owned sector (Ma & Lu, 2005). After observing the advantages and disadvantages of this new organizational form, Chinese government adopted the landmark strategy of "holding on to the large and letting go of the small" to restructure and improve the performance of the SOEs. Somewhat later, a number of privately owned enterprises emerged and also adopted a business group structure.

Since the late 1990s, the overall scale and performance of China's business groups further developed when central and local governments introduced numerous policies to build national teams consisting of large business groups as an engine for economic growth (Nolan, 2001). With the establishment of the State-owned Assets Supervision and Administration Commission (SASAC) in 2004, the main shareholders of large state-owned business groups were clearly stated. The Chinese business groups are characterized by a simple hierarchy structure, with a parent company at the top and the affiliates at the next tier; in most, 100% or more than 50% are owned by the parent company (Lee & Wing, 2001). SASAC took the role of claiming property rights on behalf of the state and is responsible for promoting, supervising, and directing the standardization and development of business groups. Local state-owned business groups are under management of the local SASAC. With supportive government policies and fierce market competition, business groups are becoming a major contributor to Chinese economy.

In the past two decades, scholars have begun to extensively explore the groups' structural characteristics, performance, and the link between the two in the transition economy from various perspectives and with different methods. With the quick expansion of business groups in China, the parent–affiliate management system has become the dominant organizational form. A parent company, which acts as the headquarters on behalf of a controlling/dominant owner, such as the state, exercises its authority on others through layers of core companies as affiliates (Fan, Wong, & Zhang, 2005; Li, Sun, & Liu, 2006). Chinese business groups were characterized by a large powerful "parent" or "core" company, otherwise known as a "group company," surrounded by other "children" companies in which the mother holds a controlling share. This is known as the "close" layer of the group. Hence, one of the focuses in the area of business groups is to study the relationship between the structure of parent companies and the performance of the affiliated firms. Based on the research of business groups in emerging markets, Khanna and Palepu (1997) argued that due to the institutional voids and imperfect external market in these countries, business groups have emerged by filling these institutional voids and contribute to better firm performance (Qian, 1996; Xu & Wang, 1999). Following Khanna and Palepu (1997), researchers have carried out a large number of empirical studies on business groups and their performance in emerging markets, including China, India, Korea, Chile, and Russia (Bertrand, Mehta, & Mullainathan, 2002; Claessens, 1997; Lins, 1999). There has been a debate on whether state ownership contributed to the performance of group-affiliated companies. Some found a negative impact of state ownership on firm performance in business groups due to the soft budget constraints and administrative intervention imposed by governments (Nolan, 2001; Yiu et al., 2005). Others found that managers in large business groups could enjoy more autonomy in their decision making, particularly when they diversified through group pyramid ownership structures: companies at the bottom of the pyramid structure were kept at an arm's length from the state or governmental control (Fan et al., 2005).

In this study, we examine the performance effect of firms affiliated with business groups using data that includes listed group affiliations in the Shandong Province of China from 2005 to 2010, including both state-owned and private business groups. Business groups in Shandong province have shared similar characteristics with groups throughout China while maintaining region and industry-specific features. Large- and medium-sized SOEs account for a large portion of the enterprises in Shandong Province.

The rest of the chapter is structured as follows. Section 2.2 begins by situating the hypotheses in the context of China's unfolding institutional development. Section 2.3 explains the study design. Data analysis and results are presented in Section 2.4. Section 2.5 concludes with a summary and implications section that also discusses the study's limitations and provides suggestions for future research.

2.2 Hypothesis development

An economics-based viewpoint argues that business groups are formed for the purpose of achieving competitiveness (Ma & Lu, 2005). In China, business groups are coalitions of firms from multiple industries that interact over long periods of time and are distinguished by elaborate inter-firm networks of lending, trade, ownership, and social relations (Keister, 1998). A business group is a result of a market economy with high development, an outcome of mass production and specialization, and an institutional arrangement or an intermediary institution between the market and the firm. Business groups are viewed as efficient responses to market failures.

As a firm's group affiliation is concerned, if its largest shareholder is a particular business group, the firm should be regarded as this groups' affiliate. Chinese business groups were formed and developed under economic transition. One of the results of economic transformation is that the state-owned economy maintains absolute control in the important industries and key areas of the national economy. Most business groups in China were transformed from previously SOEs, which hold a large portion of shares of affiliated firms. Further, consistent with the classification of ownership type, China's listed firm's largest shareholder is considered to be state-owned if it falls in one of the following three "state-owned" categories: government agencies, state-owned nongroup enterprises, or state-owned business groups (Ma, Yao, & Xi, 2006).

At the society level, China has been experiencing the transition from a planned economy to a market economy (Boisot & Child, 1996). According to an institutional perspective, the market forces and formulation of the formal regulations are underdeveloped in countries experiencing transition (Peng, 2002). It takes time for the transition countries to establish and improve the formal institutions not qualitatively different from industry-specific characteristics in the West. The governments are directly involved to promote the business groups before the formal institutional environment is well developed. Thus, a fundamental characteristic of the Chinese market is that the government's power has streamlined economic sections on one hand (Hassard, Sheehan, & Morris, 1999); on the other hand, the government is still involved in direct intervention in economic affairs in many aspects. Under this circumstance, state-owned business groups can enjoy governmental support by receiving favorable conditions, such as funds, capital, licenses for specific businesses, technology, land, and information (Guthrie, 2005; Nolan, 2001). In this way, it is easier for state-owned business groups to save transaction costs while dealing with the relationship with the government than it is for the nonstate-owned counterparts (Demsetz, 1983). Meanwhile, compared to the nonstate counterparts, state-owned business groups enjoy more favorable policy support from the government, which provides their affiliations with better access to scarce resources, such as capital, material inputs, and skilled personnel that will improve firm performance. Thus, evidence supports a positive group affiliation effect:

Hypothesis 1: In China's transition economy, state-owned business groups have a positive impact on the performance of affiliated firms.

However, there are both benefits and costs associated with group affiliation, and it is far from clear whether all affiliated firms participate in the distribution of group benefits and costs.

As the dominant owner, the parent company both pursues maximum benefits of the whole group and exerts control on affiliated firms if necessary. Thus, the ownership structure of parent business groups contributed to the performance of group-affiliated firms. Empirical studies in developed countries show that other things being equal, the more control there is over affiliated firms, the worse their financial performance is. When a parent company has dominant ownership, it gains respective voting rights in the company's board and therefore could influence the latter's decision. A parent company, as the dominant owner, could use these control rights to leverage a large amount of assets by investing in a small fraction of ownership in others to achieve its objectives or interest. This is achieved when a company uses deviations from one-share-one vote, pyramiding ownership structure, and cross-holdings as means to control a target firm (Morck, Wolfenzon, & Yeung, 2005; Scharfstein & Stein, 2000). Empirical studies in Asian corporations have suggested that higher control rights would cause a serious agency problem when diversification increases because a parent company could extend its control to large number of companies (Claessens, Djankov, Fan, & Lang, 1999; Lins, 1999; Lins & Servaes, 2002). However, listed affiliated firms with the dominant ownership owned by parent companies are unable to take part in corporate governance as independent market participants. Therefore, under the unique property rights system and imperfect financial market mechanism, the listed affiliated firms may follow the malpractices of the state-owned parent companies. Unlike their Western counterparts, whose ownership structure is decided by the capital input, Chinese business groups were formed in a distinctive governance style; that is, parent companies hold a majority of equity stake and absolute control in an affiliate. The governance structure of affiliated firms performs no function since it is unable to counterbalance the absolute control of parent companies. In this group system with less check-and-balance power, deviation of control and residual claims lead to expanding ultimate shareholders' preference of control benefits, which creates negative externalities and allocate resources inefficiently.

Due to the dominant control of the parent companies in the groups, it is difficult to design incentive, monitoring, and control mechanisms in the affiliated firms with this ownership structure. Therefore, the right-balancing function of corporate governance in the group affiliations fails, especially when parent group companies expropriate affiliations' value by utilizing its status as a dominant shareholder (Clarke, 2003; Nee, Opper, & Wong, 2007; Yiu et al., 2005). While state-owned business groups maybe advantageous in the early stages of reform, the lack of connection between principals and agents and the lack of supervision of the principals may create inefficiencies that have negative long-term consequences (Keister, 2001). We therefore posit a negative group affiliation effect:

Hypothesis 2: During the China's transition economy, state-owned business groups have a negative impact on the performance of affiliated firms.

Different from the viewpoint of "all state-owned enterprises are intrinsically less effective" raised by the ownership school, the management school does not believe that there is anything intrinsically inefficient about state ownership itself. In accordance with management school, the reason the enterprises have low efficiency is that government, as the largest shareholder, had ineffective management on its investments. State-controlled firms are not different from those listed firms in market economies that have wide spread public ownership, and a firm's performance depends on its management culture and the clarity of its goals and objectives (Chang & Singh, 1997; Wortzel & Wortzel, 1989).

The management school argues that granting subsidiaries certain degree of autonomy may bring many advantages, including the more efficient utilization of information. As to the SOEs, the efficiency of the firms will be improved since the governments grant more autonomy to employees and managers. Chinese governments are striving to create a liberalized institutional environment for economic development. As a result, the affiliations of state-owned business groups are not different from those of nonstate-owned business groups. We therefore develop the following hypothesis:

Hypothesis 3: In China's transition economy, the performance of affiliations of state-owned and nonstate-owned business groups is not obviously different.

While business groups may be advantageous early in reform, the advantage of business groups will diminish as market system and soft market infrastructure are well developed (Carney, Shapiro, & Tang, 2009). Soft market infrastructure consists of a variety of organizations and actors, such as technical standards committees, consumer watchdogs, market research firms, executive recruitment agencies, and financial institutions that facilitate economic specialization and market efficiency (Khanna & Palepu, 1997). Firstly, the benefits associated with affiliated firms will gradually erode as market institutions are established (Khanna & Palepu, 1997; Khanna & Yafeh, 2007). The financial intermediaries in emerging markets are either absent or not fully evolved. Under this situation, the efficiency of allocating scarce capital and financing resources is low (Khanna & Palepu, 1997). The poorly developed financial system makes it difficult to convert bank savings to external investment. A banking system to a great extent has been a government intervention. The loan and value contribution does not scale linearly, so that the capital is unable to flow to the efficient sectors, which reduces the efficiency of resource allocation. In this regard, an internal capital market within the business groups offers a competitive advantage over independent firms in the absence of a well-developed national financial market. In particular, firms need capital to survive and develop, especially when they face increasing market size, technology updating, and mergers and acquisitions. If a firm is independent, it is difficult to get access to scarce capital where markets are inadequate at allocating funds (Keister, 2001) and obtaining needed loans from the bank. Thus, the reserves of the capital in different affiliated firms within business group are crucial.

The business groups establish finance companies as an intermediary institution to manage cash flows among affiliated firms (Goto, 1982; Keister, 1998). Insider lending within the group appears to give firms access to otherwise scarce capital and achieve better economic benefit in circumstances of poor-quality institutions and extensive market failure (Keister, 2001). Firms with excessive cash flow can invest in weak affiliated firms with a shortage of capital that face investment opportunity both within and outside the group. However, as the financial market and the situation of resource allocation improve, the efficiency of capital allocation is enhanced, and the advantages of the intermediary finance companies will lessen.

Secondly, the development of market institutions facilitates the emergence of more specialized independent firms that will compete away the excess returns of group affiliated firms. Khanna and Yafeh (2007) argue that the efficiency of capital accumulation and allocation in internal capital market within the group decrease as external capital market improves. If the resource allocation in the securities market is strong-form efficient, the effectiveness of professional investment banks and the diversified investment portfolio of institutional investors is higher than the diversification of the business groups, and the effectiveness of the internal market no longer exists. The business groups will disappear with the progress of soft market infrastructure and market institutions. Institutionalizing market mechanisms is conducive to entry by unaffiliated and independent firms, which poses pressures on affiliated firms. Thus, we propose:

Hypothesis 4: The role of the business group to improve the performance of the affiliated firms will weaken with time.

2.3 Study design

2.3.1 Sample selection and data source

As suggested by Yiu et al. (2005), a single country appears to be a sensible approach to an examination of the comparative performance of business group affiliations and independent firms, as it eliminates the confounding effect of different economies. Accordingly, this study used a sample of China's publicly listed companies. We studied the financial performance of group-holding listed enterprises to reflect the value of listed firms. There are two reasons for this. First, given the difficulty of data collection in emerging economies (Wright et al., 2005), we believe that the financial results of the listed group affiliations are the most consistent, accurate, and transparent among the information available for Chinese firms. In order to examine the above hypothesis, the selected sample from the years 2005 to 2010 listed affiliations of large business groups in Shandong Province. After 20 years' development, by the end of 2010 there is a relatively effective and improved outside supervision mechanism for the stock markets in Shenzhen and Shanghai. Since 2000, the State Statistics Bureau has published China's large enterprises (business groups) development annual reports. Scholars can attain the information on affiliated firms from the reports. Second, a majority of the listed affiliations were core companies associated with large business groups (Keister, 1998, 2000; Nolan, 2001).

The definition of "business group" in this chapter is based on Business Group Regulations of Registration and Management released by the National Industrial and Commercial Bureau: "an economically collected organization that consists of a parent company, as the main entity, and numerous independent enterprises and nonenterprise organizations that are linked by investing and production/operation collaboration" (The State Statistics Bureau of the People's Republic of China, 2001, p. 18).

There are three requirements for being a business group: (1) the registered capital owned by core affiliated firms or the parent company is required to exceed RMB 50 million, and the group must own at least five affiliated firms; (2) the total registered capital owned by the parent company and all affiliated firms is required to exceed RMB 100 million; and (3) each affiliated firm in the business group takes a legal person status.

We derived the basic sample from the official websites of the Shanghai and Shenzhen Stock Exchanges as well as listed companies' annual reports and websites. Because the presence of foreign shareholders would significantly influence a listed company's corporate governance and performance in emerging economies (Khanna & Palepu, 2000b), and also because companies with three consecutive years of net profits are eligible to issue shares to foreign investors according to the regulations of China Securities Regulatory Commission (CSRC), we only included those having no B-shares and H-shares in our sample. This study focuses on listed companies with only A-shares in Shanghai and Shenzhen Stock Exchanges for five sample years from 2005 to 2010.

To minimize potential problems, we eliminated the following sample companies: (1) financially distressed listed firms; (2) listed firms in the financial sector due to the heterogeneous accounting practices; (3) listed firms that are collectively owned, foreign owned, social group owned, and employee stock-owned plan association owned, according to the last controllers; and (4) listed firms whose information is not accessible or partially missing.

The final sample is 80 out of 121 publicly listed companies that use A-shares in the two stock exchanges. Of these, 40 are listed on the Shanghai Stock Exchange and 40 on the Shenzhen Stock Exchange.

2.3.2   Variables

We measured the dependent variable as return on asset (ROA), calculated as net income divided by total assets. ROA has been the most widely used performance measure in related studies of business group performance (e.g., Caves & Uekusa, 1976; Khanna & Palepu, 2000a; Lincoln & Gerlach, 2004; Nakatani, 1984). ROA may be more reliable than stock market-based alternatives (such as Tobin's Q) when stock markets are in their early stages of development. For China, this is particularly true of the early period. Since there exists a large amount of nontradable shares and stock market segmentation in China, the stock price severely deviates from the firm performance. The credibility of the firm performance is doubtful if Tobin's Q is used as the performance measure.

2.3.2.1 Dummy variables

Dummy variables are also called nominal variables representing the nature of other factors. This variable takes the value of 0 or 1: solely state-owned = 1; state-foreign/ private partnership firms and others = 0. The dummy variables are introduced because the governance structure and equity nature have a distinct impact on the performance of listed firms. Dummy variables are used as devices to improve the accuracy of the model, to sort data into mutually exclusive categories, and to enlarge sample size and reduce errors.

2.3.2.2 Data screening

Prior to the statistical analyses, we evaluated our study samples to make sure our data set satisfies basic statistical assumptions. We screened the data in two ways. First, our study sample is reasonably large for hypothesis testing. Second, we collected large enough samples to increase the data reliability.

2.3.2.3 Data standardization

Since data from various sources have different characteristics and dimensions, this present study standardized the data. We fixed the data between 0 and 1 through defining maximum and minimum value.

2.4 Data analysis and result

With the deepening of economic reform, there is an equal number of state-owned and nonstate-owned business groups for our sample (Table 2.1).

This hypothesis examines if there is significant difference between the performance of listed firms affiliated with nonstate-owned business groups in different years. The symbols "≤" and "≥" in this table describe the null hypothesis. A stands for "accept" and R stands for "refuse." The decimals indicate P value (the significance level is 0.05). Table 2.2 indicates the performance of listed firms affiliated with nonstate-owned business, with the best in 2007 and the second best in 2007. There is little difference for the rest of the years.

This hypothesis examines if there is a significant difference between the performance of listed firms affiliated with state-owned business groups in different years. The symbols "≤" and "≥" in this table describe the null hypothesis. A stands for "accept" and R stands for "refuse." The decimals indicate P value (the significance level is 0.05). Table 2.3 indicates the performance of listed firms affiliated with nonstate-owned business, with the best in 2007 and the second best in 2010. There is little difference for the rest of the years.

This hypothesis examines if there is a significant difference between the performance of listed affiliated firms of state-owned and nonstate-owned business groups

Table 2.1 Data screening and data standardization

	Stock code	Equity nature	Z2005	Z2006	Z2007	Z2008	Z2009	Z2010
1	600157	0	0.16	0.01	0	0.009	0.3	1
2	600162	0	0	0.17	1	0.72	0.7	0.37
3	600735	0	0.37	0	1	0.66	0.73	0.55
4	600966	0	0.58	0.55	0.67	1	0.29	0
5	000407	0	0	0.18	0.02	1	0.83	0.8
6	000416	0	0.57	0	0.03	0.1	0.51	1
7	000506	0	0.57	0.85	1	0.99	0.35	0
8	000639	0	0.47	0.4	0.41	0.25	0	1
9	000726	0	0.6	0.48	1	0	0.01	0.4
10	000739	0	1	0.96	0.12	0.08	0.13	0
11	000811	0	0.24	0.13	0.28	0	0.56	1
12	000830	0	1	0.26	0.94	0.87	0	0.5
13	000869	0	0	0.25	0.57	0.89	1	1
14	002026	0	0.92	0.39	1	0	0.1	0.88
15	002041	0	0.57	0.02	0.03	0	0.54	1
16	002073	0	1	0	0.29	0.6	0.24	0.29
17	002078	0	1	0.29	0.4	0	0.39	0.5
18	002083	0	0.96	1	0.17	0.08	0	0.32
19	002088	0	1	0.33	0.45	0.38	0.02	0
20	002094	0	1	0.3	0.28	0.08	0	0.31
21	002107	0	1	0.92	0.64	0.59	0.57	0
22	002111	0	1	0.96	0.21	0.29	0	0.02
23	002217	0	1	0.52	0.52	0.27	0.02	0
24	002242	0	0	0.15	0.19	0.88	1	0.98
25	600076	0	0.37	0.69	0	0.6	1	0.77
26	600180	0	0.95	0.85	0	1	0.94	0.9
27	600212	0	0.94	0.85	0	1	1	0.97
28	600219	0	0.36	0.16	1	0.41	0	0.38
29	600308	0	0.63	0.54	0.51	0.47	1	0
30	600385	0	0.58	0	1	0.6	0.97	0.72
31	600586	0	0	0.13	0.81	0.12	0.04	1
32	600766	0	1	0.9	0.9	0	0.9	0.82
33	600777	0	1	0.88	0	0.86	0.82	0
34	600898	0	0.93	0.83	0.8	0	0.52	1
35	600986	0	0.15	0	0.01	0.08	1	0.08
36	660467	0	0.4	0.3	1	0.35	0	0.35
37	600532	1	1	0.95	1	0	0.94	0.34

Continued

Table 2.1 Continued

	Stock code	Equity nature	Z2005	Z2006	Z2007	Z2008	Z2009	Z2010
38	600698	1	1	1	0.05	0.96	0	0.23
39	600760	1	0.65	0	0.84	1	0.87	0.74
40	600960	1	0	0.05	0.23	0.14	0.38	1
41	600027	1	1	1	0.95	0	0.98	0.8
42	000338	1	0	0.5	0.78	0.46	0.67	1
43	000423	1	0	0.27	0.61	0.91	0.51	1
44	000488	1	0.99	0.81	1	0.58	0	0.36
45	000554	1	0.14	0.5	0.42	1	0.01	0
46	000599	1	0.16	0.05	0.22	1	0.63	0
47	000617	1	1	0.75	0.5	0.46	0.18	0
48	000655	1	0	0.62	0.87	1	0.54	0.79
49	000677	1	0.71	0.81	1	0.42	0.8	0
50	000680	1	0	0.52	1	0.68	0.4	0.9
51	000682	1	1	0	0.29	0.2	0.3	0.31
52	000720	1	0.99	1	0.66	0	1	0.92
53	000756	1	0	0.2	0.27	0.33	1	0.95
54	000822	1	1	0.97	0.94	0.82	0	0.7
55	000880	1	0	0.22	0.92	1	0.74	0.69
56	000915	1	0	0.1	0.12	0.14	0.52	1
57	000951	1	0.39	1	0.45	0.32	0.46	0
58	000957	1	0.16	0	0.74	0.7	1	0.3
59	000977	1	0.2	0.22	0.31	0.7	0	1
60	002072	1	1	0.92	0.91	0.54	0	0.84
61	002193	1	0.25	1	0.33	0.32	0	0.38
62	600017	1	0	0.31	0.08	1	0.58	1
63	600022	1	0.71	0.67	1	0.33	0	0
64	600188	1	0.41	0.15	0.34	1	0	0.47
65	600223	1	0.72	0	0.67	0.32	1	0.87
66	600309	1	0.26	0.58	1	0.96	0	0.19
67	600319	1	0.2	0.17	0.08	0.04	1	0
68	600350	1	0	0.5	1	1	0.37	0.6
69	600426	1	0.69	0.58	1	0.87	0.8	0
70	600448	1	0.92	0.97	0.36	0.89	0	1
71	600529	1	0	0.06	0.11	1	0.53	0.74
72	600547	1	0	0.33	0.35	1	0.62	0.72
73	600587	1	0	0.26	0.12	0.47	0.97	1
74	600727	1	0.96	0.95	0.95	0	0.88	1

Table 2.1 **Continued**

	Stock code	Equity nature	Z2005	Z2006	Z2007	Z2008	Z2009	Z2010
75	600756	1	0.78	0	0.44	1	0.65	0.6
76	600783	1	0.23	0.16	0.2	0.17	0	1
77	600784	1	0	0.18	0.05	0.07	0.22	1
78	600789	1	0.19	0	0.58	0.63	0.6	1
79	600858	1	1	0.96	0.27	0.4	0.36	0
80	600882	1	0.96	0.99	1	0	0.9	0.23

Table 2.2 **Hypothesis testing of matched sample**

	Nonstate-owned				
Nonstate-owned	2006	2007	2008	2009	2010
2005	≤R 0.000493	≥A 0.067495	≤R 0.022162	≥A 0.063094	=A 0.19211
2006		=A 0.544333	=A 0.544333	=A 0.701781	=A 0.325052
2007			=A 0.536471	=A 0.838974	=A 0.642911
2008				=A 0.61768	=A 0.297735
2009					=A 0.401197

Table 2.3 **Hypothesis testing of matched sample**

	State-owned				
State-owned	2006	2007	2008	2009	2010
2005	=A 0.503883	≥R 0.038094	=A 0.228688	=A 0.652734	≥R 0.018884
2006		=A 0.160472	=A 0.370357	=A 0.973143	=A 0.287222
2007			=A 0.957536	=A 0.255263	=A 0.859041
2008				=A 0.391308	=A 0.819983
2009					=A 0.213842

Table 2.4 **Hypothesis testing of double sample heteroscedasticity**

Years	2005	2006	2007	2008	2009	2010
Equity nature	Nonstate-owned					
State-owned	≥R 0.027474	=A 0.461781	≤R 0.014443	=A 0.096582	=A 0.740013	=A 0.51593

in the same years. We used a double-sample heteroscedasticity hypothesis. The symbols "≤" and "≥" in this table describes the null hypothesis. A stands for "accept" and R stands for "refuse." The decimals indicate P value (the significance level is 0.05). Table 2.4 indicates that the performance of listed firms affiliated with nonstate-owned business groups is better than the listed firms affiliated with nonstate-owned business groups in 2005. The performance of listed firms affiliated with state-owned business groups is better than the listed firms affiliated with nonstate-owned business groups in 2007. There is little difference for the rest of the years.

2.5 Conclusion

We examined five years (2005–2010) of time span data on 80 business groups. Through analyzing statistics of listed firms, we gained an overall insight into the performance of listed affiliated firms of state-owned and nonstate-owned business groups. First, the performance between the state-owned and nonstate-owned listed affiliated firms does not differentiate much. This supports Hypothesis 3, in which ownership does not have much impact on firm performance. Second, the longitudinal comparison between the listed affiliated firms of state-owned and nonstate-owned business groups does not differentiate much. This does support Hypothesis 4, which states that the capital market in Shandong Province needs to be improved.

Rather than focusing merely on state-owned business groups in previous studies (Lu & Yao, 2006; White, Hoskisson, Yiu, & Bruton, 2008; Yiu et al., 2005), the present study also explores nonstate-owned business groups. Based on the comparison of firm performance of listed affiliated firms between state-owned and nonstate-owned business groups, the study presents the idea of reform on business groups, that is, the improvement of macroeconomic policy has been acknowledged as one important way to improve the market performance of SOEs. This result enriches theories of business groups, supports the ideas of management school, and provides a new point of view for corporate governance.

Our research findings have political implications for the development of business groups in Shandong Province. Large- and medium-sized SOEs account for a large portion of SOEs in Shandong Province, and they are a pillar of the national economy. Due to the Chinese contextual specificity, the privatization of SOEs in China is sensitive; thus, the reform on property rights cannot be adopted widely in China. In the late 1990s, the government in Shandong Province formulated many market-based policies, which have great influence on firm reform and economic development. With regard to state-owned business groups, governments need to further improve their management style, such as granting employees more autonomy in respect to production and marketing. The governments need to further gradually streamline their economic agencies/sections and change the functions from a direct administrative role of monitoring subordinate enterprises to a more indirect role of formulating regulations and policies. As the largest shareholder of SOEs, governments need to provide motivations to make managers strive to improve the performance and effectiveness of SOEs through market scanning and responsive strategy making. In addition, the small performance difference of the listed affiliated firms of business groups in different years implies that the well-developed financial market and other formal institutions have to be established to support economic activities with low transaction costs.

Our research limits discussion to the listed affiliated firm of business groups located in Shandong Province. The sample should be extended by including nonlisted firms that are affiliated with business groups: their data should provide us an with in-depth insight into management practices of affiliated firms and their relations to the dominant owner as well as to others. Last but not least, we have not considered geographic/international expansion, which is likely to be a cutting-edge topic both in practice and research concerning Chinese business groups.

References

Bertrand, M., Mehta, P., & Mullainathan, S. (2002). Ferreting out tunnelling: An application to Indian business groups. *Quarterly Journal of Economics, 117*(1), 121–148.

Boisot, M., & Child, J. (1996). From fiefs to clans and network capitalism: Explaining China's emerging economic order. *Administrative Science Quarterly, 41*, 600–624.

Carney, M., Shapiro, D., & Tang, Y. (2009). Business group performance in China: Ownership and temporal considerations. *Management and Organization Review, 5*(2), 167–193.

Caves, R., & Uekusa, M. (1976). *Industrial organization in Japan*. Washington, DC: The Brookings Institution.

Chang, S., & Hong, J. (2000). Economic performance of group-affiliated Companies in Korea: Intra-group resource sharing and internal business transactions. *Academy of Management Journal, 43*(3), 429–448.

Chang, H., & Singh, A. (1997). Can large firms be run efficiently without being bureaucratic. *Journal of International Development, 9*(6), 865–875.

Claessens, S. (1997). Corporate governance and equity prices: Evidence from the Czech and Slovak Republics. *Journal of Finance, 52*(4), 1641–1658.

Claessens, S., Djankov, S., Fan, J. P. H., & Lang, L. H. P. (1999). *Expropriation of minority shareholders in East Asia*. SSRN working paper.

Clarke, D. (2003). Corporate governance in China: An overview. *China Economic Review, 14*(4), 494–507.

Demsetz, H. (1983). The structure of ownership and the theory of the firm. *Journal of Law and Economics, 26*(2), 375–399.

Fan, J. P. H., Wong, T. J., & Zhang, T. (2005). *The emergence of corporate pyramids in China.* Working paper, Chinese University of Hong Kong.

Goto, A. (1982). Business groups in a market economy. *European Economic Review, 19*, 53–70.

Guthrie, D. (2005). Organizational learning and productivity: State structure and foreign investment in the rise of the Chinese corporation. *Management and Organization Review, 1*(2), 165–195.

Hassard, J., Sheehan, J., & Morris, J. (1999). Enterprise reform in post-Deng china. *International Studies of Management & Organization, 29*(3), 54–83.

Keister, L. (1998). Engineering growth: Business group structure and firm performance in China's transition economy. *American Journal of Sociology, 104*(2), 404–440.

Keister, L. (2000). *Chinese business groups: The structure and impact of interfirm relations during economic development.* Oxford, NY: Oxford University Press.

Keister, L. (2001). Exchange structures in transition: Lending and trade relations in Chinese business groups. *American Sociological Review, 66*, 336–360.

Khanna, T., & Palepu, K. (1997). Why focused strategies may be wrong for emerging markets. *Harvard Business Review, 75*(4), 41–51.

Khanna, T., & Palepu, K. (2000a). The future of business groups in emerging markets: Long-run evidence from Chile. *Academy of Management Journal, 43*, 268–285.

Khanna, T., & Palepu, K. (2000b). Is group affiliation profitable in emerging markets? An analysis of diversified Indian business groups. *Journal of Finance, 55*, 867–892.

Khanna, T., & Rivkin, J. (2001). Estimating the performance of business groups in emerging markets. *Strategic Management Journal, 22*, 45–74.

Khanna, T., & Yafeh, Y. (2007). Business groups in emerging markets: Paragons or parasites? *Journal of Economic Literature, 45*(2), 331–372.

Lee, K., & Wing, W. T. (2001). Business groups in China compared with Korean Chaebols. *The Post-Financial Crisis Challenges for Asian Industrialization, 10*, 721–747.

Li, Y., Sun, Y., & Liu, Y. (2006). An empirical study of SOEs' market orientation in transitional China. *Asia Pacific Journal of Management, 23*, 93–113.

Lincoln, J. R., & Gerlach, M. L. (2004). *Japan's network economy: Structure, persistence, and change.* Cambridge, UK: Cambridge University press.

Lins, Karl (1999). *Equity ownership and firm value in emerging markets.* Manuscript, University of North Carolina.

Lins, K., & Servaes, H. (2002). Is corporate diversification beneficial in emerging markets. *Financial Management, 31*, 5–31.

Lu, Y., & Yao, J. (2006). The impact of state ownership and control mechanisms on the performance of group affiliated companies in China. *Asia Pacific Journal of Management, 23*(4), 485–503.

Ma, X., & Lu, J. (2005). The critical role of business groups in China. *Ivey Business Journal, 69* (5), 1–12.

Ma, X., Yao, X., & Xi, Y. (2006). Business group affiliation and firm performance in China's transition economy: A focus on ownership voids. *Asia Pacific Journal of Management, 23*, 467–483.

Morck, R. K., Wolfenzon, D., & Yeung, B. (2005). Corporate governance, economic entrenchment, and growth. *Journal of Economic Literature, 43*, 655–720.

Nakatani, I. (1984). The economic role of financial corporate grouping. In M. Aoki (Ed.), *The economic analysis of the Japanese firm* (pp. 227–258). Amsterdam: North Holland.

Nee, V., Opper, S., & Wong, S. (2007). Developmental state and corporate governance in China. *Management and Organization Review, 3*(1), 19–53.

Nolan, P. (2001). *China and the global economy.* Basingstoke, UK: Palgrave.

Peng, M. (2002). Towards an institution-based view of business strategy. *Asia Pacific Journal of Management, 19,* 251–267.

Qian, Y. (1996). Enterprise reform in China: Agency problems and political control. *Economics of Transition, 4*(2), 427–447.

Scharfstein, D. S., & Stein, J. C. (2000). The dark side of internal capital markets: Divisional rent-seeking and inefficient investment. *Journal of Finance, 55*(6), 2537–2564.

The State Statistics Bureau of the People's Republic of China (2001). *China's Statistical Yearbook.* Beijing: The Chinese Statistics Press.

White, R. E., Hoskisson, R. E., Yiu, D., & Bruton, G. D. (2008). Employment and market innovation in Chinese business group affiliated firms: The role of group control systems. *Management and Organization Review, 4*(2), 225–256.

Wortzel, H., & Wortzel, L. (1989). Privatization: Not the only answer. *World Development, 17*(5), 633–641.

Wright, M., Filatotchev, I., Hoskisson, R. E., & Peng, M. W. (2005). Strategy research in emerging economies: Challenging the conventional wisdom. *Journal of Management Studies, 42*(1), 1–33.

Xu, X., & Wang, Y. (1999). Ownership structure and corporate governance in Chinese stock companies. *China Economic Review, 10*(1), 75–98.

Yiu, D., Bruton, G., & Lu, Y. (2005). Understanding business group performance in an emerging economy: Acquiring resources and capabilities in order to prosper. *Journal of Management Studies, 42*(1), 183–296.

Labor litigation in China

3

J. Shen
Shenzhen University, Shenzhen City, Guangdong Province, China

3.1 Introduction

Labor litigation is the last recourse for settling labor disputes in China. Legal action becomes extremely important for maintaining justice in employment relations as employment relations become more and more complicated and a large number of labor disputes cannot be settled through consultation and arbitration. China's labor litigation has been popular practice over the last decade, but not yet looked at in the literature of human resource management and industrial relations. This may be because labor litigation is a new thing and usually regarded as a subject of law. As a result, little is known about China's labor litigation.

This chapter aims to provide a better understanding of labor litigation in order to facilitate an assessment of the overall labor dispute resolution system in today's China. It looks at the characteristics and functions of labor litigation as well as issues such as the development of the labor litigation system, the factors associated with its growing use, its process, and its role in settling labor disputes. The limitations of the labor litigation system and the practical implications are also discussed.

3.2 Labor litigation

Labor litigation generally includes all labor disputes that are formally submitted to a court about any subject in which one party is claimed to have violated labor codes or labor law, but not committed a crime. Labor litigation is regarded to be effective in maintaining justice in employment relations as this process inherently involves forces that, once invoked, are hard for an individual litigant to keep under control. Ideally, labor litigation should comply with the principles of being easily assessable, informal, speedy, and inexpensive compared with other judicial systems, as Donovan Commission Report mentioned (MacMillan, 1999), making the system available to both employees and employers. In reality, among these four principles, only has inexpensiveness been realized. Individual labor litigation is also beneficial to employers in market economies where there are independent trade unions, as legal cases are likely lead to less collective bargaining and strike actions.

Over the last decade, labor litigation has become more important for employees when compared with collective bargaining and strike actions (Schneider, 2001). The legal regulations on employment relations contributed to the development of labor litigation. Schneider (2001) argues that the frequent legal complaints from German workers are because of the strongly regulated labor market. In addition, the frequent use of labor litigation is also usually associated with the following four factors:

The Strategies of China's Firms.

- The frequent occurrence of labor disputes resulted from flexible terms of employment (Schneider, 2001). Naturally, the more labor disputes, the more legal cases.
- A lack of effective alternative dispute resolution mechanisms as filters of labor disputes, such as weak unions (Brown, Bernd, & Sessions, 1997; Earnshaw, Goodman, Harrison, & Marchington, 1998; Towers, 1997). Normally, a range of prelegal mechanisms are introduced in order to reduce the court cases, so the less effective the prelegal mechanisms, the more legal cases.
- The high unemployment rate, making it harder to find alternative employment (Schneider, 2001). This is relevant to many employment relations issues, but particularly to dismissals.
- The legal framework enhancing workers' rights (Schneider, 2001). Legal frameworks of employment relations make both employers and employees aware of their rights and provide guidance for courts to settle disputes.

Considerable variations in court cases between European nations are apparently associated with these factors. Figure 3.1 shows the number of court cases that a typical large private European company employing at least 1000 employees in the countries concerned expects in a year. Belgium ranks with Poland and the Netherlands as one of the three litigation capitals of Europe, while employers in Sweden and Finland are rarely involved in court cases. A typical large company in Belgium usually needs

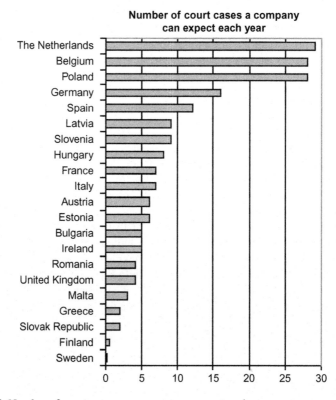

Figure 3.1 Number of court cases a company can expect each year.
Source: The Federation of European Employers (2004), http://www.fedee.com/litigation.shtml (accessed 13.05.06).

to defend 28 court cases brought by present or former employees every year, but a similar firm in Sweden faces an average of only 1 case in every 10 years. There are a large number of dismissal disputes in Belgium where it is relatively easy for employers to dismiss employees and no there is formal system for dispute resolution outside the courts. Employers in Sweden and Finland rarely need to enter a courtroom because in Scandinavia, despite the mass of employment legislation, there are many ways for employees to resolve disputes without the need for court action (The Federation of European Employers, 2004).

Due to the fact that going to court is normally a costly and time-consuming process, labor litigation is normally not the first choice of labor dispute resolution for employees or employers. The volume of cases is lower in some European nations, such as the Slovak Republic, Poland, Spain, Greece, and Italy, where the legal procedure takes longer. For example, in the Slovak Republic, it takes an average of 22 months to get through the court procedure. And if formal conciliation processes do not work, further delay in litigation is likely (The Federation of European Employers, 2004). "There are a succession of institutions that mediate the conflict before it reaches the litigation stage" in many countries, such as Britain, Germany, and Scandinavia (Schneider, 2001, p. 269). Even if a dispute has been brought before the court, further attempts are made to reach pretrial settlement. In fact, only a small fraction of labor disputes eventually make it to the trial hearings.

As labor litigation is normally regarded as a subject of law, it has generally not been much considered in the industrial relations or employment studies literature. Little is known about how effective the labor litigation system is in dealing with labor disputes and how supplementary it is to other labor resolution institutions.

3.3   The development of labor litigation in China

Resolving labor disputes through litigation is a postreform phenomenon. With the deepening of economic reform, employment relations have become more and more complicated, provoking widespread labor conflict. The prelegal channels have gradually shown an inability to resolve a considerable number of difficult labor disputes. Hence, like the Chinese saying, "only strong medicine cures serious illnesses," a more radical and effective legal mechanism is in great need. Meanwhile, China also seeks to regulate the labor market using the legal framework. "The position of the courts in the mechanism for resolving labor disputes can be understood from two perspectives: the ultimate right of the parties to take legal actions and the rights of the parties to apply for the enforcement of a valid labor arbitral award" (Mo, 2000, p. 36).

Recently, Chinese people have the right to settle their labor disputes through litigation, although they are always encouraged to take other channels, such as consultation and arbitration. The Labor Law states that the party that has objections to the ruling of the labor arbitration committee can bring the case to a people's court (Article 79, Chapter 5, the 1994 Labor Law). From the government's point of view, regulating industrial relations through the legal channels may even serve to avert a crisis situation where workers might actively seek to set up alternative trade unions or engage in mass protest (Chan, 2004). Rapidly increasing unemployment has also contributed to the growing use of labor litigation.

In March 22, 2001, the Supreme People's Court issued explanations on several issues regarding litigation of labor disputes (The Supreme People's Court, 2001) (hereafter SPC Explanations). Labor litigation is regulated mainly by the 1994 Labor Law and SPC Explanations. Supplemented by other judicial guidance, SPC Explanations provide detailed instructions for handling labor disputes in people's courts. According to SPC Explanations, if the disputants have rejected labor arbitration rulings, they can bring their cases before courts. People's courts deal with labor disputes, including:

(a) labor disputes arising from employment relations without signed labor contracts;
(b) labor disputes which occur in the course of implementing labor contracts; and
(c) disputes regarding retirees' pension, medical fees, injury insurance, and social insurance to which the original employers did not contribute.

Industry accident lawsuits normally fall within the category of civil litigation. Some local courts have re-categorized industry accidents as ordinary accident lawsuits in order to more effectively settle labor disputes.

3.4 Court

China does not have a specialist industrial or employment court. Labor disputes are dealt with by civil courts, following all civil court procedures. The composition of the Chinese civil court is different from that of employment tribunals or industrial courts in industrialized nations, such as Britain and Germany. In China, the court panel is comprised of professional judges; while the panel of employment tribunals or industrial courts is made up of a professional lawyer acting as chairperson and two lay judges who are drawn from a list of candidates nominated by trade unions and employers' organizations, respectively. Therefore, while the Western employment tribunal or industrial court has a structure and process that are similar to labor arbitration; the Chinese civil court is more legalistic and has fewer labor characteristics. The regulations regarding a Chinese civil court's jurisdiction are similar to that of a labor arbitration commission, that is, a court has jurisdiction over labor disputes where employees' salaries are formally paid. Chinese courts allow employees who work for overseas companies that are not situated in Mainland China to submit labor disputes.

Due to the fact that tripartite consultation committees and arbitration committees are largely controlled by the governments, Chinese civil courts are more independent (Fu & Choy, 2004). Courts have necessary power to render a final decision concerning labor disputes, such as freezing properties. The court fees for dealing with labor disputes are fixed to between RMB 30 and 50 Yuan, which are much lower than the fees for dealing with commercial cases. This is similar to labor litigation in Western market economies. For example, in order to make labor courts or employment tribunals highly accessible for claimants, legal costs in industrialized nations, such as the UK and Germany, are much lower compared to the ordinary courts (Schneider, 2001). Consequently, people's courts are generally reluctant to accept labor disputes because of the lack of capacity and poor financial incentives for dealing with labor disputes (Mo, 2000).

3.5 Legal services

Lawyers are an important component of the labor litigation system. Legal services are widely available in today's China and provided by three forms of law firms, including state ownership with limited liability, joint ownership with limited liability, and partnership with unlimited liability. Some of the lawyers operate from within the legal aid centers of university law schools or the trade unions while others have started their own private practices (Chen, 2004). The liability of the law firm with limited liability is limited to its total assets. The partners who established the law firm with unlimited liability, however, are responsible for the whole debt and liability of the firm. A state-owned law firm is established by an SOE, a university, or an institution. The other two forms of law firms are normally established by individuals. However, it is not clear about the advantages and disadvantages of each type of law firms (Mo, 2000).

Most law firms promote their business in local newspapers and other media, and have homepages on the Internet. In principle, legal service fees are regulated by local pricing bureaus. Under most circumstances, lawyers' fees are decided through discussions between the applicants and the lawyers. Similar to legal costs in the court, the lawyer's fees for dealing with labor disputes are usually relatively lower than for settling commercial disputes. Lawyers represent disputing parties not only at court but also in the process of mediation and labor arbitration.

The passage of the 1994 Labor Law has increased worker's awareness of their rights to use legal channels to seek justice in employment relations and also led to a substantial number of lawyers and paralegals offering services to workers who seek legal assistance. Nevertheless, it should be noted that Chinese workers' general awareness of China's laws, particular labor law, and regulations still remains low. Among the workers interviewed by The Hong Kong Christian Industrial Committee, a group that organizes and provides assistance to workers in Hong Kong and China, "Less than half of interviewees said they knew about labor law." None of the workers knew about other regulations concerning labor rights. Workers had no idea how to use the laws to defend their rights (Hong Kong Christian Industrial Committee, 2001). The management of lawyers is mainly regulated by the 1996 Law on Lawyers and is administered by the Ministry of Justice. The Ministry of Justice is responsible for stipulating the qualifications of lawyers, setting out the entry requirements for and issuing certificates to lawyers, approving the establishment of law firms and supervising the activities of lawyers and law firms. To obtain a practicing certificate for being a lawyer in China, a person must meet the following requirements:

- have at least a college law degree or equivalent education in law;
- pass the national professional exam for lawyers;
- have Chinese nationality, including citizens of Hong Kong and Macau; and
- a track record of good behavior (Mo, 2000).

Lawyers can establish their associations, which are regulated by government civil affair administration. Associations of lawyers have no power to issue practicing certificates. Instead, associations of lawyers at different levels provide training and establish networks for lawyers. Associations of lawyers "are meant to play an intermediary role between legal profession, the government and other sectors of the Chinese society" (Mo, 2000, p. 53).

3.6   The labor legislation procedure

According to the 1994 Labor Law, labor arbitration is the precondition for labor litigation. A court will not accept a case that has not gone through arbitration, or has been withdrawn or abandoned by disputants when it has been accepted for arbitration, or if a mediation agreement has been reached by disputants during the process of arbitration. A court will accept a case only if the arbitral award has been rendered and one or both parties do not accept the award. If any party is unhappy about the award made by a labor arbitral tribunal, s/he is entitled to submit the dispute to a court to litigate the matter within 15 days without having to prove the invalidity of the award. Therefore, labor litigation is actually the re-trial of the matters determined by the labor arbitral award made previously in labor arbitration (Mo, 2000). Such regulation has considerably reduced the number of labor disputes dealt with by courts. In order to facilitate handling labor disputes in courts, some have been converted by local people's courts into ordinary civil disputes, bypassing the arbitration committee. For example, in Shenzhen, industrial accidents have been re-categorized as ordinary torts and failure to pay salaries as ordinary debts (Fu & Choy, 2004).

The 1994 Labor Law Article 83 specifies the role of the court and the timeline for submitting disputes to the court. It stipulates that if any of the parties involved in a labor dispute have objections to an arbitration ruling, it can raise a lawsuit with a people's court within 15 days after receiving the ruling. If one of the parties involved neither raises a lawsuit nor implements the arbitration ruling within the legal period of time, the other party can apply to a people's court for forced implementation. Article 84 stresses that the procedure for submitting disputes relating to the implementation of collective contracts is the same as other labor disputes, showing the high extent to which collective contracts have been poorly implemented.

The plaintiff has to submit the dispute to a low-level court first. Both parties need to provide supporting evidence during the court hearing (Wang, 2004). If one party does not accept the ruling made by the low-level court, s/he can bring the case before a higher-level court. The normal legal process begins with filing a complaint in court by the plaintiff. If the lawsuit is regarded to be eligible, it will be accepted by the court. Then, the defendant gets notice of the complaint and an opportunity to answer, and a trial is scheduled. Even when a case has been brought before the court, the court will usually still attempt to settle the dispute through conciliation.

3.7   The role of litigation in dealing with labor disputes

Chinese labor litigation serves two purposes in terms of resolving labor disputes: enforcement of the arbitration award and handling disputes at a court of law. If any party refuses to implement the award that has been accepted previously in the process of arbitration, a lower court should enforce the award. An application for enforcing a labor arbitration award should be made in writing to a lower court where it has the jurisdiction. If the court accepts the application for enforcing the arbitration award, it should write to the other party to comply with the award within a stipulated time, or further legal actions may occur, such as freezing accounts and seizing property, etc.

Although the caseload of the courts has been significantly reduced by the adoption of compulsory labor arbitration before filing a lawsuit, the cases settled through litigation have increased substantially over the last decade. Table 3.1 shows that the number of labor law cases in China increased by 257%, from 28,285 to 100,923 from 1995 to 2001. In Shanghai, 30% of labor disputes had been dealt with through litigation from 1996 to 2001 (SHMTUC, 2002). From 1995 to 2004, labor lawsuits increased sevenfold to more than 18,000 cases (Shanghai Municipal Statistical Bureau, 1996–2005). However, the official statistics did not indicate the proportion of collective labor disputes and cases put forward by employers.

It is worth noting that although the court cases have increased rapidly over the last decade; the average court cases per large firm are very modest compared to the average European standard (see Figure 3.1).

According to the statistics released by SPC, in the cases dealt with by the people's court between 1995 and 2001, overall the laborers won 62.46%, 55.88%, and 55.32% in Shangdong, Guangdong, and Heilongjiang Provinces, respectively. In some courts, such as Ningbo in ZheJiang Province and Zhongshan in Guangdong, the workers have won more than 90% of cases.

It has not been possible for the researcher to obtain the details of either nationwide or regional court cases, as they are regarded to be secret documents by courts. It, therefore, becomes impossible to know to what extent courts have maintained justice in employment relations. Compromisingly, here we analyze some of cases that were available on the official websites of labor arbitration and litigation administration or national media when the study was conducted.

Case 1. Harbin Embroidery dismissed nine workers who did not attend a meeting regarding superannuation. The award of the labor arbitration sustained the dismissals.

Table 3.1 **Labor legal cases between 1995 and 2001**

	Cases handled at courts
1995	28,285
1996	37,558
1997	50,124
1998	59,118
1999	73,340
2000	78,373
2001	100,923

Source: China Law Yearbooks (1996–2002).

The workers did not accept the ruling and filed a lawsuit to Harbin Nanggang District Court in the beginning of 2004. The court overturned the arbitral ruling and awarded reinstatement (source: www.ldzc.com/law/jgct/11522.html, accessed 28.02.06).

Case 2. Mr. Liang started working for Guangdong Shende Plastic Metal Window Company (GSPMW) in June 2000 without signing a labor contract. Mr. Liang was dismissed during the company's restructuring in November 2004. The company refused to pay him unemployment compensation, stating that he did not have a labor contract. In March 2005, Mr. Liang filed a lawsuit in Guandong Ronggui Court. The court ruled that the company had to pay Mr. Liang unemployment compensation (source: www.ldzc.com/law/jgct/203921.html, accessed 28.02.06).

Case 3. After Mrs. Li's request that her former employer pay unemployment compensation after her resignation was not sustained by the arbitral award, she filed a lawsuit in Shenzhen Nangshang District Court in March 2004. She claimed that her resignation was not voluntary but that she misled by the management. The court's ruling supported the award of labor arbitration (source: www/ldzc.com/law/jgct.html, accessed 28.02.06).

Case 4. Mr. Lee's work-related illness became worse after he signed a one-off compensation agreement with his company. He requested continuing compensation, but labor arbitration did not sustain his request. He then filed a lawsuit in Shenzhen Baoan District Court. The district court did not sustain his request, either. He then filed a lawsuit in Shenzhen Municipal Court. The municipal court sustained his request (source: www.ldzc.com/law/gsal/200050320.htm, accessed 26.02.06).

Case 5. Mr. Dan was injured at work in January 2002 and became mentally incapacitated. Due to a disagreement regarding the amount of compensation Mr. Dan should receive, the case was not settled through labor arbitration. The case was then brought to the court in September 2002. The court's ruling is that the company should pay Mr. Dan 440,000 Yuan RMB.

Case 6. Feng Xingzhong, a 33-year-old Sichuan native, contracted life-threatening silicosis at work because of unsafe working conditions. On November 17, 2002, he lodged a compensation claim with Haifeng (LDAC), but his application was rejected on the grounds that he had exceeded the 60-day time limit. Feng then pursued a compensation lawsuit against Gaoyi Gems, first at the Haifeng County Court and later (on appeal) at the Shanwei Municipal Intermediate Court. Both courts dismissed Feng's case on the ground that there had been "no employment relationship" between him and the Gaoyi Gems Factory. On January 24, 2005, Feng lodged a second application for arbitration of his compensation claim, this time at the Huidong County LDAC and named the Gaoya Jewellery Manufacturing Plant (the factory's original name and location) as the respondent. On May 20, 2005, the Huidong LDAC instructed Gaoyi Jewellery to pay Feng a lump sum work-related disability award of 19,350 Yuan, plus 12,900 Yuan in reimbursement for medical fees, and also a disabled person's allowance of 806.25 Yuan per month for the rest of his life. However, LDAC rulings are nonbinding in nature, and since Gaoyi Jewellery had already relocated its production facilities to another jurisdiction, there was virtually no chance that this ruling would be enforced. On June 24, therefore, Feng brought a civil lawsuit against Gaoyi Jewellery in the Huidong County Court. The hearing took place on September 27, 2005.

On December 22, the court awarded him the above-mentioned total of 463,761 Yuan in compensation (China Labour Bulletin, 2006). Although justice was not served in the early stages of Feng vs. Gaoyi, the labor law was eventually upheld.

Case 7. Wuhua started working for Xi Chuan Palace Food Co (XCPF) in 2001. After a short time, he signed a 10-year labor contract as deputy general manager of the company. Wuhua left for another restaurant before the labor contract was due to end. He also poached chefs to join him at the new restaurant. Moreover, he took the cooking recipes that he developed when he worked for Xi Chuan Palace Food Co. The company's business was seriously affected. Therefore, the company brought the case to the Changdu Labor Arbitration Committee on August 30, 2004, requesting Wuhua to pay 5,000,000 Yuan RMB for breaching the labor contract. The company won the case. Wuhua did not accept the award and filed a lawsuit in Qingyang People's Court on May 20, 2005. The court supported the ruling of the labor arbitration committee.

In the case of Harbin Embroidery vs. nine workers, the award of reinstatement is consistent with the labor law. In the case of Mr. Liang vs. GSPMW, labor law was partly upheld. Reinstatement should have been awarded as the case was unfair dismissal. It is hard to assess whether the court upheld the labor law in the case of Mrs. Li vs. her employer. This is because of the difficulty in ascertaining the credibility of the plaintiff's claim that she was misled to resign. In the case of Mr. Lee vs. his company, Mr. Lee received unfair awards at the stage of arbitration and the low-level court. The employee's right was eventually protected by the higher-level court. In the case of Mr. Dan vs. his company, labor law was upheld. This case has set a precedent for future compensation cases involving occupational illnesses at least in the Guangdong jewelry industry. From the employer perspective, the foci of legal disputes are employee resignation (normally skilled workers or managers) before the labor contract is due and damage of factory equipment by workers. Wuhua vs. XCPC is a typical case. In this case, the legal award basically upheld the labor law although the compensation was over-awarded.

3.8 Conclusions

Labor litigation is one of the most important developments in China's employment relations since the economic reform. Although there is no specialist employment tribunal in China, labor litigation has become a key institution and an increasingly popular option for resolving labor disputes, indicated by the upsurge in the court cases during the last decade. Low-cost legal services are widely available to Chinese employees and employers. The frequent legal complaints from workers are due to several factors. First, there are an increasing number of labor disputes resulting from the fact that employment relations have become more complicated and almost unlimited power over employment has been given to employers. Naturally, more labor disputes occur as more are passed through filters and finally brought before courts. Second, the existing nonlegal channels, including traditional administrative and political means and newly emerged tripartite consultation and labor arbitration, are ineffective to settle these widespread and difficult labor disputes. A lack of enforcement of workers' rights is a reason for workers' unwillingness to reach settlements before litigation. The benefit of labor litigation is that the enforcement of a court ruling is basically ensured. Third, the use of labor litigation is a result of a gradually regulated labor market. The legal framework enhances legal dispute resolution. Fourth, the frequent legal complaints from workers are due to a lack of collective bargaining through which a large number of general and critical labor issues are resolved in market economies. As collective actions are illegal in China, employers do not regard the reduction in collective bargaining and strike actions as a benefit of labor litigation.

However, compared with many European nations, Chinese employers still face a modest number of court cases. This could be explained by many factors. First, labor arbitration is compulsory and has significantly reduced the number of court cases. Second, labor litigation is a complicated and time-consuming process. It is too difficult for many Chinese workers who lack the knowledge of law to go through the legal process. Third, individual labor litigation does not receive union support, and it usually becomes very hard for individual workers who lack resources to obtain adequate supporting evidence, which is required by the court.

A high proportion of court cases are found in the employee's favor; based on the limited number of published cases, labor law has basically been upheld. Even so, it is difficult to draw the conclusion that Chinese labor litigation is a fair and impartial adjudication of disputes. First, the national reinstatement rate in unfair dismissal cases is unknown because the related information is not accessible. Second, given that Chinese workers have a weak position, they normally do not request reinstatement; instead, they compromise by requesting unemployment compensation. Hence, even if they have won the case, justice is not done. The light penalty for violating workers' rights means that employers are not too concerned about litigation. China's current labor litigation has several limitations. First, "The most significant limitation on the court's jurisdiction is to shy away from policy-related cases…urban courts refuse cases that relate to redundancies and failure to pay employees resulting from the restructuring of government-led SOEs" (Fu & Choy, 2004, p. 20). Courts have limited their jurisdiction. The limited jurisdiction hinders the civil court from functioning as an effective labor dispute resolution institution.

Second, current labor disputes are dealt with by using the procedure of civil litigation. The civil litigation procedure is not always applicable to resolving labor disputes. Settling labor disputes is sometimes beyond the capacity of and has little financial benefit to civil courts. Consequently, civil courts are generally unwilling to deal with labor disputes. Also, settling labor dispute at the civil court is unfair to employees. Disputants involved in civil litigation usually have equal positions. However, employees are in a weaker position than that of employers in employment relations; the compromising claim is a reflection of workers' weaker position. Moreover, employees do not usually have resources to obtain adequate evidences required by the court for supporting claims. By using the same procedure as that of the civil court, workers' rights may not be effectively protected. In addition, because labor litigation is a long, drawn-out process and labor arbitration is compulsory, China's current labor litigation cannot be considered accessible or expeditious.

There are significant practical implications for improving labor litigation. There is a great need for establishing specialist industrial tribunals or employment tribunals. Chinese scholars such as Chang (1995) and Wang (2004) have argued that specialist labor courts are necessary in order to more effectively settle labor disputes and maintain justice in employment relations. Such a call is justifiable. Those dealing with labor disputes need specialized knowledge of labor law and other employment regulations. Labor disputes have different characteristics and regulations from civil disputes and therefore need a different court procedure. An undifferentiated procedure may hinder the effective and fair resolution of labor disputes. Moreover, dealing with labor disputes is a burden to civil courts that do not have the necessary personnel resources. In Western industrialized economies, industrial tribunals or labor courts play an important role in resolving labor disputes and minimizing social instability; Germany established industrial tribunals as early as 1890. Establishing labor courts mainly made up of lay judges is likely to achieve the goal of easy accessibility, informality, speediness, and low cost. Moreover, in industrialized nations, although there is a range of prelegal labor dispute resolution mechanisms as filters of conflict, disputants are free to bring cases directly before courts. Therefore, the current policy banning the bypassing of labor arbitration should also be reviewed if a specialist labor court is to be established.

The discussions have research implications as well. So far it has not been possible for the researcher to access nationwide statistical evidence of the extent to which employees' rights have been enforced by courts. Appropriate data are, however, vital for assessing the efficacy of the labor litigation system and drawing considered conclusions. Researchers may make efforts in that direction. Future studies should also look at whether and how employees compromise when they bring labor conflicts before the courts, in order to assess the extent to which workers' rights are protected and to improve labor regulations and labor dispute resolution. As the contributing factors of the extensive use of labor litigation are likely to remain unchanged in the near future, it is also likely that we will continue to see a constant and rapid increase in the number of labor disputes being brought to courts. Labor litigation will continue to play an irreplaceable role for resolving labor disputes in the long run while prelegal channels of labor dispute remain ineffective.

References

Brown, S., Bernd, F., & Sessions, J. (1997). Unemployment, vacancies and unfair dismissals. *Labour, 11*(2), 329–349.

Chan, A. (2004). Recent trends in Chinese labour issues: Signs of change. *China Perspectives, 57*, 23–31.

Chang, K. (1995). *Labour relations, labourers and labourers' rights: Labour issues in today's China.* Beijing: China Labour Press.

Chen, F. (2004). Legal mobilisation by the Chinese trade unions: The case of Shanghai. *The China Journal, 52*, 27–45.

China Labour Bulletin. (2006). *Press release: Silicosis victim wins record compensation after three-year fight for justice.* Press Release No. 11, 27th January.

China Law Yearbooks. (1996–2002). *China Law Yearbooks.* Beijing: China Law Yearbook Press.

Earnshaw, J., Goodman, J., Harrison, R., & Marchington, M. (1998). Industrial tribunals, workplace disciplinary procedures and employment practice. *Labour Market Trends, 106,* 479–481.

The Federation of European Employers. (2004). *Which country tops the employment litigation league in Europe?* http://www.pressbox.co.uk/Detailed/17809.html (accessed 13.05.06).

Fu, H. L., & Choy, D. W. (2004). From mediation to adjudication: Settling labour disputes in China. *China Rights Forum, 3,* 17–22.

Hong Kong Christian Industrial Committee. (2001). *How Hasbro, McDonald's, Mattel and Disney manufacture their toys?* Report on the labor rights and occupational safety and health conditions of toy workers in foreign investment enterprises in Southern mainland China, http://www.mcspotlight.org/media/press/releases/mcspot190202.html (accessed 18.05.06).

MacMillan, J. K. (1999). Employment tribunals: Philosophies and practicalities. *Industrial Law Journal, 28*(1), 33–56.

Mo, J. (2000). Probing labour arbitration in China. *Journal of International Arbitration, 17*(5), 19–83.

Schneider, M. R. (2001). Employment litigation on the rise? Comparing British employment tribunals and German labour courts. *Comparative Labour Law & Policy Journal, 22*(2/3), 266–280.

Shanghai Municipal Statistical Bureau. (1996–2005). *Shanghai statistical yearbooks.* Shanghai: Shanghai Municipal Statistical Bureau.

SHMTUC. (2002). *Lao Dong Guang Xi Diao Cha (Labour Relations Survey).* Shanghai: Shanghai Municipal Trade Union Council (in Chinese).

The Supreme People's Court. (2001). *Explanations on several issues regarding litigation of labour disputes.* http:ldbzt.jl.gov.cn/ldzyzc/sscs/t20060113_110667.htm (accessed 28.02.06).

Towers, B. (1997). *The representation gap: Change and reform in the British and American workplace.* Oxford: Oxford University Press.

Wang, Y. L. (2004). An analysis of the labour litigation system in China. *Journal of Wu Han University of Science and Technology, 17,* 354–357.

Location patterns of Chinese transnational corporations: A comparative study of Chinese and foreign transnational corporations

4

M. Chen
King's College London, London, UK

4.1 Introduction

The rapid international expansion of big firms has become very striking in recent decades, and those transnational corporations (TNCs) that operate in more than one country are playing increasing influential roles in the world economy. According to the World Investment Report 2000 of the United Nations Conference on Trade and Development (UNCTAD), there were 15,000 TNCs and 35,000 branches in 1980; these figures grew to 63,000 and 690,000, respectively, in 2000. Additionally, TNCs' foreign direct investment (FDI) accounted for 90% of the total amount of global direct investment in 2000. The total value of transnational mergers and acquisitions (M&As) increased from $75 billion in 1987 to $1.1 trillion in 1999 and reached its peak of $2.7 trillion in 2007; TNCs' sales amount rose from $3 trillion in 1980 to $14 trillion in 1999, and in the meantime, the trade volume of TNCs represented 40% of the total amount of global trade (United Nations Conference on Trade and Development, 2000; WilmerHale, 2014). Significantly, through economic cooperation and international trade, TNCs have facilitated the communication between different countries, and stimulated the cross-border capital flows, connected markets in different countries, and accelerated economic globalization.

Subsequently, the causes and effects of big companies' internationalization and TNCs' location patterns have become the focal point of research. The mainstream literature sees the international division of labor as the initial factor that has driven the internationalization of big companies. With the purpose of getting cheaper human resources from labor pools in overseas markets to reduce production costs, large firms transferred low-skilled, or labor-intensive works to other countries (Frobel, Heinrichs, & Kreye, 1980; McCallum, 1999). Thereafter, as the potentiality of markets in cheap-labor countries was recognized by foreign firms, they started to produce in and for countries with a cheap work force and a large potential market. Additionally, apart from the labor, price differences also exist in other aspects and the accessibility of resources in foreign markets is also an important cause of TNCs' internationalization. Seo (2011) argues that being embedded in this world economy with time differences and spatial distance, the systematic price gaps between different markets not only exist in the labor force but also in land, mineral resources, etc. In terms of the accessibility of resources, besides the availability of certain natural resources, such as rare-earth metals, the asymmetric information also concerns some selected TNCs.

Hence, the factors that motivate firms to internationalize are various and complicated and are closely linked with the risks and contextual factors in foreign markets, companies' investment motives, and characteristics.

Section 4.2 will tease out the general location strategies that could be applied to both Western and Chinese TNCs, based on analyzing risks in foreign markets and various investment motives. Section 4.3 will specifically focus on Chinese transnational corporations (CTNCs) through gaining an insight into the problems of CTNCs' internationalizing process and identify Chinese corporations' special location patterns by highlighting CTNCs' national-interests-oriented internationalization. The final section will summarize the key differences between Western and Chinese companies' location strategies and point out the gaps in current research.

4.2   General location strategies of TNCs

Establishing branches overseas is high cost and high risk. If a city could reduce companies' cost of operating businesses in foreign countries and satisfy their investment motives (such as reducing resource costs, gaining market share, and widening brand awareness) at the same time, this would be a key attraction (Goerzen, Asmussen, & Nielsen, 2013). This indicates a fundamental trade-off between risks and benefits in the process of international expansion. In addition, firms that are driven by different transnational investment motives will differ from other firms on the location patterns. Thus, in order to understand the main factors that concern TNCs in the process of choosing locations, it is necessary to explain the risks companies will face when they enter a foreign market. In this section, risks in foreign countries will be outlined first. Location strategies will be outlined on the basis of combined analyses of risks and motives.

4.2.1   Risks in foreign markets

TNCs' internationalization is not easy due to many obstacles, including different languages, economic systems, cultures, and different governmental and institutional regulations (Hymer, 1968). When foreign corporations first enter a totally unfamiliar market, the unfamiliarity with host countries will bring many risks. Goerzen et al. (2013, p. 431) have summarized those risks as the "liability of foreignness" (LOF). It is the general definition of challenges and risks that TNCs have to face when they are in overseas markets as a foreign investor. The key factors of LOF are "complexity, uncertainty, and discrimination" (Goerzen et al., 2013, p. 431).

Complexity refers to the complex problems that are brought by running business across national boundaries. For example, the information asymmetries between headquarters and subsidiary offices may present difficulties for parent companies to control and prevent branches from appropriation of profits and moral hazard

(Bergen, Dutta, & Walker, 1992; Gómez-Mejia & Palich, 1997; Sassen, 2001). *Complexity* will result in higher costs for TNCs in communicating and coordinating with overseas subsidiaries than keeping businesses in the same country. *Uncertainty* is brought by the unfamiliarity with different environments in host counties, including different cultures, languages, and laws. This requires foreign firms to spend additional money and time on getting to know the uncertain factors; and the inexperience of operating cross-border businesses is likely to bring losses to corporations if they make any mistakes (Goerzen et al., 2013).

Discrimination stems from the closed-minded attitude of host countries. This "discrimination" will come from all of the actors in economy, i.e., governments and clients. Undoubtedly, the arrival of TNCs' branch firms will be a great threat for local corporations in the same industry. So, by aiming to protect domestic companies, government may place different regulations on foreign firms (Kostova & Zaheer, 1999). The regulations include those of investment industries, taxes, annual incomes, a certain number of local employees, etc. Additionally, when clients are choosing products in the market, they usually prefer the brands or corporations with which they are familiar (Goerzen et al., 2013). Such behavior of government and clients may put TNCs in an unfavorable position in the competition with local companies and bring more risks to TNCs.

Many academics argue that by aiming to reduce the above risks, world cities with "global interconnectedness, cosmopolitanism and abundance of APS (advanced producer services)" (Goerzen et al., 2013, p. 427) are the best choices for TNCs. To be specific, possessing advanced communication facilities and playing the role of information centers in the world (Hymer, 1968; McCallum, 1999; Sassen, 1991; Wang, Zhao, & Wang, 2007), world cities are well integrated in the global city network and they are able to help solve the *complexity* issue to some extent by helping headquarters monitor their subsidiary companies with reduced communication costs. Moreover, the cosmopolitan environment in world cities enables TNCs to decrease *discrimination* and *uncertainty* risks. World cities have diversified cultures and more open-minded attitudes, which could guide TNCs to a fairer arena (Goerzen et al., 2013). *Discrimination* and *uncertainty* could also be decreased by acquiring specialized business services (e.g., accountancy, advertising, law, and consultancy) of APS companies that are also agglomerative in world cities (Goerzen et al., 2013; Sassen, 2001). APS firms have important significance to help support foreign companies' localization: accounting firms know local tax regulations very well, they can help foreign enterprises avoid duty reasonably; advertising firms are helpful to widen TNCs' brand awareness; law and consultancy firms can help investors get familiar with the host environment. As the concentration point of APS firms, world cities are able to offer TNCs the most professional services to reduce LOF and be involved into host markets as soon as possible. Compared to seeking help from the APS partners in the TNCs' own countries, Seo (2011, p. 73) argues that APS firms in host countries have the advantage of getting access to "opaque information." The modern economy is an information-based economy, and getting informational advantage is very important for companies. APS firms in host countries are more familiar with the market and have more corporate/individual relations with local government or institutions so that they have better access to "opaque information" than outside APS firms. Undoubtedly, world cities are the best choice of location for overseas corporations to reduce LOF; however, they have negative aspects for attracting foreign investors as well, such as the high business operating costs—notably rents and salaries. Not all companies would like to locate in world cities. Because risks in foreign markets are not the only thing that concern TNCs, their investment motives are the decisive factor of location patterns.

4.2.2 Investment motives

Generally, these motives can be classified as market seeking, resource seeking, efficiency seeking, and strategic asset seeking (Dunning, 1998; Goerzen et al., 2013). Investment motives are the key considerations of TNCs to select locations, but not the only factor. In the process of deciding locations, different companies will consider very similar groups of factors, but different investment motives affect the weight that firms give to the various factors (Han & Qin, 2009). In other words, there is little difference between the groups of considerations, but the emphases are different. Therefore, when it comes to analyze location strategies of different companies, only the key factor will be discussed.

4.2.2.1 Market seeking → cities' regional/global connectivity

Foreign companies with market-seeking objectives usually are looking for either local or regional (sometimes global) markets. Establishing branches in an overseas city is an easy way to enter the host country's market, while the geographic size of the market depends on the city's connectivity with surrounding cities or regions (Dunning, 1998; Goerzen et al., 2013). Some well-connected cities, such as world cities like London, Tokyo, and New York, are even regarded as "distribution hubs," which are able to distribute goods to different small markets (Goerzen et al., 2013, p. 433). As they have extensive connections with other cities and are integrated in the world economy, this attribute of world cities enables them to link corporations with surrounding countries' markets. The more intensive the city's connectivity, the larger market it can potentially offer to TNCs. To some extent, this can explain why major TNCs have located different levels of offices in different cities: global or regional headquarters in world cities, and low-level offices in subordinate cities.

4.2.2.2 Resource seeking → natural resources, cheap human resources, infrastructures (transportation and telecommunication), information, knowledge, etc.

At the early stages of globalization, most companies' internationalization was driven by shortage of natural resources and cheap labor. Since there are many different labor pools in the world, global integration is able to help manufacturing TNCs exploit the wage differences to reduce labor costs by moving the manufacturing process of labor-intensive production overseas (Buckley & Ghauri, 2004; Frobel et al., 1980;

McCallum, 1999). Consequently, the production process has been divided into different stages to allocate to multiple factories, and labor-intensive or low-skilled stages are always sent to areas with cheap labor. Those tasks can be performed with little training and have few requirements about workers' skills, experience, or education. After the manufacturing process, goods are transported to other places for either assembly or sale. For most natural-resource-intensive and labor-intensive firms, apart from considering the qualities and prices of natural resources or labor force, transport cost is usually one of the key factors with which they will be concerned (Fujita & Thisse, 1996). Driven by resource-seeking motives, apart from firms that are looking for special natural resources, most firms will prefer cities with both cheap natural resources/labor and proper transport facilities. As Dunning (1998, p. 51) stated, TNCs would like to locate in places with the "best economic and institutional facilities for their core competencies to be efficiently utilized."

Another important infrastructure element for TNCs is telecommunications, since the world economy has become increasingly information-based. Many academics believe that the economy has been shifted from "goods production" to "information handling" (Hall, 1998, p. 21), and regard telecommunication as the root of "the construction of a global economy" (Castells & United Nations Research Institute for Social Development, 1999). The efficiency of gaining information determines whether firms could make efficient and effective business decisions in competition. In particular, in some "information-sensitive" industries like the financial industry, which rely almost entirely on telematics, the accessibility of information will directly affect whether financial firms can act earlier with less cost (Wang et al., 2007, p. 104). In addition, with the purposes of getting access to foreign markets, enlarging global office network and managing production chains more efficiently, companies desire advanced telematic facilities to decentralize economic activities for them (Yusuf & Wu, 2002). In general, "the more complex and developed the industry, the more important is information," while "information is not costless" and asymmetric (Drennan, 1996, p. 361; Wang et al., 2007). Consequently, information-seeking TNCs are more likely to concentrate in "teleport" cities, which have the most advanced telecommunication industry and are able to reduce costs and risks for firms (Wang et al., 2007; Warf, 1989).

Furthermore, there are some TNCs pursuing advanced knowledge, such as advanced skills and technologies, they usually place emphasis on accessibility to knowledge. Therefore, most knowledge-seeking firms will either form a spatial cluster or locate near universities (Goerzen et al., 2013). Silicon Valley is a case in point. It is one of the world's most famous high-tech agglomerations located in the South Bay portion of the San Francisco Bay Area in Northern California, just outside of San Francisco. The key contribution of this location is that there are several top universities in Silicon Valley (including Stanford University, San Jose State University, and Carnegie Mellon University) that can offer highly educated graduates and research facilities to those knowledge-seeking companies. Once knowledge-seeking companies form a cluster economy, it is more convenient for them to build business corporations, and they could share the communal facilities and resources to improve fund utilization and business efficiency.

4.2.2.3 Efficiency seeking → easy access to natural resources, highly skilled human resources, open economic environment, government policy support, cluster economies, etc.

The natural resources and labor force sought by efficiency-seeking TNCs are different from those sought by resource-seeking companies. The efficiency-based resources-seeking motive emphasizes accessibility to natural resources and the quality (e.g., creativity, diversified skills, experiences) of human resources (Dunning, 1998; Goerzen et al., 2013), rather than focusing on the prices and availability of natural resources and labor. For example, the South China Sea has a large amount of petroleum and gas reserves; it has been estimated that petroleum reserves are between 23 and 30 billion tons and that gas reserves are around 16 trillion m^3, accounting for 30% of China's total petroleum and gas reserves (Yu, 2012). However, 70% of the reserves are located in a deep-sea area and requires high-tech exploitation methods that China lacks. The inaccessibility of reserves in the South China Sea drove Chinese companies to seek petroleum and gas overseas; even though they have to pay more transportation expenses, they could exploit petroleum and gas more efficiently. In terms of labor, locations of APS firms are the case in point. Transnational ASP firms usually tend to locate in world cities where they can get easy access to clients and highly skilled human resources that are capable of producing highly professional services. It is indubitable that world cities have larger market and larger amounts of well-educated/trained work force than subordinate cities. Locating in world cities could reduce foreign corporations' difficulties, time, and costs of expanding local markets and recruiting and it also will reduce the time to find replacements. Consequently, the efficiency of APS firms' operations could be improved.

Dunning (1998) demonstrates that government has taken an increasingly important place in enhancing the quality of human resources by providing upgraded education/training programs and facilitating economic activities by removing obstacles for FDI. The openness of the economic environment is closely related to government support. Trade barriers are lowered or eliminated, taxes reduced, grants distributed, special economic zones built, while various preferential policies conducted by governments could open the host countries' market and offer a low-obstacle investment environment for TNCs. Referring to the open-minded attitudes in the section on risks, governmental support will bring foreign investors a fair competition as well.

A cluster economy is a specialized spatial cluster of economic activities that companies concentrate into sharing particular resources, factor inputs, opportunities, or economic environment. For those "competence-creating" and "supply-driven" firms, world cities are less attractive, but they need to make a trade-off between cluster economies and transport costs in the global market system (Dunning, 1998; Fujita & Thisse, 1996; Goerzen et al., 2013, p. 343). But with the fall of transportation costs, intensifying the agglomeration of "supply-driven" firms has been another way to improve the efficiency for companies and reduce their fixed costs.

4.2.2.4 Strategic asset seeking → firms' business strategies, knowledge-related assets, brand awareness, market share, etc.

Apart from the attributes of cities, TNCs' business strategy is also an important factor to influence their locations (Goerzen et al., 2013; Jin, 2009). Some transnational firms that only focus on local markets in host countries tend to expand their office networks in host countries as widely as possible. In this case, compared to locating in one or two world cities in a certain country, establishing branches in many subordinate cities may allow companies to be involved in local markets more intensively. However, a strategy of global integration encourages TNCs to spread branches in world cities: first of all, as mentioned in the section on risks, world cities could reduce TNCs' LOF and the relative costs by providing APS and advanced communication facilities to keep branch offices well integrated in their office networks. Second, in terms of the information issue, offices in world cities are acting as information collectors (Hymer, 1968; Wang et al., 2007); they have a greater informational advantage than subordinate cities. Establishing subsidiary companies as tools to transmit information honestly and efficiently from overseas world cities becomes necessary for TNCs targeting global markets.

Usually, seeking knowledge-related assets, widening brand awareness, and expanding market share will not influence transnational companies' location patterns directly, since TNCs could purchase most mobile knowledge-related assets (such as the latest technologies), and brand awareness and market could be widened by advertising. However, locations might be affected if the knowledge-related assets are immobile, or companies chose an M&A strategy to acquire particular assets (Zhong, Peng, & Liu, 2013). Foreign companies can obtain the existing technologies, brand awareness, and market share of a local company by M&A, and the reorganization of the corporation after acquisitions will impact the office locations.

4.3 Special location strategies of CTNCs

In the world economic system, China's economy is special and distinct from the economy of other countries—it has an incomplete market economy in which government intervention is playing a vital role (Han & Qin, 2009) and the majority of CTNCs are state-owned enterprises (SOEs). Given these attributes, there are other special factors that Chinese firms need to consider when they select office locations. This section will explain those special considerations by analyzing government intervention, CTNCs' operational problems, and corporation strategies.

4.3.1 Current problems of the CTNCs

China's markets opened to foreign investors after the announcement of the Open Door policy by Xiaoping Deng in 1978; when China joined the World Trade Organization in 2001, it gave overseas firms another valuable chance to enter its market. These two events brought a huge amount of overseas capital and led to China's economic boom (Chen, 2009; Li, 2009a). In addition to this facet of encouraging foreign investment, the Open Door policy contained another facet: encouraging Chinese companies to internationalize (Chen, 2009). However, these two facets have been seriously unbalanced: in 2003, Chinese companies' outward FDI was only $1.4 billion, while China replaced the United States as the largest recipient of FDI in the world with a massive $115.1 billion (Apoteker & Barthéléry, 2009; Ministry of Commerce of the People's Republic of China, 2003; Perkowski, 2012). During the past 9 years, China's outward FDI had increased rapidly and reached to $87.8 billion in 2012 (Jin, Teow, & Rui, 2013); however, compared to the inward FDI, which amounted to $120 billion and suffered an annual fall by 3.4% (United Nations Conference on Trade and Development, 2013), the outward FDI still lagged behind. CTNCs' entered the world arena only a few decades ago, and companies' internationalization strategy is a young discipline in China. Most Chinese companies are guided by foreign literature, which has developed in a different context (Chen, 2009).

The history of the stages of development of Chinese companies was summarized by Yang and Ke (2004, quoted by Jin, 2009, p. 2):

> *The 1980s. In this period, the dominant economic system was the planned economy and the strategies of Chinese SOEs were generally specialized in production for a specific industry.*
>
> *The 1990s. In this period, China embarked on the transformation from a planned economy towards a market economy. Chinese enterprises made a major change in their corporate strategies: diversification became the leading strategy in the 1990s.*
>
> *Since 2000. The market economy has become the dominant economic system in China. Corporate strategies in China started to diverge: diversification remained the dominant pattern even if some companies started reducing their number or core businesses and if a few companies developed successful focused strategies.*

During the planned economy period, China's economy was controlled by the central government, and all Chinese companies' overseas investments had to be examined and approved by the State Council, irrespective of the amount and projects that companies were going to invest. As a result, at this stage, China's outward FDI was quite limited—only $9.2 million/year (Li, 2009a). Moreover, Chinese enterprises had no right to make important business decisions, and most big companies' managers were nominated by the government. Thus, business strategy did not exist in this period (Jin, 2009). Even when China's economic system was transforming from a planned economy to a market economy, the business decisions of Chinese companies were greatly affected by government planning. Generally, business strategy has only been studied since 2000, so current research results are too immature to give CTNCs advice on their internationalization. Affected by this, the CTNCs are currently quite immature in the global market and have many problems in their internationalization performance.

Apart from the influence of the economic development process, most Chinese transnational enterprises are SOEs, and their state-owned nature has also affected their internationalization. The protection of government has made CTNCs less competitive (Jin, 2009). Due to the long-term protection of the Chinese government, SOEs and other non-SOEs have been competing unfairly in the domestic market. Obviously, SOEs have priority in this competition because they have dominated China's pillar industries: entities include China Huaneng Corporation in the electric utility industry; PetroChina and Sinopec-China Petroleum in the oil and gas utility industry; China Railway Group in the railroad industry; Baoshan, Heibei, and Wuhan Iron & Steel Corporations in the iron and steel industry, etc. In the industries mentioned above, SOEs either share the whole market or take the major share of the market. In addition to pillar industries, SOEs are also leaders in the financial industry, including securities, insurance, and banks. For example, China's top security companies (Citic Securities and Haitong Securities), top insurance firms (China Life Insurance, the People's Insurance Company of China, and New China Life Insurance), and four commercial banks (Bank of China, China Construction Bank, Industrial and Commercial Bank of China, and Agricultural Bank of China) are all SOEs. Many financial SOEs have been reformed and turned into listed companies in recent years—such as New China Life Insurance and four commercial banks—but the majority of the shares are held by Central Huijin Investment Company, which is wholly owned by the state. Benefitting from the policy and capital support from the central government, SOEs received priority in China's national market at the beginning of the competition; the governmental support gave SOEs little experience with competition, which contributed to their limited competitiveness in international market.

Moreover, a lack of experienced staff is another limitation of CTNCs. The experience of leaders can affect companies' business strategy, problem management, and opportunity-seizing capabilities in unfamiliar overseas investment environments (Shambaugh, 2012). The Chinese companies' internationalization requires experienced multilingual and multicultural managers in order to become familiar with host countries' environments and to reduce the LOF. Among current CTNCs, most private enterprises, such as Lenovo and Huawei Technologies, are aware of this problem and have hired non-Chinese management professionals to lead overseas branches in an exploration of foreign markets (Nguyen, Okrend, & Tang, 2013). Reorganizing management teams in transnational SOEs is much more difficult than in private enterprises due to SOEs' "politicized" character: the SOEs have many Communist Party members in the management teams, and most SOE CEOs are appointed by the Organization Department of the Chinese Communist Party (Shambaugh, 2012). This factor has increased the chance of corruption and has made transnational SOEs difficult to acquire the management professionals they really need.

Although Chinese companies have put many efforts into global integration, there is poor awareness of Chinese brands (Jin, 2009; Shambaugh, 2012). According to a survey by the United Nations Industrial Development Organization, cited by Jin (2009), companies owning famous brands shared over 40% of the overall market with only 3% proportion of brand names. However, no Chinese brands were among the annual ranking of global top 100 brands in 2011 (Backaler, 2012). Additionally, because of the poor global brand presence of CTNCs, their products are not easily accepted by clients in foreign markets. Thus, the major CTNCs may choose to decrease prices to increase sales. However, this is not a long-term strategy (Nguyen et al., 2013). Widening brand awareness through sustained advertising is very costly; however, the Chinese government is eager to internationalize Chinese firms as soon as possible (Shambaugh, 2012). As a result, most CTNCs have chosen to merge existing foreign companies with a solid brand presence.

Lacking advanced technology and innovation is another costly challenge faced by CTNCs (Li, 2009a; Nguyen et al., 2013). Currently, Chinese companies do not have any core comparative advantages in the global market; most of their investments in foreign countries are "labor-intensive projects with low added value and technology" (Jin, 2009, p. 28) but this kind of project is "at the bottom of the industrial structure" and the market demand for such project is quite limited in today's advanced economy (Li, 2009a, p. 33). Additionally, due to China's well-known one child policy, Chinese society is facing the problem of an aging population; therefore, labor prices in the Chinese market may increase in the future and will not have the competitive advantage in this aspect compared with other countries in South East Asia. McCallum (1999) disclosed that the complexity of products and services had been able to indicate the skill level of human resources in a country and also indicate the "sophistication" of that country's economy. Investing funds in research and development to increase the value added of Chinese companies' investment projects is necessary for improving CTNCs' international competitiveness.

Hence, the most important contributing factors to the above problems for CTNCs are China's special characteristics in terms of its institutional, social, and cultural background (Guger, 2008), such as central government protection, difficulty of restructuring management teams in SOEs, and the one-child policy. There is almost no difference in investment motives between overseas TNCs and CTNCs; however, in order to deal with these problems in the internationalizing process, CTNCs' corporation strategies will differ from overseas TNCs and bring some differences in location strategy.

4.3.2   Corporate strategies and location patterns of CTNCs

To a large extent, a country's international competitiveness is determined by the power of its own TNCs (Jin, 2009). This means competitive companies play key roles in realizing the economic globalization ambition of countries. Particularly in the context of China's collectivistic culture, CTNCs are acting as "national champions" with a responsibility to enhance the economic competitiveness of China in the world economy instead of just internationalizing for themselves; even some independently private enterprises, like Huawei, that have gained strong power in global scale, will be transferred to a "state direct/military connected company acting as a private agent for state interests" (Apoteker & Barthéléry, 2009, p. 29); Thus, CTNCs' strategies link with national interests and strategic objectives closely, and their internationalizing development is affected by political factors greatly (Guger, 2008; Li, 2009a).

As national champions, besides the resource-seeking Chinese companies, other enterprises focus on investing in core industries (including the financial and electronics industries) in foreign countries and are eager to occupy the market.

Thus, they prefer the most efficient way—cooperation, or even M&A—to acquire the related experiences and strategic assets in order to fill their weaknesses (Zhong et al., 2013). Most experience of operating transnational businesses is at the individual level; however, replacing party members with experienced non-Chinese professionals in SOEs is very difficult. To some extent, those party members in a management level are tools of the central government to monitor and control SOEs. Given this political factor, cooperating with partners in host countries may be the best way to reduce LOF, maintain China's special personnel structure in the management level of SOEs, and allow them to internationalize more effectively (Li, 2009a; Zhong et al., 2013).

"The more the emerging multinational corporations experience cooperation with partners from the developed market, the higher their internationalization performance [will be]" (Zhong et al., 2013, p. 2480). This is not only because partners could guide Chinese firms in host countries but also because the benefits from cooperation could be leveraged and learned by CTNCs to better prepare for challenges in the future. Mathews' "linkage-leverage-learning" framework (2006, quoted by Zhong et al., 2013, p. 2483) states that the sources of TNCs' competitive advantages are "first the resources accessed through linkage with external firms, then the extent to which partners' resources can be leveraged, and finally organizational learning through repeated application of linkages and leverages process which allows [the TNCs to improve internationalizing capabilities]."

Essentially, Chinese corporations could gain these resources from cooperation partners: more professional employees, partners' linkages with external companies, more competent suppliers, and customers' trust (Zhong et al., 2013). However, CTNCs still have shortages that cannot be solved efficiently by cooperation, such as lack of core technologies and poor brand presence. M&A has been regarded as "a short cut" to acquire other enterprises' current market share, distribution network, latest technologies, well-known brands, and other intangibly strategic assets (Guger, 2008; Nguyen et al., 2013). Due to the inexperience of CTNCs and a lack of professionals, building the above competitive advantages will be a long and hard process; thus, buying shares of a mature foreign company is much easier in order for Chinese firms to realize internationalization. Chinese companies' outward FDI has increased sharply since 2005, and M&A has been the dominant method to internationalize (Apoteker & Barthéléry, 2009; Guger, 2008). Another catalyst of this phenomenon was the push from China's central government: according to the announcement of the State Asset Supervision and Administration Commission in 2000, China aimed to create 30–50 CTNCs before 2010 (Apoteker & Barthéléry, 2009). But the Chinese economic system was not dominated by a market economy until the 2000s, and it was quite ambitious that the central government wanted to realize this goal in just 10 years. In order to do so, the government has provided both policy and financial aid to Chinese companies (Guger, 2008; Rein, 2010), and the central government's pursuit of rapidly international expansion explains the recently increasing amount of M&A deals: for instance, the acquisition of IBM's PC division by Lenovo; the Canadian oil and gas company Nexen by China National Offshore Oil Corporation; and Volvo by Geely Automobile company.

Generally, in terms of the groups of factors that concern companies when they are selecting locations, politically sensitive Chinese companies have to consider political factors that foreign companies generally do not. This gives the location strategies of CNTCs these special characteristics.

4.3.2.1 Asia-oriented preference

With the purposes of seeking stable cooperation with overseas companies, China's outward FDI mainly orients to neighboring countries in Asia (Apoteker & Barthéléry, 2009). Based on the analysis of China's overseas investment in 2005 carried out by Li (2009b), 71% of the total amount was invested in Asia, followed by Latin America with 20%, then Africa and Europe both with 3%, North America with 2%, and Oceania with 1%. The outward FDI of China has become country-diversified since it joined the WTO; although Asia still remains its main investment target, the amount of FDI in western developed countries is increasing (Li, 2009b). On one hand, compared with Europe and American continents, neighboring countries have the advantage of geographical positions (a closer physical distance and location in the similar time zone), which could reduce transport costs and offer much more convenience for CTNCs. Whereas, on the other hand, the proximate culture and the widespread Chinese diasporas may be helpful for decreasing the barriers of trans-boundary business cooperation and contributing useful relationship to facilitate it. In Chinese foreign investment history, the cooperating partner of China's first foreign investment, which happened in 1979 (in the context of the planned economic system), was a Japanese company called Tokyo Maruichishoji Co. Ltd., which built China's first joint enterprise in Tokyo with Beijing Friendship Commercial Service Corporation. Additionally, because some of the residents of those countries speak Mandarin (e.g., Taiwan and Singapore), it is likely to make business cooperation easier (Apoteker & Barthéléry, 2009; Guger, 2008).

4.3.2.2 Different M&A targets for SOEs and non-SOEs

When Chinese companies show an Asia-oriented preference during the process of seeking cooperating partners, central government and national interests seem to play the decisive roles in China's cross-border M&As (Li, 2009b). Generally, M&A deals can be divided into natural resources seeking M&A and strategic assets seeking M&A. After reviewing China's M&A cases in the past 30 years collected by one of China's well-known media companies, IFeng News (2009), all of the companies doing resources-seeking M&As were SOEs, with the purposes of "reducing the risk of resource shortage, increasing the nation's strategic resource reserves, and helping safeguard the nation's economic stability and security" (Li, 2009b, p. 67). For example, Shougang Group bought Hierro Peru iron ore mine in 1992, which was the first M&A deal in Chinese history; Hunan Valin Iron and Steel Group became the second-largest shareholder of Australian Fortescue Metals Group (the world's fourth-largest iron ore supplier); and Sinopec acquired Addax Petroleum, which had rich oil and gas resources in East Africa and the Middle Asia. Li (2009b) explained that since China had become the global factory, the gap between demand and supply of natural resources had widened; thus, acquiring resources had become one of main objectives of China's transnational M&As. The strategic assets seeking M&As were mostly done by non-governmental companies at that time, such as Suning Appliance Co., Ltd., which took over Laox Co. (a Japanese home appliance retailer with 80 years history); Geely Automobile Company, which acquired Australian Drivetrain Systems International, one of the two enterprises producing automatic gearboxes in the world in addition to typical carmakers; and Shanghai Automotive Industry Corporation (SAIC), which purchased both Korean Ssang Yong Motor Corporation and the British Rover Company.

4.3.2.3 Different targeted industries in developing and developed countries

In terms of investing industries, Chinese companies have showed different targets in developing and developed countries (Apoteker & Barthéléry, 2009). CTNCs focused on investing in natural-resource-based or low-value-added projects in developing countries; while in developed countries, they concentrated on core industries (e.g., finance, mechanical engineering, metal processing). For instance, according to the information on the official website of Bank of China (BOC), it has locations in 13 cities in 9 developing counties (namely Cambodia, Vietnam, Russia, Malaysia, Panama, Thailand, Indonesia, Zambia, and Brazil), and in 32 cities in 15 developed countries/regions. Among the nine developing countries, city are located around China; thus, those office locations may be affected by Asia-oriented preference. Additionally, BOC shows a greater desire to establish branches in developed countries than in developing countries. Besides Russia and Indonesia, BOC only chose one city in each developing country. It selected three to four cities, respectively, in top developed countries, such as Glasgow, Manchester, Birmingham, and London in the UK; Los Angeles, Chicago, and New York in the United States; Nagoya, Kobe, Osaka, Yokohama, and Tokyo in Japan; and Vancouver, Calgary, Montreal, and Toronto in Canada. Li (2009a) demonstrates that investing in big cities is an easy way to create distribution channels and build sales networks for Chinese companies. CTNCs have a lack of experience in transnational business operations, wide brand awareness, and global sale networks, but they are eager to internationalize. As the concentration points of various firms, big cities in developed countries have many more connections with both local and overseas firms than other cities, which is very helpful for Chinese companies in expanding sale networks.

Compared to this, China's investments in developing areas like Africa mainly focus on infrastructure construction, natural resources, and manufacturing industry. China has signed many economic cooperation agreements with Africa that covers various resources, like new energy, minerals, and electricity; and infrastructure construction has accounted for 25% of China's direct investments in Africa (IFeng News, 2014). In terms of manufacturing industry, the stock of investment in Africa had increased to $2.48 billion at the end of 2011, representing 15.3% of China's total investment in Africa; and the investment goal shifted from circumventing trade barriers and using preferential trade agreements to expanding local market and moving the whole production chain to Africa (Wei, 2014).

4.4 Coda: Key differences between foreign and Chinese TNCs' location patterns and the gaps in current research

Generally, the location patterns of TNCs are based on the basis of achieving firms' motivations with minimized LOF and costs. Investment motives can be mainly classified as market seeking, resource seeking, efficiency seeking, and strategic asset seeking. Based on these motives, companies will give varying weights to a group of factors when they are considering locations. Compared to foreign corporations, which are only concerned with economic factors and context factors in host countries, affected by distinct context, Chinese companies are more politically sensitive, especially SOEs, which are the main forces of Chinese transnational enterprises. They have one more responsibility than foreign companies in international expansion process: that of national interests. The national targets and government intervention have affected the location patterns of Chinese companies. The office locations of foreign firms are just individual choices, but the location of Chinese firms may be decided by both firms and the government.

According to the examples of behavior of CTNCs, they have showed different preferences from foreign companies on locations. The spatial distribution of Chinese corporations is Asian-oriented, targeting different industries in developed and developing countries. But those special preferences are phenomena that only can be seen by example and cannot be deeply explained by theory, due to the lack of research on the location patterns of Chinese companies. Currently, there is a small amount of literature on the location strategies of Chinese enterprises; however, it is just based on quantitative analysis, and very few academics have used qualitative research methods to study the location patterns of CTNCs in depth. In order to tease out the importance of national interests and government in the location strategies of Chinese companies, simply analyzing Chinese economic policies, news, and Chinese companies' behaviors to see if Chinese firms have followed government policies is not enough; rather, it is necessary to use qualitative approaches. However, the difficulty of interviewing Chinese government officials and managers in SOEs will be a big challenge. The methodology of studying this topic will be the biggest problem for academics to think about in the future. Once the research methods can be solved, the location patterns of CTNCs can be demystified.

References

Apoteker, T., & Barthéléry, S. (2009). *The emergence of Chinese multinational companies (CMCs): Reality, issues and challenges.* Social Science Research Network website. Available at: http://papers.ssrn.com/sol3/papers.cfm?abstract_id=2169224 (accessed 10.05.14).

Backaler, J. (2012). Viewpoint: Why do so few Chinese brands go global? *BBC News.* Available at: http://www.bbc.co.uk/news/business-17998321 (accessed 12.05.14).

Bergen, M., Dutta, S., & Walker, O. (1992). Agency relationships in marketing: A review of the implications and applications of agency and related theories. *Journal of Marketing, 56*(3), 1–24.

Buckley, P., & Ghauri, P. (2004). Globalisation, economic geography and the strategy of multinational enterprises. *Journal of Internal Business Studies, 35*(2), 81–89.

Castells, M., & United Nations Research Institute for Social Development. (1999). *Information technology, globalization and social development.* Available at: http://www.unrisd.org/unrisd/website/document.nsf/70870613ae33162380256b5a004d932e/f270e0c066f3de7780256b67005b728c/$FILE/dp114.pdf (accessed 10.05.14).

Chen, G. (2009). Introduction and organization of the book. In J.-P. Larçon (Ed.), *Chinese multinationals.* Singapore: World Scientific Publishing Company.

Drennan, M. P. (1996). The dominance of international finance by London, New York and Tokyo. In B. Berry, E. Conkling, & D. Ray (Eds.), *The Global Economy in Transition.* Upper Saddle River: Prentice Hall.

Dunning, J. (1998). Location and the multinational enterprise: A neglected factor? *Journal of International Business Study, 29*(1), 45–66.

Frobel, F., Heinrichs, J., & Kreye, O. (1980). *The new international division of labour: Structural unemployment in industrialised countries and industrialisation in developing countries.* Cambridge: Cambridge University Press.

Fujita, M., & Thisse, J.-F. (1996). Economics of agglomeration. *Journal of the Japanese and International Economies, 10*, 339–378.

Goerzen, A., Asmussen, C., & Nielsen, B. (2013). Global cities and multinational enterprise location strategy. *Journal of International Business Studies, 44*, 427–450.

Gómez-Mejia, L., & Palich, L. (1997). Cultural diversity and the performance of multinational firms. *Journal of International Business Studies, 28*(2), 309–336.

Guger, P. (2008). *Chinese companies worldwide.* VOX website. Available at: http://www.voxeu.org/article/how-are-chinese-multinational-enterprises-different (accessed 15.05.14).

Hall, P. (1998). Globalization and the world cities. In F. Lo, & Y. Yeung (Eds.), *Globalization and the world of large cities.* New York: United Nations University Press.

Han, S. S., & Qin, B. (2009). The spatial distribution of producer services in Shanghai. *Urban Studies, 46*(4), 877–896.

Hymer, S. (1968). The large multinational 'corporation'. In M. Casson (Ed.), *Multinational corporations.* Hants: Edward Elgar (1990).

IFeng News. (2009). *The M&A history of Chinese companies in the past 30 years.* IFeng News website. Available at: http://finance.ifeng.com/leadership/cygc/20090813/1082909.shtml (accessed 28.04.14).

IFeng News. (2014). *An analysis of China's investments in Africa.* IFeng News website. Available at: http://finance.ifeng.com/news/special/picture42/ (accessed 18.07.14).

Jin, Z. (2009). Corporate strategies of Chinese multinationals. In J.-P. Larçon (Ed.), *Chinese multinationals.* Singapore: World Scientific Publishing Company.

Jin, X., Teow, R., & Rui, S. (2013). *2013 Chinese outbound investment trends overview.* Lexology website. Available at: http://www.lexology.com/library/detail.aspx?g=37fb616c-1253-4f30-8bfe-8b5d74076bb9 (accessed 01.07.14).

Kostova, T., & Zaheer, S. (1999). Organizational legitimacy under conditions of complexity: The case of the multinational enterprise. *Academy of Management Review, 24*(1), 82–98.

Li, Z. (2009a). China's go global policy. In J.-P. Larçon (Ed.), *Chinese multinationals.* Singapore: World Scientific Publishing Company.

Li, Z. (2009b). China's outward foreign direct investment. In J.-P. Larçon (Ed.), *Chinese multinationals.* Singapore: World Scientific Publishing Company.

McCallum, C. (1999). *Globalisation, developments and trends in the new international division of labour.* Munich Personal RePEc Archive. Available at: http://mpra.ub.uni-muenchen.de/20579 (accessed 18.04.14).

Ministry of Commerce of the People's Republic of China. (2003). *The statistics of foreign direct investment from January to December in 2003*. Ministry of Commerce of the People's Republic of China website. Available at: http://www.mofcom.gov.cn/article/ton gjiziliao/v/200401/20040100171259.shtml (accessed 12.04.14).

Nguyen, K., Okrend, M., & Tang, L. (2013). Are Chinese companies the next generation of multinational corporations? Lenovo vs. Sony in the global PC industry. *American International Journal of Contemporary Research, 3*(2), 1–10.

Perkowski, J. (2012). *China leads in foreign direct investment*. Forbes website. Available at: http://www.forbes.com/sites/jackperkowski/2012/11/05/china-leads-in-foreign-direct-investment/ (accessed 02.05.14).

Rein, S. (2010). *Three big trends changing China for multinationals*. Forbes website. Available at: http://www.forbes.com/2010/08/24/china-multinationals-branding-leadership-careers-rein.html (accessed 28.04.14).

Sassen, S. (1991). *The global city*. Princeton: Princeton University Press.

Sassen, S. (2001). *The global city: New York, London, Tokyo*. Oxford: Princeton University Press.

Seo, B. (2011). Geographies of finance: Centers, flows, and relations. *Hitotsubashi Journal of Economics, 52*, 69–86.

Shambaugh, D. (2012). *Are China's multinational corporations really multinational?* Brookings website. Available at: http://www.brookings.edu/research/articles/2012/07/10-china-multinationals-shambaugh (accessed 30.04.14).

United Nations Conference on Trade and Development. (2000). *The world investment report 2000*. UNCTAD website. Available at: http://unctad.org/en/Docs/wir2000_en.pdf (accessed 01.07.14).

United Nations Conference on Trade and Development. (2013). *Global investment trends monitor*. UNCTAD website. Available at: http://unctad.org/en/PublicationsLibrary/webdiaeia2013d1_en.pdf (accessed 01.07.14).

Wang, D. T., Zhao, X., & Wang, D. (2007). 'Information Hinterland'—A base for financial centre development: The case of Beijing versus Shanghai in China. *Economische en Social Geografie, 98*(1), 102–120.

Warf, B. (1989). Telecommunications and the globalisation of financial services. *The Professional Geographer, 41*(3), 257–271.

Wei, J. G. (2014). *The best time for manufacturing industry to enter Africa*. Huanqiu website. Available at: http://opinion.huanqiu.com/opinion_world/2014-01/4800322.html (accessed 18.07.14).

WilmerHale. (2014). *2014 M&A report*. WilmerHale website. Available at: http://www.wilmerhale.com/uploadedFiles/Shared_Content/Editorial/Publications/Documents/2014-WilmerHale-MA-Report.pdf (accessed 18.08.14).

Yu, X. (2012). *The petroleum reserves in the South China Sea*. China News website. Available at: http://news.china.com.cn/2012-05/07/content_25321229.htm (accessed 14.08.14).

Yusuf, S., & Wu, W. (2002). Pathways to a world city: Shanghai rising in an era of globalization. *Urban Studies, 39*(7), 1213–1240.

Zhong, W., Peng, J., & Liu, C. (2013). Internationalization performance of Chinese multinational companies in the developed markets. *Journal of Business Research, 66*, 2479–2484.

Research on the relationship among large shareholders and its economic consequences of listed companies in China

T. Liu, S. Yang, Q. Shi
Beijing University of Technology, Beijing, China

5.1 Introduction

The influences of the interest conflict and the coordination among shareholders have been a topic of concern, either from the practical or theoretical perspective. More attention has been paid to the stake division between large and small shareholders as well as differences between shareholders. In reality, the conflict generated by the pure differences of the number is easier to be coordinated. What is worse is that if the transaction varies greatly, it is difficult to figure out the simple standard of equilibrium point of shareholder interests (Hansmann, 1996). Therefore, the current status of the stakeholder structure is far from enough to support the financial research (Cai & Wei, 2011).

The social culture of China refers to a typical "relationship" quality. The debate represented here is: "Does the special culture exist in the listed companies?" To find the answer, we selected data from 2008 to 2011 in the listed companies in China as samples. (This is mainly because since 2007, China has begun to implement new accounting standards, which may result in quite different financial indicators.) Some detailed investigations and analyses of the relationship characteristics of the top ten shareholders in the listed companies will be explored. Table 5.1 shows that a relationship among the large shareholders is common.

Apparently, except for the proportion of the shareholding, some other economic or social relations among the shareholders of the listed companies do exist, such as the shareholding relationship, the concerted action relationship, and the kinship that may exist in natural people, etc. It has been described that the relationship among the large shareholders of listed companies does not only exist objectively but is also a high proportion. We divide listed companies into two categories based on relationships among large shareholders: one is relational shareholder listed companies (RSLC), in which relationships exist among the top ten shareholders, and the other is independent shareholder listed companies (ISLC), whose shareholders are fully independent of each other. Are there any significant differences between them? What effect would the types and numbers of relationships among large shareholders bring to listed companies? These are the exact research motivations of this chapter. According to the relationship of large shareholders, the listed companies have been classified on the basis

Table 5.1 **2008–2011 The relationship statistics of large shareholders**

Year	The number of listed company	The number of relation company	Proportion (%)
2008	1620	678	41.85
2009	1771	748	42.24
2010	2118	1016	47.97
2011	2356	1240	52.63
Total	7865	3682	46.82

of the statistics; the differences between different types of companies in corporate performance, agency cost, and quality of earnings will be examined.

This chapter is structured as follows: Section 5.1 presents background and the motivation. Section 5.2 describes the classification of the relations of the large shareholders in listed companies in China; a literature review and the theoretical foundation are presented in Section 5.3; the research design follows in Section 5.4; and Section 5.5 includes the conclusion and inadequate of the study.

5.2 The classification of the large shareholders' relationship

5.2.1 The distribution of types and quantity of relationship among large shareholders

Through the investigation, it has been found that the relationships among the large shareholders of listed companies mainly include these types: shareholding relationship (Sh-re), association relationship (As-re), trusteeship relationship (Tr-re), authorization relationship (Au-re), concerted action relationship (Ca-re), and kinship relationship (Ki-re). Considering that As-re, Tr-re, Au-re, and Ca-re are relationships through formal or informal contracts; they are referred to as contractual relationships (Co-re). Thus, we divide the relationships among the large shareholders of listed companies into three categories: shareholding relationship (Sh-re), contractual relationship (Co-re), and kinship relationship (Ki-re).

As can be seen from Table 5.2, the main types of relationship among the major shareholders are a shareholding relationship and a contractual relationship. From a comprehensive perspective, 40.39% of the companies have major shareholders with a shareholding relationship, and 57.74% have a contractual relationship. However, the percentage of the shareholding relationships and contractual relationships had a downward trend recently, while the share of the kinship relationship has had a clear upward trend. In addition, multiple shareholder relationships do exist in some companies: two or more kinds of relationships may exist in several major shareholders. For example, the largest shareholder of the China Merchants Property Development (000024),

Table 5.2 **Quantity and proportion of different types of relationships among the large shareholders of listed companies**

Year	Sh-re	Co-re	Ki-re	Sh&Co	Multi-Co	Total
2008	282	416	60	32	18	808
	(41.59%)	(61.36%)	(8.85%)	(4.72%)	(2.65%)	(119.17%)
2009	320	429	103	38	18	908
	(42.78%)	(57.35%)	(13.77%)	(5.08%)	(2.41%)	(121.39%)
2010	403	584	189	50	28	1254
	(39.67%)	(57.48%)	(18.60%)	(4.92%)	(2.76%)	(123.43%)
2011	482	697	250	79	52	1560
	(38.87%)	(56.21%)	(20.16%)	(6.37%)	(4.19%)	(125.81%)
Total	1487	2126	602	199	116	4530
	(40.39%)	(57.74%)	(16.35%)	(5.40%)	(3.15%)	(123.03%)

which is the China Merchants Shekou Industrial Zone Co. Ltd. (40.38% of shares held by the listed company), not only holds 100% shares of the fourth-largest shareholder, the Dafeng International Holdings Co. Ltd. (2.87% of shares held by the listed company), but also has a concerted action relationship. In addition, 16 other contractual relationships also remain in the large shareholders.

Table 5.3 shows the distribution of shareholders' relationships in listed companies. In general, most large shareholders of listed companies have one type of relationship; about 15% companies contain two or three relationships. Interestingly, the percentages of the companies with six to ten relationships are just behind those with two to three relationships.

5.2.2 Analysis of shareholder relationships in different types of companies

By tracing the chain of equity, according to the nature of the actual control, the listed companies have been divided into state-owned listed companies and the private control of listed companies. In addition, there remain a small number of noncontrolling companies. State-owned and controlled companies include state-owned enterprises, local governments, or public institutions; private-controlled companies include private enterprises, individuals, village committees, and other civil society organizations. The distribution of the number of the two main controlled companies is illustrated in Figure 5.1.

Further tests confirmed that the relationship between the number of large shareholders and the nature of the company is significantly correlated, as shown in Tables 5.4 and 5.5.

Table 5.3 **Quantitative distribution of the relational shareholder from 2008 to 2011**

Year	1	2	3	4	5	6–10	11–20	≥21	Total
2008	313	125	92	46	24	65	10	3	678
	(46.17%)	(18.44%)	(13.57%)	(6.78%)	(3.54%)	(9.59%)	(1.47%)	(0.44%)	(100.00%)
2009	366	118	99	51	23	71	15	5	748
	(48.93%)	(15.78%)	(13.24%)	(6.82%)	(3.07%)	(9.49%)	(2.01%)	(0.67%)	(100.00%)
2010	473	136	148	75	31	116	25	12	1016
	(46.56%)	(13.39%)	(14.57%)	(7.38%)	(3.05%)	(11.42%)	(2.46%)	(1.18%)	(100.00%)
2011	569	178	191	68	30	148	27	29	1240
	(45.89%)	(14.35%)	(15.40%)	(5.48%)	(2.42%)	(11.94%)	(2.18%)	(2.34%)	(100.00%)
Total	1721	557	530	240	108	400	77	49	3682
	(46.74%)	(15.13%)	(14.39%)	(6.52%)	(2.93%)	(10.86%)	(2.09%)	(1.33%)	(100.00%)

Number

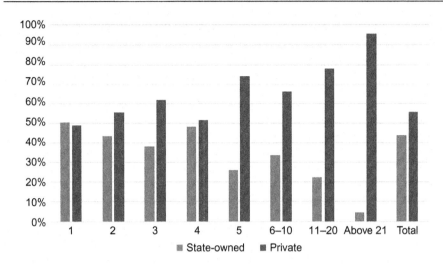

Figure 5.1 The proportion of number of relationships in state-owned and private companies.

Table 5.4 **Chi-square test of the relationship number of state-owned and private companies**

Number	Type of actual control		Total
	State-owned (%)	**Private (%)**	**Total**
1	53.88	40.94	46.63
2	15.08	15.06	15.07
3	12.54	15.98	14.47
4	7.20	6.04	6.55
5	1.74	3.90	2.95
6–10	8.32	12.91	10.89
11–20	1.12	3.07	2.21
Above 21	0.12	2.10	1.23
Total	100.00	100.00	100.00

Chi-square and correlation coefficient test

Chi-square	*Value*	*Diff.*	*P-value*
Pearson's chi-square	117.5853	7	0.000
Likelihood-ratio chi-square	128.0792	7	0.000

Correlation coefficient			
Cram's V	0.1792		
Gamma	0.2303 (ASE = 0.024)		
Kendall's τ-b	0.1372 (ASE = 0.015)		

Table 5.5 **Number of links associated with large shareholders *T*-test**

Group	N	Mean	Std. err.	Std. dev.	[95% Conf. interval]	
State-owned	1611	2.3563	0.0576	2.3135	2.2432	2.4694
Private controlled	2052	3.7510	0.1735	7.8573	3.4108	4.0911
Combined	3663	3.1376	0.1011	6.1164	2.9395	3.3357
Diff.		−1.3947	0.2023		−1.7913	−0.9980

Note: $t = -6.8934$, $Pr(T < t) = 0.0000$.

As can be observed in Table 5.4, there is a significant correlation between the number of the relationship and the nature of the company. By *T*-test, we can further confirm that the number of state-owned companies is significantly smaller than the number of private companies, as can be seen in Table 5.5.

5.3 Literature review and theoretical foundation

The literature of shareholders' homogeneity primarily focuses on the perspective of property rights, the type of ultimate controller, shareholding ratio, and ownership structure, but does not refer to the various implicit association among the major shareholders (Cai & Wei, 2011), which may result in shareholder heterogeneity. Within further study of the ownership structure, some scholars pay attention to the heterogeneity problem of the major shareholder. Recent literatures, like Maury and Pajuste (2005) show that although equal voting rights among large shareholders have a positive impact on corporate performance, the effect is subject to shareholder type. Cornett et al. (2007) claimed that the investment companies are more willing to monitor managers than banks and insurance companies because they have a relatively small business association with the manager. Bratton (2006), Kahan and Rock (2007), Briggs (2007), Brav, Jiang, Partnoy, and Thomas (2008), and Klein and Zur (2009) provide evidence that hedge funds are more likely to persuade companies to reform in order to improve their corporate performance, because then the manager's remuneration is directly linked with fund performance. Chen, Harford, and Li (2007) believe that conflicts of interest would exist among the shareholders and further test the effects of the shareholder heterogeneity on investment policies, stock transactions, and enterprise value. Cronqvist and Fahlenbrach (2009) agree with Shleifer and Vishny (1986) that the heterogeneity of major shareholders is partly due to conflicting interests of shareholders, arguing that the literatures almost does not refer to shareholders' heterogeneity as factors influencing corporate decision making. Holderness (2009) examines U.S. listed company data and validates the existence of shareholder heterogeneity: different types of shareholders show different professional backgrounds and investment motives. Cronqvist and Fahlenbrach (2009) suggest that executive style would influence corporate policy framework, dividing large shareholders into 11 categories based on different cognitive skills, investment style, and other preferences, and finally concluding that large shareholders with more impact and influence have a strong effect on company policies and performance. Harris et al. (2010) divide shareholders into active monitoring ones and moderate monitoring ones, basing the divisions on management's monitoring efforts, to find that effects of different types of shareholders on corporate financing decisions will show significant differences. Colpan, Yoshikawa, Hikino, and Esther (2011) examine the significant differences of corporate strategic decision among foreign securities investment shareholders, domestic corporate shareholders, and domestic financial institutions, pointing out that foreign investors tend to concentrate on the products' portfolio and conservative capital commitments; in contrast, domestic shareholders prefer to continue holding share to maintain a business relationship with the commercial partners when the company's performance decreases.

The relationship among shareholders is one of the important factors that bring about shareholder heterogeneity. A number of foreign scholars focus on political relations among large shareholders, verifying that these relations can improve company value; this is mainly because a politically associated company can easily acquire state-owned bank loans, achieving long-term interest rates and other preferential conditions, and thereby promoting the company's performance. For example, Boubakri, Cosset, and Saffar (2008) argue that a government with strong supervision would get involved with private companies by sending officials as their administrator. Charumilind, Kali, and Wiwattanakantang (2006) examined Thailand's listed companies during the Asian financial crisis, revealing that the company that maintains a good relationship by bringing in investment banks or other financial institutions will offer fewer collateral assets to secure long-term loans. Domestic scholars also confirm that the company value of China's listed companies with a local government background would be significantly overwhelm that with the central government background (Wu et al., 2008). Companies with political relations also have advantages in accessing bank loans (He, 2011).

A feature of "Guanxi management" is remarkable in China's commercial actions (Xu & Liu, 2012), especially in incomplete and unconstrained markets; relationships play an important role in access to scarce resources. This phenomenon is more prominent in private enterprise, driven by altruism and basic moral sentiment. It has been verified that the company with kinship shareholders, who share the same values and goals, can usually reduce agency cost at a maximum level (Karra et al., 2006; Wang & Zhou, 2006). Although some research has shown that along with the continuous improvement of the institutional environment, the governance model in family business, characteristic of kinship relationship, has generated a weakened management adaptability such as friction-prone (Wang & Zhou, 2006) and lower organizational efficiency (He et al., 2008; Pérez-González, 2006). However, this does not weaken the conjunction in the organizational structure; on the contrary, as this chapter has verified, the corporate control of the relational company is a growing trend. By the end of 2011, large shareholders with economic, contract, or kinship relationships exist in more than 50% of listed companies. It can be inferred that the relationship among the large shareholders has already broken the limits of kinship among family members in private enterprises. What is more, to some extent, the existence of economic and contractual relationships is a reflection of continuous development and improvement of the legal and institutional environment. In the modern corporate governance system, a single shareholder can exert influence over decisions only when his voting rights exceed a certain proportion; in accordance with the rules of the majority system proposed resolution system, that proportion of shareholding determines control power. However, the condition of the control power mechanism decided by pure shareholding ratio has been changed in the attendance of the shareholders' relationship. Relational shareholders could vote together to achieve specific control objectives. The structural allocation of control power is the result of the game of relational shareholders. What is more, it is more likely to weaken the control power mechanism by deciding through a pure shareholding ratio when complex relationships exist among large shareholders.

Relationship management is a unique internal governance practice in Chinese traditional culture (Yang, 2009), particularly in family business, where much attention is given to internal family relations. This results in management and operations that are more dependent on a company's internal relationship, but not on the management systems and mechanisms. Cooperation among family members is less dependent on social capital and social trust, due to reputation in internal network helping them maintain relation, whereas people would lose reputation as long as they become dishonest, further losing abundant profit opportunities. In addition, mutual trust between individuals in company networks can effectively reduce agency cost while eliminating speculative behavior and prompting the efficiency of resources utilization and overall level of operations (Gao & Guo, 2004). Putnam (1993) introduces "citizen participation" into the analysis of social capital. They believe that social organizations are characterized by social capital, such as norms, trust, and networks, which can improve the efficiency of society function by facilitating coordination and action. Fukuyama (1998) summarizes the meaning of social capital into the group's values and social norms, namely general social trust. Thus, it can be inferred that with the existence of shareholding relationships, contractual relationships, and kinship relationships among the large shareholders, independent shareholders together form an integrated large-shareholder alliance. The social networks of the alliance would reduce the coordination cost of shareholders, thereby increasing the social capital. Because the relationships among the shareholders reduce the coordination cost and increase the balance, it can be inferred that the increase in the social capital of the shareholders' network would bring further beneficial impacts. We address this view by testing the following hypotheses:

H1: Listed companies with relationships among the large shareholders have a better performance.

H2: Listed companies with relationships among the large shareholders have a relatively low cost.

H3: Listed companies with relationships among the large shareholders have a higher earnings quality.

5.4   Research design

5.4.1   Sample and data

Our sample is drawn from China's listed companies on the CSMAR database during 2008–2011. We exclude 122 financial companies, 320 special treatment companies, and companies lacking data. Thus, we have data available for 7423 cases.

5.4.2   Corporate performance

In order to examine whether the financial performance between relational and nonrelational shareholders is different, we have chosen for comparison a representative ten indicators in four areas to reflect the company's market value, profitability, risk, and operational efficiency. Table 5.6 lists the descriptive statistics of financial data in sample companies.

Then, we conduct a *T*-test of financial performance proxies between ISLC and RSLC, with results as follows.

From the Table 5.7, it can be seen that some significant differences in the financial performance between large ISLC and RSLC do exist. The market value reflects the sum of market capitalization and net debt of listed companies (the net asset stands for the nontradable market capitalization). The market value of RSLC is significantly higher than that of ISLC. In terms of the asset size, RSLC is significantly higher than ISLC. BVM (total assets/market value) reflects the relationship between the amounts of assets and market value; increases in this ratio to some extent indicates a coincidence of the market value and book value, revealing a high security of company assets. As can be seen from Table 5.7, BVM of RSLC is significantly higher than that ISLC. In addition, ROS and ROE (stand for profitability) of RSLC are significantly higher than those of ISLC. In contrast, LOA and COLEV of RSLC are significantly lower than those of ISLC, indicating that the total financial risk and operational risk of RSLC are significantly lower. As to operational efficiency, TATurn of RSLC is significantly higher.

In summary, compared to ISLC, RSLC has significantly larger operating assets, higher market value, better operational efficiency, and lower operating risk.

5.4.3   Agency cost

This chapter chooses management expenses ratio as a proxy of agency cost, which has widely been used in previous studies (Li, 2007; Luo & Zhu, 2010; Song & Han, 2005; Wan & Qu, 2012). Management cost is the total cost for operation and function, including reasonable expenditure and expense in-office, whereas expense in-office is the main access to resource embezzlement, So management expense rate (MER, ratio of operating expense to operating income) is the most appropriate indicator to observe and measure expense in-office. Table 5.8 lists the descriptive statistics of MER.

Further, according to the number and type of relationships among large shareholders, *T*-test is conducted to verify differences of agent cost among groups.

Table 5.6 Descriptive statistics of company performance proxies

	N			Mean			Standard error		
	Total	ISLC	RSLC	Total	ISLC	RSLC	Total	ISLC	RSLC
MV	7423	3900	3523	12,200	10,100	14,500	26,700	22,800	30,300
TQ	7423	3900	3523	2.1094	2.1125	2.106	1.7852	1.735	1.8395
BVM	7423	3900	3523	0.6715	0.6612	0.683	0.2689	0.2742	0.2625
ROS	7423	3900	3523	0.0882	0.0695	0.109	0.1888	0.2063	0.1648
ROE	7423	3900	3523	0.0917	0.0743	0.111	0.1315	0.1406	0.1176
EOS	7423	3900	3523	0.1836	0.191	0.1754	0.1742	0.1878	0.1573
LOA	7423	3900	3523	0.4692	0.5018	0.4332	0.2552	0.263	0.2413
COLEV	7423	3900	3523	3.4332	3.7339	3.1003	4.7782	5.3377	4.0448
TATurn	7423	3900	3523	0.7501	0.7354	0.7665	0.5253	0.5289	0.5208
LNASSET	7423	3900	3523	21.6268	21.554	21.7072	1.2769	1.2602	1.2905

Notes: MV: market value (in millions); TQ: Tobin's Q; BVM: ratio of book value to market value; ROS: sales profit margin; ROE: return on equity; EOS: ratio of expenses to sales; LOA: asset-liability ratio; COLEV: comprehensive lever; TATurn: total assets turnover; LNASSET: asset size.

Table 5.7 **Financial performance *T*-test of ISLC and RSLC**

	ISLC	RSLC		
	Mean	Mean	*t*-Value	Sig.
MV	10,100	14,500	−7.1827	0.0000***
TQ	2.1125	2.106	0.1575	0.5626
BVM	0.6612	0.683	−3.4968	0.0002***
ROS	0.0695	0.109	−9.0365	0.0000***
ROE	0.0743	0.111	−12.1226	0.0000***
EOS	0.191	0.1754	3.84	0.0000***
LOA	0.5018	0.4332	11.6715	0.0000***
COLEV	3.7339	3.1003	5.717	0.0000***
TATurn	0.7354	0.7665	−2.5484	0.0054**
LNASSET	21.5541	21.7072	−5.1674	0.0000***
N	3900	3523		

Notes: ** and *** Indicate statistical significance at the 5% and 1% levels two-tailed, respectively.

Table 5.8 **Descriptive statistics of MER**

		MER			
	N	Min	Max	Mean	Standard error
Number					
0	3900	0.0102	1.7933	0.1193	0.2228
1	1634	0.0102	1.7933	0.1062	0.197
2	529	0.0102	1.7933	0.1066	0.1921
3	517	0.0102	1.7933	0.0897	0.1011
4	233	0.0102	0.3278	0.0768	0.0561
5	105	0.0102	0.2572	0.0847	0.0594
6–10	383	0.0102	1.7933	0.1087	0.2075
11–20	77	0.0115	0.2963	0.0815	0.0508
Above 21	45	0.0156	1.7832	0.1162	0.2572
Total	7423	0.0102	1.7933	0.1107	0.2021
Type					
0	3900	0.0102	1.7933	0.1193	0.0036
1	814	0.0102	1.7933	0.1101	0.0078
2	1438	0.0102	1.7933	0.0981	0.0045
3	349	0.0135	1.7933	0.0982	0.0059
4	93	0.0153	0.2955	0.0861	0.0065
5	59	0.0102	1.7933	0.1418	0.031

Continued

Table 5.8 **Continued**

		MER			
N		Min	Max	Mean	Standard error
12	411	0.0102	1.7933	0.0934	0.0079
13	134	0.0172	0.6638	0.0947	0.0082
14	4	0.0309	0.0859	0.0678	0.0125
15	10	0.0209	0.1205	0.0711	0.013
23	72	0.0151	0.3295	0.108	0.0085
24	57	0.0192	1.7933	0.1052	0.0305
25	11	0.0102	0.2955	0.0848	0.0261
34	3	0.0437	0.0441	0.0439	0.0001
35	3	0.1081	0.2963	0.1894	0.0558
45	15	0.0302	1.7933	0.235	0.1207
123	35	0.0256	0.258	0.0746	0.0093
124	5	0.039	0.1978	0.1063	0.028
125	4	0.0229	0.1623	0.0755	0.0301
135	1	0.0555	0.0555	0.0555	
234	2	0.055	0.1443	0.0996	0.0447
245	3	0.0517	0.0836	0.0637	0.01
Total	7423	0.0102	1.7933	0.1107	0.0023

Notes: Number: the number of relationships among large shareholders; type: the type of relationships among large shareholders.

The result is shown in Table 5.9. It can be inferred that the types and number have a significant effect on agency cost, indicating that relationships among large shareholders change the effect of pure ownership on agency cost.

State-owned control is an important component of China's listed companies. There has been much research on the efficiency of a state-owned company, whereas the view of state-owned enterprises with a higher agency cost is generally agreed upon in previous studies (Li, 2007; Ping, Fan, & Chaoyan, 2003). Therefore, in this chapter, samples are divided into two groups based on their nature for T-test. Results are as follows (Table 5.10).

It can be seen that in general, the agency cost of state-owned companies is significantly lower than that of private companies in 2008–2011. This is not consistent with previous findings. Further, regardless of the nature of company, it can be found that the agency cost of RSLC is significantly lower than that of ISLC, showing that the intrinsic relationships among large shareholders reduce agency cost. This can be explained by the theory of social capital: the involvement of social capital improves the efficiency of corporate governance and reduces agency cost. A cross-examination of relationship is then conducted between state-owned and private groups, as shown in Table 5.11.

As can be seen from the table, even in the RSLC, the agency cost of state-owned enterprises is significantly lower than that of private enterprises, similar to ISLC.

Table 5.9 **MER rank sum test**

	N	MER
Number		
0	3900	0.0735
1	1634	0.0694
2	529	0.0653
3	517	0.0688
4	233	0.0617
5	105	0.0672
6–10	383	0.0724
11–20	77	0.0788
Above 21	45	0.0752
Chi-square		17.6820
P-value		0.0240
Type		
0	3900	0.0735
1	814	0.0640
2	1438	0.0677
3	349	0.0797
4	93	0.0710
5	59	0.0825
12	411	0.0680
13	134	0.0760
14	4	0.0772
15	10	0.0610
23	72	0.0884
24	57	0.0734
25	11	0.0404
34	3	0.0439
35	3	0.1638
45	15	0.0664
123	35	0.0516
124	5	0.0879
125	4	0.0585
135	1	0.0555
234	2	0.0996
245	3	0.0558
Chi-square		61.7280
P-value		0.0000

Table 5.10 T-test of the agency cost

Group	N	Mean	Std. err.	Std. dev.	[95% Conf. interval]	
State-owned and private						
State-owned	3784	0.0908	0.0025	0.1509	0.0859	0.0956
Private	3622	0.1309	0.0040	0.2406	0.1231	0.1387
			$t=-8.5563$, $\Pr(T<t)=0.0000$			
State-owned RSLC and ISLC						
State-owned RSLC	1524	0.0833	0.0033	0.1281	0.0772	0.0904
State-owned ISLC	2260	0.0958	0.0035	0.1643	0.0890	0.1026
			$t=-2.6023$, $\Pr(T<t)=0.0093$			
Private RSLC and ISLC						
Private RSLC	1986	0.1136	0.0045	0.1643	0.1047	0.1225
Private ISLC	1636	0.1519	0.0070	0.2814	0.1374	0.1649
			$t=-4.6381$, $\Pr(T<t)=0.0000$			

Table 5.11 T-test of agency cost (cross-sample)

Group	N	Mean	Std. err.	Std. dev.	[95% Conf. interval]	
State-owned RSLC and private RSLC						
State-owned RSLC	1524	0.0833	0.0033	0.1281	0.0772	0.0898
Private RSLC	1986	0.1136	0.0045	0.1993	0.1048	0.123
			$t=-5.4472$, $\Pr(T<t)=0.0000$			
State-owned ISLC and private ISLC						
State-owned ISLC	2260	0.0958	0.0035	0.1643	0.089	0.1027
Private ISLC	1636	0.1519	0.007	0.2814	0.1395	0.166
			$t=-7.2303$, $\Pr(T<t)=0.0000$			

The aim of our chapter is to examine how relationships among the large shareholders influence corporate performance (Section 5.4.1), agency cost (Section 5.4.2), and the level of discretionary accruals of earning (Section 5.4.3). In order to evaluate the influence of the relationship among the large shareholders on agency cost, in the first stage we divide the sample into state-owned and private based on the nature of company. In the second stage, to survey the relation between the relationship among the large shareholders and agency cost (MER), we regress agency cost, relationship among the large shareholders, and control variables. As proxies for the relationship among the large shareholders we use whether relational large shareholders exist in the company and the number of relationships among large shareholders, which we call RE and RENUM, respectively. The control variables, which may also affect agency cost, are leverage, managerial ownership, growth, equity restriction ratio (S), industry, and year, widely used in previous research.

In this analysis, the following models are estimated:

$$MER = \beta_0 + \beta_1 \times RE + \beta_2 \times LEVER + \beta_3 \times MANST + \beta_4 \\ \times GROWTH + \beta_5 \times S + \beta_6 \times IND + \beta_7 \times YEAR + \varepsilon \tag{5.1}$$

$$MER = \beta_0 + \beta_1 \times RENUM + \beta_2 \times LEVER + \beta_3 \times MANST + \beta_4 \\ \times GROWTH + \beta_5 \times S + \beta_6 \times IND + \beta_7 \times YEAR + \varepsilon \tag{5.2}$$

Table 5.12 reports the result of the regression of agency cost on relationships among large shareholders. In Model 5.1, a negative relationship between whether relational large shareholders exist and agency cost, shows that in both state-owned and private companies, agency of RSLC is significantly lower than that of ISLC. What is more, with the increase in quantity of relationships among the large shareholders, agency cost shows a significant reduction trend to prove that negative relationship between the number of relationship and agency cost. And it also proves that the relationship among the large shareholders conducts a function of balancing.

5.4.4 Earnings quality

Earnings quality has recently received increasing attention by regulators and the popular press. In this chapter, following previous research, we employ the absolute value of discretionary accruals as earnings quality. In the first stage, to preliminarily investigate the relationship between earnings quality and relationships among the large shareholders, we conduct a single factor variance analysis of earnings quality on the number of relationships, as shown in Table 5.13.

From Table 5.13, it can be found that significant differences exist in earnings quality of different groups. In the second stage, examining further the relationship between earnings quality and relationships among the large shareholders, we made regression on earning quality (discretionary accruals), relationship among the large shareholders (RE and RENUM), and control variables. The control variables that may also influence earnings quality are the nature of company (STATE, state-owned and private), the proportion of direct controlling shareholders (ZS), ownership proportion of actual controller (SSS), control proportion of actual controller (SSK), leverage, whether bearing a loss during two years (LOST), board size, the ratio of independent director (INDPER), whether the general manager or the chairman is one person (SZ), the asset, year, and industry, widely used in previous studies. The models are as follows; regression results are shown in Table 5.14.

Table 5.12 **Regression results of agency cost**

Variable	State-owned		Private	
	Regression coefficients			
	P-value			
RE	−0.015***		−0.014**	
	−0.001		−0.022	
RENUM		−0.004***		−0.003**
		−0.003		−0.016
LEVERAGE	0.001	0.001	0	0
	−0.161	−0.141	−0.811	−0.799
MANST	0	0	−0.000***	−0.000***
	−0.692	−0.691	0	0
GROWTH	0.014***	0.014***	0.011***	0.011***
	0	0	0	0
S	−0.001***	−0.001***	−0.002***	−0.002***
	0	0	0	0
IND	0.002***	0.002***	0.010***	0.010***
	−0.007	−0.007	0	0
YEAR	−0.002	−0.003	0.001	0.001
	−0.228	−0.196	−0.81	−0.81
_cons	4.937	5.281	−1.165	−1.165
	−0.217	−0.186	−0.831	−0.831
Adjusted R^2	0.052	0.052	0.063	0.063
F-value	30.621	30.34	34.873	34.971

Note: ** and *** Indicate statistical significance at the 5% and 1% levels two-tailed, respectively.

Table 5.13 **Earnings quality under a single factor variance analysis of relationship**

	Squares sum	df	Mean	F	Significance
Between groups	0.137	8	0.017	5.306	0.000
In groups	23.927	7414	0.003		
Total	24.064	7422			

Note: We divide the sample into nine groups based on the number of relationships, 0, 1, 2, 3, 4, 5, 6–10, 11–20, and above 21, respectively.

Table 5.14 **Regression results of relationship and earnings quality**

Variable	Regression coefficients/P-value	
RE	−0.005***	
	(0.001)	
RENUM		−0.001**
		(0.014)
STATE	−0.001	−0.001
	(0.721)	(0.714)
ZS	−0.000**	−0.000**
	(0.023)	(0.037)
SSS	−0.000*	−0.000*
	(0.055)	(0.063)
SSK	0.000**	0.000*
	(0.044)	(0.068)
LEVER	0.001***	0.001***
	(0.010)	(0.009)
LOST	0.020***	0.020***
	(0.000)	(0.000)
BZ	−0.001*	−0.001*
	(0.078)	(0.071)
INDPER	−0.008	−0.008
	(0.532)	(0.533)
SZ	−0.003*	−0.003*
	(0.077)	(0.068)
ASS	0.000	0.000
	(0.200)	(0.214)
YEAR	−0.001**	−0.002**
	(0.017)	(0.014)
IND	0.003***	0.003***
	(0.000)	(0.000)
_cons	3.039**	3.137**
	(0.015)	(0.012)
Adjusted R^2	0.043	0.043
F-value	23.761	23.419

Note: *, **, and *** Indicate statistical significance at the 10%, 5%, and 1% levels two-tailed, respectively.

$$DAC = \beta_0 + \beta_1 \times RE + \beta_2 \times STATE + \beta_3 \times ZS + \beta_4 \times SSS + \beta_5$$
$$\times SSK + \beta_6 \times LEVER + \beta_7 \times LOST + \beta_8 \times BZ + \beta_9 \times INDPER$$
$$+ \beta_{10} \times SZ + \beta_{11} \times ASS + \beta_{12} \times YEAR + \beta_{13} \times IND + \varepsilon \qquad (5.3)$$

$$DAC = \beta_0 + \beta_1 \times RENUM + \beta_2 \times STATE + \beta_3 \times ZS + \beta_4 \times SSS + \beta_5$$
$$\times SSK + \beta_6 \times LEVER + \beta_7 \times LOST + \beta_8 \times BZ + \beta_9 \times INDPER$$
$$+ \beta_{10} \times SZ + \beta_{11} \times ASS + \beta_{12} \times YEAR + \beta_{13} \times IND + \varepsilon \qquad (5.4)$$

The regression results further confirmed that after controlling for other key factors that affect earnings quality, earnings quality of RSLC is significantly higher than that of ISLC. What is more, with a large increase in the number of relationships, earnings quality show a significant positive trend, thus proving that the more relationships, the more shareholders balance and check, the more abundant social capital in company level, and, ultimately the higher the earnings quality.

5.5   Discussion and conclusion

Because the "Guanxi" culture has deep roots in China, it is inevitable that this relationship exists in the commercial actions among the listed companies. It has been verified that there remains a link between the top ten shareholders in approximately 50% of listed companies. In the long run, this kind of bonding relationship will change the impact brought about by the simple stake. In this research, based on social network theory, the impact on corporate performance, agency cost, and the earnings quality generated by relationship among the large shareholders and the number have been examined.

Some viewpoints have been verified in this research: (1) The overall financial performance of the abundant Guanxi network is significantly better than the company that lacks Guanxi. In the meanwhile, it is the common rule that the relational shareholders would provide more social capital to listed companies, resulting in different financial performance. (2) The relational large shareholders of listed companies have a considerably lower agency cost than the independent ones. Besides, in the relational large shareholders of listed companies, the state-owned company's agency cost is significantly lower than the private company. Among private controlled companies, companies with kinship relationships have a significantly lower cost than those with contractual and shareholding relationships. From the perspective of the regression results, it is certain that agency cost of RSLC is significantly lower than ISLC, and the more relationships they maintain, the lower agency cost they spend. This result can be found both in state-owned and private companies. (3) After controlling for other key factors, which affect earnings quality, earnings quality of RSLC is significantly higher than ISLC. Besides, earnings quality has a significant positive trend if the network of the stakeholder relationship is abundant. As a consequence, the more plentiful relations they hold, the more restrictions they experience; thus, the more abundant social capital they could provide, the higher earnings quality can be achieved. The implication of this study is that social capital is a positive factor for stakeholders, and relationships among shareholders is one path on which to build social capital. Other avenues for the social capital of shareholders is a direction for future research.

Acknowledgments

This chapter offers its appreciation of the following foundations: Youth Project of National Social Science Foundation of China (No. 11CGL026), Key Project of National Social Science Foundation of China (No. 13AGL003), and The Regular Visiting Scholar Program Subordinated to The Beijing Education Committee's Academic Human Resources Development Project (No. 067135300100).

References

Boubakri, N., Cosset, J. C., & Saffar, W. (2008). Political connections of newly privatized firms. *Journal of Corporate Finance, 14*(5), 654–673.

Bratton, W. (2006). *Hedge funds and governance targets.* Working paper. Available at SSRN: http://ssrn.com/abstract=928689.

Brav, A., Jiang, W., Partnoy, F., & Thomas, R. (2008). Hedge fund activism, corporate governance, and firm performance. *The Journal of Finance, 63*, 1729–1775.

Briggs, T. (2007). Corporate governance and the new hedge fund activism: An empirical analysis. *Journal of Corporation Law, 32*, 681–737.

Cai, N., & Wei, M. H. (2011). Shareholders relationship, collusion and tunneling: Evidence from the reduction of originally non-tradable shares. *Economic Management Journal, 33*(9), 63–74.

Charumilind, C., Kali, R., & Wiwattanakantang, Y. (2006). Connected lending: Thailand before the financial crisis. *Journal of Business, 79*(1), 181–217.

Chen, X., Harford, J., & Li, K. (2007). Monitoring: Which institutions matter? *Journal of Financial Economics, 86*, 279–305.

Colpan, A. M., Yoshikawa, T., Hikino, T., & Esther, B. D. B. (2011). Shareholder heterogeneity and conflicting goals: Strategic investments in the Japanese electronics industry. *Journal of Management Studies, 48*(3), 591–618.

Cornett, M. M., Marcus, A. J., Saunders, A., & Tehranian, H. (2007). The impact of institutional ownership on corporate operating performance. *Journal of Banking & Finance, 31*(6), 1771–1794.

Cronqvist, H., & Fahlenbrach, R. (2009). Large shareholders and corporate policies. *Review of Financial Studies, 22*, 3941–3976.

Fukuyama, F. (1998). *Trust—The creation of social ethics and prosperity.* Hohhot: Distant Press.

Gao, J. M., & Guo, J. G. (2004). The Analysis of mechanism and differentiation of trust in interfirm network. *Nankai Business Review, 3*, 63–68.

Hansmann, H. (1996). *The ownership of enterprise.* Cambridge, MA: The Belknap Press of Harvard University Press.

Harris, O., Madura, J., & Glegg, C. (2010). Do managers make takeover finance decisions that circumvent more effective outside blockholders?. *The Quarterly Review of Economics and Finance, 50*, 180–190.

He, J. (2011). Political connections, financial development and discrimination in bank loan cost. *Journal of Shanxi Finance and Economics University, 33*(6), 36–45.

He, X., Chen, W. T., & Li, X. C. (2008). Share or pan-family—An empirical study of professional manager governance in family firm. *China Industrial Economics, 5*, 109–119.

Holderness, C. (2009). The myth of diffuse ownership in the United States. *The Review of Financial Studies, 22*(4), 1377–1408.

Kahan, M., & Rock, E. (2007). Hedge funds in corporate governance and corporate control. *University of Pennsylvania Law Review, 155*, 1021–1093.

Karra, N., Tracey, P., & Phillips, N. (2006). Altruism and agency in the family firm: Exploring the role of family, kinship, and ethnicity. *Entrepreneurship Theory and Practice, 30*(11), 861–877.

Klein, A., & Zur, E. (2009). Entrepreneurial shareholder activism: Hedge funds and other private investors. *Journal of Finance, 64*, 187–229.

Li, S. (2007). Ownership, agency cost and agency efficiency. *Economic Research Journal, 1*, 102–113.

Luo, W., & Zhu, C. (2010). Agency costs and corporate voluntary disclosure. *Economic Research Journal, 10*, 143–155.

Maury, B., & Pajuste, A. (2005). Multiple large shareholders and firm value. *Journal of Banking and Finance, 29*(7), 1813–1834.

Pérez-González, F. (2006). Inherited control and firm performance. *American Economic Review, 96*, 1208–1228.

Ping, X. Q., Fan, Y., & Chaoyan, H. (2003). An empirical analysis of agent cost in China SOEs. *Economic Research Journal, 11*, 42–53.

Putnam, R. (1993). The prosperous community: Social capital and public life. *The American Prospect, 13*, 35–42.

Shleifer, A., & Vishny, R. (1986). Large shareholders and corporate control. *Journal of Political Economy, 95*, 461–488.

Song, L., & Han, L. L. (2005). An empirical analysis of influence on agency cost from holding proportion of large shareholders. *Nankai Business Review, 1*, 30–34.

Wan, P., & Qu, X. H. (2012). Chairman personal characteristics, agency costs and the voluntary disclosure of operating revenue plan: Evidence from stock market in China. *Accounting Research, 7*(15–23), 96.

Wang, M. L., & Zhou, S. C. (2006). The controlling family type, double three-tier principal-agent problems and enterprise value. *Management World, 8*, 83–93.

Wu, W. F., Wu, C. F., & Liu, X. W. (2008). Political connection and market valuation: Evidence from China individual—Controlled listed firms. *Economic Research Journal, 7*, 130–141.

Xu, X. X., & Liu, X. (2012). Founder's authority, allocation of control rights and governance transformation in family business—A case study based on the control conflict of GOME Ltd. *China Industrial Economics, 2*, 141–150.

Yang, G. F. (2009). Relation governance: The new assumptions of internal governance in Chinese family enterprise. *Inquiry into Economic Issue, 9*, 81–85.

Efficiency evaluation of listed real estate companies in China

Y. Wang, Y. Zhu, M. Jiang
Xi'an University of Architecture and Technology, Xi'an, China

6.1 Introduction

The real estate industry is a fundamental industry for social development, which makes up 23% of the total fixed asset investments in China. It has also been an important industry stimulating national economic growth since the 1990s. Therefore, the development of the real estate industry directly affects the national economy and social stability. The Chinese real estate industry boomed with the rising housing price and strong demand in large and medium cities over the past decade. The total investment in real estate industry was 8601 billion Chinese Yuan in 2013, which represents an increase of 19.8% over the previous year, according to the National Bureau of Statistics of the People's Republic of China. Meanwhile, the total sale of private housing was 130,551 million m^2 with 8143 billion Chinese Yuan, an increase of 17.3%. However, under the tightening governmental control on real estate industry and the implementation of a "housing purchasing limit"[1] in 2011, industry competition has become more intense and real estate companies should improve their efficiency for greater competitiveness. Therefore, to evaluate the efficiency of real estate companies and explore the efficiency differences between companies requires not only mastering the basic efficiency features of Chinese real estate companies but also presenting countermeasures for companies and policy suggestions to strengthen the real estate industry.

The most common methods to evaluate company efficiency are the parametric model and nonparametric model. The Stochastic Frontier Analysis (SFA), which was proposed by Aigner, Lovell, and Schmidt (1977) and Meeusen and van den Broeck (1977), analyzing efficiency of the building production function of the company, was the most commonly used parametric method. Data envelopment analysis (DEA) is a typical nonparametric method that measures relative efficiency by comparing it with the possible production frontiers of decision-making units (DMUs) with multiple inputs and outputs using linear programming (Farrell, 1957). This can handle

---

[1] Following the State Council's No. 10 Document (the full title is the "State Council's Notification on Firmly Curbing the Surge in Housing Prices in Some Cities") promulgated in April 2010, some big cities have developed policies to restrict the number of properties that are purchased; this is known as the "housing purchase limit" and is aimed at curbing speculation and excessive investment and promoting a stable and healthy real estate industry in the long term. As of October 31, 2011, more than 46 cities have implemented the "purchase limit," for example, Beijing stopped selling housing to local residents who already own two or more properties, and nonlocal residents who have paid social insurance or personal income tax for five years (or more) continuously can only buy one property.

multiple inputs and outputs conveniently without defining the production function nor the cost function; thus, many scholars use the DEA method to conduct research on efficiency. Hui, Wong, and Chiang (2005) evaluated the efficiency of the construction industry using the DEA model; the results showed that production efficiency in the construction industry was low. Both the quality of personnel and education levels were low, and the production technology was not advanced enough. Horta, Camanho, and Costa (2010) analyzed the efficiency of the Portuguese construction industry with two types of DEA models and advanced a corresponding competition strategy. Further, the DEA method was also widely used to measure the efficiency of enterprises in the services sector (Lee, 2013), banks (Mostafa, 2009), telecommunications (Resende, 2008), and power plants (Sarica & Or, 2007).

Efficiency research on real estate companies in China generally began in 2000. Zhang (2006) proposed a two-stage DEA model to evaluate the performance of the real estate companies, which evaluated the operational performance of 26 listed real estate companies for efficiency and effectiveness, and found that there was no significant correlation between these two indicators. Liu and Sun (2006) and Yuan and Gao (2009) analyzed the efficiency of listed Chinese real estate companies using the DEA method, and held that the overall efficiency of Chinese real estate industry was relatively high. However, Ren and Qian (2009) thought that most of the real estate developers were in diseconomies of scale, and resource utilization level was low when measuring the efficiency of 47 Chinese listed real estate companies in 2007 with the DEA method. Wang, Lin, and Han (2009) conducted similar research using the DEA method and concluded that Chinese real estate industry has entered a stage of rapid development with a substantial increase in productivity; meanwhile, the efficiency index of the real estate companies did not significantly positively correlate with the annual composite stock price index. Lu and Zuo (2010) estimated the efficiency of 45 listed real estate companies with panel data in the Tobit model. The empirical results showed that the efficiency of China's listed real estate companies was at a middle level; the proportion of large shareholders was positively correlated with technical efficiency (TE) and scale efficiency (SE), while market concentration and nonoperating expenses were negatively correlated with efficiency. Wang and Yang (2010) measured the dynamic investment efficiency of 57 real estate enterprises: the results showed the growth in efficiency of Chinese real estate enterprises mainly came from SE rather than pure technical efficiency (PTE), and the dynamic investment efficiency of real estate enterprises was consistent with regional economic development. Zhao and Li (2011) and Zheng, Han, and Pan (2013) made a comprehensive comparison of efficiency and total factor productivity (TFP) of real estate companies in China from a regional perspective. They concluded that the overall production efficiency of Chinese real estate enterprises was low, mainly due to the irrational industrial structure and diseconomies of scale, and the value of efficiency varying by region. Ran and Xu (2013) used the DEA-PNN method to study the efficiency of Chinese listed real estate companies and showed that not only the general efficiency but the comprehensive competitiveness of Chinese real estate companies was relatively weak.

In summary, the majority of Chinese research has focused on the efficiency of real estate companies from the static angle, most of which classify the real estate companies on their efficiency, ignoring the premise that similar units should have same goal, external environment, and input and output indicators. Although a few researchers did conduct a dynamic analysis using the DEA method, it supposed that production technique was constant by default, which was inconsistent with reality and weakened the explanatory power of the model. Further, in much of the literature, the sample capacity was small, and some samples contained companies whose main business was not property development. In this chapter, the data of 33 listed real estate companies whose property development business accounted for more than 80% in 2004–2011 were collected and screened rigorously, in order to make the conclusion more scientific and reasonable. Further, TE and TFP of real estate companies from the perspective of both static and dynamic were analyzed using DEA and the Malmquist index.

This chapter is organized into five sections. Section 6.1 is introduction. Section 6.2 describes the development conditions of Chinese listed real estate companies from five aspects. Section 6.3 offers model research, presenting the empirical results of efficiency of Chinese listed real estate companies. Section 6.4 discusses suggestions to improve the efficiency of the real estate companies. Section 6.5 concludes the paper.

6.2 Development of Chinese listed real estate companies

The real estate industry has been one of the pillar industries of the national economy in China since the early 1990s. The rapid development of the real estate industry has created a number of outstanding listed real estate companies, so the development of listed real estate companies reflects the basic situation and trend of the real estate industry directly. Chinese real estate companies from 2009 to 2013 were surveyed and featured the following characteristics.

6.2.1 Market concentration

Statistics showed that market share of both top 100 and top 10 real estate companies from 2009 to 2013 increased year by year, and the concentration of Chinese real estate industry improved steadily. As of 2013, market share of top 10 real estate companies reached 12%, accounting for 39.1% of total sales of the top 100 enterprises. On the one hand, only the annual sales of China Vanke Co. Ltd. were above 100 billion Chinese Renminbi before 2012, but seven real estate companies reached that mark in 2013, and the trend that following companies approached the top rank continues. On the other hand, the real estate industry has been also involved in a wave of merger and acquisition, and nearly 200 A-share listed companies (companies in Mainland China listed in the Shanghai or Shenzhen Stock Market) were involved in merger cases of real estate projects in 2013, such as Vanfund Real Estate Co., Beijing Capital Group Co., COFCO Property Co., etc. Moreover, real estate companies focus on a certain regions; it is more common that several enterprises occupy a large share of a city's development market. For example, Country Garden Co., Poly Real Estate Co., Agile Co., China Vanke Co., and R&F Properties Co. together had 25% of the market share in Guangzhou in 2011, and 12 listed real estate companies had two-thirds of the residential land market in Beijing in 2012, including China Vanke Co., Beijing Capital Development Co., Overseas Chinese Town Co., Poly Real Estate Co., China Merchants Co., etc. Resources will be further concentrated in large enterprises with the real estate industry becoming more mature and standardized; meanwhile, small real estate developers will gradually be squeezed out of the market.

6.2.2 Acquisition of land

The overall land acquisition scale of Chinese real estate developers was had been rising over the years, and prices trending in the same direction with the quantity of the traded land. However, the volume of land transactions fell significantly in 2012, but the land price of per square area still rose. Land is an important production factor for development, and real estate listed companies became a major force in the land market due to its strong capital strength and financing capability. Further, as stringent regulation policies for the real estate market in 2011 directly led to a reduction in land supply for construction, real estate developers reduced the development scale and expansion rate that had resulted from the alleviated sales growth rate and profit margins. To enact such changes, most real estate companies made a prudent strategy in acquiring land in 2012, and more attention was paid to enhance the quality of land reserves. In 2013, due to the land market boom driven by the heated sales again, the average land price of real estate developers reached 2555 Chinese Renminbi per m^2, which is the highest in recent years. Actually, the slowdown in land reserves also showed that the real estate companies were on the way to adjusting from extensive development to intensive development.

6.2.3 Financing channels

Chinese listed real estate companies have actively expanded financing channels by fine-tuning monetary policies and an improved financing environment. Common financing channels for listed real estate companies mainly include bank loans, overseas bonds, investment trusts, etc., and overseas bonds have gradually become the preferred financing mode for leading real estate companies because of their larger scale, longer-term, and lower average interest rate; small- and medium-sized real estate companies still rely on bank loans. In 2013, top 100 real estate companies' overseas bonds amounted to nearly 125 billion Chinese Renminbi, with a dramatic increase of 130%; the cost advantage is outstanding, with an average interest rate of less than 10%. Specifically, China Vanke Co., Poly Real Estate Co., China Overseas Property Co., and Greenland Group Co. controlled the financing cost to be under 9%. Further, state-owned real estate enterprises have a significant advantage in financing: the average financing cost is 7.2%, which is 2.2% lower compared with private enterprises. Accordingly, strong and large-scale real estate companies' financing channels are wide, and financing costs are relatively low, while small- and medium-sized real estate companies have narrow channels and high costs restricted by their own conditions.

6.2.4 Sales performance

With the adverse circumstances of the 2008 financial crisis, the size of real estate transactions fell sharply; transactions have quickly rebounded since 2009 because of government stimulus. In particular, the growth rate in housing sales volume of listed real estate companies reached 97.1%, a new record, dropped again significantly after 2010, and then made small gains in 2013. Affected by the State Council's No. 5 National Notice in 2013 and a series of regulation policies, the overall growth rate of the industry has slowed down and exhibited a rational trend. Sales revenue and net profit of listed real estate companies have generally been boosted from 2009 to 2013. 2013 saw an average of 5.6 billion Chinese Renminbi for listed real estate company revenue, with an increase of 30.10%, the highest in history. The net profit margin, however, is in a declining trend. The decrease of net profit margin has mainly resulted from the rising costs in land acquisition, construction and installation, marketing expenses, management expenses, and financial expenses. The costs of land, in particular, rose more than 30% in 2013, resulting in the downward trend of profit margin.

6.3 Methodology

In this chapter, in terms of characteristics of China's listed real estate companies, the BCC model (introduced by Banker, Charnes, and Cooper (1984), also named the VRS model) was used to compute the efficiency of listed real estate companies, which is the DEA model from input-oriented with the assumption of variable returns to scale. The BCC model added the factor of returns to scale on the CCR model introduced by Charnes, Cooper, and Rhodes (1978) (constant returns to scale, also known as the CRS model). The CCR model could only evaluate TE; however, the TE could be broken down into PTE and SE with the BCC model; that is, $TE = PTE \times SE$. Thus, the BCC model was more comprehensive compared with the CCR model.

6.3.1 Data

6.3.1.1 Indicators framework and sample selection

In order to fully reflect the efficiency of the listed real estate companies and meet the requirements of the BCC model, the input and output index system was created based on the following principles: (1) evaluation indicators should reflect and follow the evaluation requirements of real estate companies, (2) ratio indicators were avoided as much as possible, and (3) controllable indicators were selected from a management

Table 6.1 **Input and output indicators selected in related literature**

Authors	Input indicators	Output indicators	Model
Zhang (2006)	Total assets, capital, number of employees	Total profit, operating profit	Two-stage DEA
Liu and Sun (2006)	Average total assets, average shareholders' equity	Prime operating revenue, prime operating profit, net profit, turnover of total capital	CCR/BCC
Meng, Xing, and Chen (2008)	Number of employees, total assets	Net profit, operating revenue	CCR/BCC
Ren and Qian (2009)	Number of employees, average shareholders' equity	Prime operating revenue, net profit	CCR/BCC
Dong (2012)	Total assets, long-term debt, number of employees, cash paid to employees, taxation and dues	Operating revenue, operating profit, total profit, net profit	BCC
Ran and Xu (2013)	Total assets, shareholders' equity	Net profit, profit rate to net worth, return on equity	BCC

point of view. Some indicators used in related recent researches on real estate companies' efficiency have been collected in Table 6.1.

Total assets (X1), prime operating cost (X2), and period cost (X3) (including sale expenses, management expenses, and financial expenses) were chosen as the input indicators, and prime operating revenue (Y1) and net profit (Y2) were selected as the output indicators with reference to other scholars' researches as well as considering access to data. Total assets represented all resources the real estate companies owned or controlled, and prime operating cost meant the direct costs paid for the necessary input factors like materials and employees. Period cost consists of financial expenses, management expenses, and sale expenses, which are the daily business expenses of the real estate companies. Maintaining a low level of costs without affecting financial results reflects the cost control ability of the real estate companies. Among the output indicators, the prime operating revenue is referred to as the primary income of recurring and main business, which reflects production capacity of the enterprises, and the net profit is an important indicator measuring final profitability.

In order to ensure the validity of the data, samples were selected in accordance with two principles to constructing DEA model:

(1) The prime business of sample companies is real estate development. In some existing literature, it is unreasonable to select sample enterprises with diverse businesses, and the returns on real estate development accounted for less than 20% total revenue, which will distort the research results.

(2) Sample companies have stable operations. Enterprises that have a longer history in the stock market and stable operation were selected. Volatile companies, the Special Treatment shares' companies (companies of poor performance in the previous year), companies of no annual report and B-share listed (foreign capital stocks listed on Shanghai and Shenzhen stock) were excluded.

Finally, 33 listed real estate companies were chosen that mainly conduct real estate development from 2004 to 2011 in China. Data were collected from China Finance Information Network (http://quote.cfi.cn).

6.3.1.2 Data description

Data for indicators of the 33 A-share listed real estate companies are presented in Table 6.2. It shows that the prime operating revenue and net profit grew in different degrees from 2004 to 2011. The mean value of prime operating revenue expanded nearly six times during this period, with the highest growth rate of 72% in 2006–2007, but the minimum value basically stayed in the low level in this period, as did the net profit indicator.

As output indicators, the input indicators of listed real estate companies also presented an increasing trend year by year. The total assets, in particular, expanded 10 times during 2004–2011, when China's real estate industry underwent significant development, and properties of the real estate companies were rapidly accumulated. Further, Table 6.2 also showed that both the growth rate of prime operating costs and period costs were less than that of prime operating revenues and net profit during this period.

When importing the data into STATA12.0, Pearson's test was selected (Table 6.3). The result showed that the input and output indicators were highly positively correlated, which met the requirement of the premise of the DEA model that input and output indicators were in a monotonic relationship. Consequently, it is reasonable that the DEA model was used to analyze the efficiency of the listed real estate companies.

6.3.2 Efficiency analysis with DEA

BCC model was used with DEAP 2.1, and the TE of 33 listed real estate companies from 2004 to 2011 are given in Table 6.4.

As Table 6.4 shows, the overall TE of Chinese listed real estate companies was low in 2004: there were only nine companies with a TE of 1, which meant the enterprises were at the industry's efficient production frontier. The number of efficient DMUs fell sharply during 2008–2009 but quickly increased during 2010–2011 because of the recovery market. In 2009, only the TE of just four companies was equal to 1, and the mean value of all sample companies' TE was also the lowest in the whole period. Affected by the financial crisis of 2008, economic depression and decline in purchasing power have a significant impact on enterprises, which led to a low efficiency of the entire real estate industry. Efficiency of Shanghai Shimao is the lowest in the samples, which showed it had weak risk resistance capacity when confronting complex changes

Table 6.2 **Descriptive statistics of the 33 listed real estate companies (2004–2011)**

Years		Prime operating revenue	Net profit	Total assets	Prime operating cost	Period cost
2004	Mean	13.54	1.37	34.36	10.44	1.29
	Maximum	76.67	8.78	155.34	57.33	6.89
	Minimum	0.76	0.11	2.39	0.12	0.15
	Standard deviation	14.48	1.76	30.55	11.42	1.29
2005	Mean	13.45	1.75	39.63	9.69	1.41
	Maximum	105.59	13.65	229.15	75.26	10.02
	Minimum	0.45	0.01	3.33	0.19	0.14
	Standard deviation	17.89	2.58	42.03	12.94	1.71
2006	Mean	18.86	2.42	60.26	13.72	1.93
	Maximum	178.48	21.55	485.08	127.75	16.25
	Minimum	0.48	0.06	3.54	0.36	0.08
	Standard deviation	30.32	3.89	85.09	21.83	2.88
2007	Mean	32.59	5.21	109.86	23.15	2.98
	Maximum	355.27	48.44	1000.94	247.23	33.18
	Minimum	1.86	0.02	2.88	1.17	0.12
	Standard deviation	60.43	8.85	180.24	42.30	5.68
2008	Mean	36.45	4.92	141.56	25.42	3.22
	Maximum	409.92	40.33	1192.37	295.39	40.48
	Minimum	0.67	0.07	2.68	0.35	0.18
	Standard deviation	72.63	7.74	220.83	52.14	6.86
2009	Mean	48.13	7.04	196.78	35.10	4.14
	Maximum	488.81	53.30	1376.09	381.17	35.29
	Minimum	0.63	0.14	2.42	0.39	0.10
	Standard deviation	90.20	10.94	280.91	69.68	6.64
2010	Mean	63.74	9.77	275.91	44.95	5.51
	Maximum	507.14	72.83	2156.38	356.98	44.30
	Minimum	0.61	0.10	2.95	0.48	0.09
	Standard deviation	106.00	15.33	442.92	76.18	8.40
2011	Mean	79.38	11.62	349.47	55.56	7.21
	Maximum	717.83	96.25	2962.08	510.07	56.45
	Minimum	0.13	0.01	2.24	0.06	0.07
	Standard deviation	144.20	19.95	596.66	103.09	11.10

Note: The unit of the measurement for data figures is 100 million Chinese Renminbi.

Table 6.3 **Pearson's correlation test**

Indicators	Prime operating revenue	Net profit
Total asset	0.8703	0.8767
Prime operating cost	0.9983	0.9633
Period cost	0.8299	0.9131

Table 6.4 **Technical efficiency of 33 listed real estate companies (2004–2011)**

Company	2004	2005	2006	2007	2008	2009	2010	2011
China Vanke	0.910	0.939	0.902	0.855	0.895	0.867	0.864	0.930
Shenzhen Zhenye	0.776	0.897	0.975	0.924	1.000	0.707	0.869	1.000
Shahe Industry	0.820	0.903	0.892	0.875	0.986	0.982	1.000	1.000
China Merchants	0.927	1.000	0.783	0.878	0.704	0.869	0.999	1.000
COFCO Property	1.000	0.940	1.000	1.000	0.781	0.554	0.560	0.830
Shenzhen Centralcon	0.846	0.872	0.820	0.808	0.816	0.816	0.815	0.953
AVIC Real Estate	0.868	1.000	0.949	0.923	0.860	0.744	1.000	0.955
Oceanwide Construction	0.831	0.642	0.828	0.989	0.615	0.694	0.655	0.881
Overseas Chinese Town	1.000	1.000	1.000	1.000	0.934	0.936	1.000	1.000
Financial Street	0.990	0.880	0.857	1.000	0.912	0.541	0.791	0.934
Shenyang Ingenious	0.876	0.729	0.838	0.880	0.988	0.747	0.749	0.799
Hainan Haide	1.000	1.000	0.976	1.000	1.000	0.760	1.000	1.000
Yicheng Real Estate	1.000	0.758	0.904	0.854	0.858	1.000	1.000	0.932
Myhome Group	0.984	1.000	0.963	1.000	0.968	0.557	0.749	0.817
Rongfeng Holding	1.000	1.000	1.000	1.000	1.000	1.000	1.000	0.789
COSMOS Group	1.000	0.878	0.841	0.888	0.789	0.591	0.894	0.986
Rise Sun	1.000	1.000	1.000	0.958	0.994	0.963	0.948	1.000
Hefei Urban Construction	0.909	1.000	1.000	1.000	0.936	0.929	0.958	0.966
Poly Real Estate	0.921	0.900	0.807	0.816	1.000	0.914	1.000	0.941
Vantone Real Estate	0.844	0.876	0.747	0.807	1.000	0.722	0.880	1.000
Beijing Urban Construction	0.781	0.802	0.830	0.851	0.827	0.824	1.000	1.000
Tianjin Reality Development	0.773	0.718	0.694	0.688	0.728	0.494	0.739	0.874

Continued

Table 6.4 **Continued**

Company	2004	2005	2006	2007	2008	2009	2010	2011
Beijing Capital Development	0.840	0.665	0.634	0.735	0.873	0.560	0.750	1.000
Gemdale	0.879	0.918	0.862	0.879	0.904	0.636	0.911	0.935
Guangzhou Donghua	0.888	0.826	0.712	0.812	0.904	1.000	0.881	0.825
Nanjing Chixia	0.893	0.817	0.903	0.922	0.870	0.689	1.000	0.941
Shanghai Wanye	0.788	0.701	0.790	1.000	1.000	0.723	0.841	0.857
Lujiazui Properties	1.000	1.000	1.000	1.000	1.000	1.000	1.000	1.000
Tande	0.796	0.791	0.751	0.746	0.816	0.776	0.810	0.904
Shanghai Shinmay	1.000	1.000	0.902	0.671	0.910	0.700	0.532	0.812
Shanghai Industrial Development	0.997	1.000	0.703	0.786	0.820	0.585	0.887	0.832
Beih-Property	0.984	0.825	0.896	0.999	0.816	0.592	0.951	1.000
Shanghai Shimao	0.991	0.874	1.000	0.896	0.838	0.420	0.815	1.000
Mean	0.913	0.883	0.871	0.892	0.889	0.754	0.874	0.930
Efficient DMUs	9	11	7	9	7	4	10	12

Note: Efficient DMUs represent the number of the companies for which the technical efficiency is equal to 1 in corresponding year.

in the market. In 2011, both the efficient DMUs and the mean value of TE reached the maximum, which indicated that the average distance between the frontier of the production function of the 33 listed real estate companies and the efficient production frontier was shortened, and the gap between the companies was reduced gradually, so higher efficiency was an inevitable result of natural selection in the market. In particular, only Lujiazui Properties was technically efficient during the sample period, reflecting its stable operation, sound corporate governance, and good risk control capacity, which could protect the interests of investors. Lujiazui Properties was rooted and cultivated in Shanghai and has formed superior brand awareness and recognition in the local market; moreover, a strong background of shareholders provides the company with solid financial support, excellent project sources, and mature experience of project development.

TE, as mentioned previously, can be broken down into the product of PTE and SE by BCC model; that is, $TE = PTE \times SE$. PTE reflects the utilization level of investment elements on the condition of existing technology. SE reflects the contribution of scale on output. Therefore, in order to find additional reasons resulting in inefficiency of the listed real estate companies, TE was broken down into PTE and SE; both were analyzed separately.

Table 6.5 provides PTE of 33 listed real estate companies over the years. Most companies demonstrated pure technical inefficiency as a whole; the mean value of

Table 6.5 Pure technical efficiency of 33 listed real estate companies (2004–2011)

Company	2004	2005	2006	2007	2008	2009	2010	2011
China Vanke	1.000	1.000	1.000	1.000	1.000	1.000	1.000	1.000
Shenzhen Zhenye	0.841	0.915	1.000	0.927	1.000	0.795	0.892	1.000
Shahe Industry	0.821	0.904	0.899	1.000	0.989	0.983	1.000	1.000
China Merchants	1.000	1.000	0.800	1.000	1.000	0.932	1.000	1.000
COFCO Property	1.000	0.949	1.000	1.000	0.783	0.624	0.724	0.842
Shenzhen Centralcon	0.934	0.893	0.830	0.813	0.820	0.861	0.891	0.957
AVIC Real Estate	0.906	1.000	0.949	0.979	0.869	0.802	1.000	0.958
Occanwide Construction	0.834	0.647	0.833	1.000	0.616	0.695	0.709	0.886
Overseas Chinese Town	1.000	1.000	1.000	1.000	1.000	1.000	1.000	1.000
Financial Street	1.000	1.000	0.913	1.000	0.978	0.689	0.921	1.000
Shenyang Ingenious	0.885	0.781	0.840	0.886	1.000	0.755	0.750	0.807
Hainan Haide	1.000	1.000	1.000	1.000	1.000	1.000	1.000	1.000
Yicheng Real Estate	1.000	0.758	0.904	0.910	0.871	1.000	1.000	0.936
Myhome Group	0.984	1.000	0.992	1.000	0.968	0.566	0.794	0.819
Rongfeng Holding	1.000	1.000	1.000	1.000	1.000	1.000	1.000	0.789
COSMOS Group	1.000	0.922	0.887	0.900	0.795	0.698	0.897	0.995
Rise Sun	1.000	1.000	1.000	1.000	1.000	1.000	1.000	1.000
Hefei Urban Construction	1.000	1.000	1.000	1.000	1.000	0.996	0.964	0.997
Poly Real Estate	0.954	0.996	0.845	1.000	1.000	1.000	1.000	1.000
Vantone Real Estate	0.860	0.889	0.771	0.857	1.000	0.823	0.882	1.000
Beijing Urban Construction	0.811	0.822	0.830	0.851	0.828	0.976	1.000	1.000
Tianjin Reality Development	0.779	0.720	0.695	0.715	0.730	0.515	0.801	0.880
Beijing Capital Development	0.844	0.675	1.000	0.844	0.937	0.640	0.897	1.000
Gemdale	0.965	0.958	0.899	1.000	0.981	0.905	0.987	0.999
Guangzhou Donghua	0.998	0.826	0.767	0.812	0.945	1.000	0.881	0.837
Nanjing Chixia	0.905	0.889	0.922	0.942	0.871	0.802	1.000	0.945
Shanghai Wanye	0.831	0.702	0.801	1.000	1.000	0.858	0.908	0.874
Lujiazui Properties	1.000	1.000	1.000	1.000	1.000	1.000	1.000	1.000
Tande	0.797	0.825	0.752	0.749	0.830	0.836	0.811	0.905
Shanghai Shinmay	1.000	1.000	1.000	1.000	1.000	1.000	0.975	0.833
Shanghai Industrial Development	0.999	1.000	0.711	0.814	0.820	0.683	0.912	0.832
Beih-Property	1.000	0.825	0.902	1.000	0.818	0.823	0.970	1.000
Shanghai Shimao	1.000	0.905	1.000	0.897	0.853	0.441	0.927	1.000
Mean	0.938	0.903	0.901	0.936	0.918	0.839	0.924	0.942

PTE declined during 2004–2009 but rose rapidly after 2009. According to statistics, annual Chinese real estate investments experienced high growth from 2004 to 2011, with a growth rate of about 20%. The sales performance of 33 listed real estate companies increased differently. The increase, however, does not mean the improvement in efficiency of the companies and numerous enterprises showed inefficient operations behind good sales. The results showed that 90% of the companies had been in the state of efficient pure technology, and the PTE index of Shenzhen Centralcon, Tande, and Tianjin Reality Development was less than 1 each year, which implied the resource utilization of the three was low and need to be improved. In contrast, PTE of China Vanke, China Merchants, Poly Real Estate, and other leading enterprises were relatively high. For China Vanke, for instance, the PTE index was always 1 during the studied years, which indicated that the enterprise was operating at an excellent level for a long time and had obvious advantages in marketing decision, internal administrative control, coordinate management, and thus operation efficiency. The number of companies with a PTE index of 1 increased from 2009 to 2011, and it was found that over 90% of the enterprises had upgraded their internal management. For example, in terms of corporate governance, the chairmen of the board of directors in China Vanke and Vantone Real Estate withdrew from daily business management to focus on strategic planning and risk control management. Meanwhile, several companies began to pay attention to the optimization of organizational structure and regulatory framework, and more than a dozen real estate enterprises collaborated with RAND Corporation (the decision-making and consultation agency) in 2011, which had a positive effect on the management level of the enterprises.

Then SE of enterprises was analyzed. Limited by space restriction, the value of SE of 33 real estate companies over the years is seen in the Appendix. The number of companies in scale inefficiency over the years is given in Table 6.6: the results show that over 60% of the enterprises were in the state of scale inefficiency during the studied years, the ratio even reached 84% in 2009, which indicates that scale inefficiency is one of the reasons leading to technical inefficiency of listed real estate companies, so TE could be improved by controlling the scale of enterprise to reasonable size. SE values of Lujiazui Properties and Rongfeng Holding were always 1 in this period, which indicate that the proportion of the inputs to outputs of the enterprises was always in a superior condition, and factors of production displayed the biggest capacity in long term.

Through the statistical analysis of returns to scale of the enterprises (see Figure 6.1), more than 20 enterprises were in decreasing returns to scale in 2009,

Table 6.6 **Number of companies in scale inefficiency (2004–2011)**

Year	2004	2005	2006	2007	2008	2009	2010	2011
Companies in scale inefficiency	23	19	25	22	25	28	22	20
Proportion (%)	69.70	57.58	75.76	66.67	75.76	84.85	66.67	60.61

Note: Scale inefficiency means the value of scale efficiency index is less than 1.

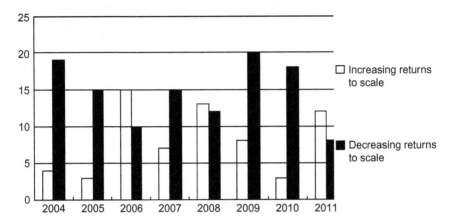

Figure 6.1 Returns to scale (the vertical axis represents the number of companies).

which reflected that most listed real estate enterprises were overinvested in a national expansion mode, while the increasing investment had not brought a corresponding increase in output. We can learn from the above that the leading real estate enterprises had higher PTE, but some strong enterprises like China Vanke, Poly Real Estate, China Merchants, Gemdale, and Financial Street were in decreasing returns to scale over the years, which also suggested that the mode of rapid expansion of the leading enterprises dragged down the TE, and that enterprises in such condition for a long period might face great risk. This has also caused the attention of some real estate companies; some said in 2010 that the growth mode would be refined from scale and speed growth into quality and efficiency growth, so the annual sales target had been lowered and more attention was paid to the quality of growth rather than the speed of expansion. However, there were also some enterprises in increasing returns to scale, such as Guangzhou Donghua and Shanghai Shinmay, which could expand scale appropriately for more output.

Annual trends of PTE and SE of the 33 listed real estate companies are shown in Figure 6.2. Both decreased and then increased; PTE and SE dropped to the minimum in 2009 but then swiftly increased. TE, as mentioned previously, is the product of PTE and SE, so the change trend in PTE and SE shown in Figure 6.2 coincided with the results that the TE showed the lowest level in 2009 but then increased in 2010–2011. In addition, the mean value of PTE was lower than SE every year, which suggested that the low TE of a real estate company mainly results from PTE and resource utilization and a need to improve management.

6.3.3 Analysis of total factor productivity

TFP of the listed real estate companies was analyzed based on the Malmquist productivity index. Over a period of time, external conditions for real estate developers changed, leading to an exploration not only of the change of TE but also the impact of technical progress.

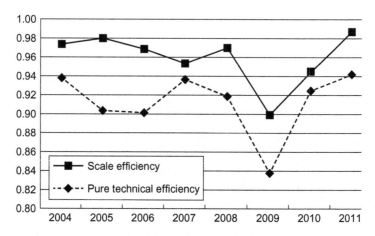

Figure 6.2 Annual trend of pure technical efficiency and scale efficiency.

Färe, Grosskopf, Norris, and Zhang (1994) analyzed the rate of productivity growth with the Malmquist productivity index; TFP expressed as Malmquist index was broken down into the product of efficiency change (Effch) and technical change (Techch). The Effch can be further broken down into the product of PTE change (Pech) and SE change (Sech); that is, TFP = Pech × Sech × Techch.

The Malmquist index represents the change degree in productivity from one period to the next. Productivity has been improved when the Malmquist index is greater than 1; the productivity of a company is in a declining trend if the Malmquist index is less than 1. Techch reflects the progress of technology and innovation. The technology of the industry advanced when Techch is greater than 1, while it shows a declining trend if Techch is less than 1. Effch represents the management and decision-making quality of the company, and there is an improvement in TE if Effch is greater than 1.

The Malmquist index was computed using panel data of the 33 companies from 2004 to 2011 in DEAP 2.1; the results are shown in Table 6.7.

Table 6.7 Malmquist productivity indexes of the listed real estate companies (2004–2011)

Year	Effch	Techch	Pech	Sech	Malmquist index
2004–2005	0.970	1.104	0.963	1.007	1.071
2005–2006	0.998	1.105	1.008	0.990	1.103
2006–2007	1.033	1.174	1.044	0.989	1.212
2007–2008	1.007	1.088	0.985	1.022	1.095
2008–2009	0.851	0.821	0.915	0.930	0.699
2009–2010	1.203	0.826	1.138	1.057	0.994
2010–2011	1.085	0.865	1.025	1.059	0.939
Mean	1.021	0.998	1.011	1.008	1.016

Malmquist indices of the 33 listed real estate companies reported significant fluctuation during 2004–2011, first increasing and decreasing subsequently. The growth of TFP was slow, with an average growth of only 1.6%. The Malmquist index is greater than 1 during 2004–2007, which meant TFP of the listed real estate companies had been improved, reflecting a significant progression in technological innovation. However, as Techch indexes during 2008–2011 are all less than 1, the declining technological innovation capability of real estate companies led to the reduction of TFP after 2008.

TFP of the Chinese real estate companies fell to its lowest level in 2008–2009 because of the decrease of both Effch and Techch. Since 2007, in order to restrain the continually rising housing prices, the government implemented strict regulations for real estate developers. Almost each commercial bank cut the credit loan on real estate enterprises, and developers faced huge financing pressures; this led to difficulties in improving technology and management levels. However, the global finance crisis temporarily rescued developers in view of its adverse effects on the whole economy, and TFP value increased in 2009–2010. But regulation orientation changed again, as the central government realized that the serious housing price bubble would damage sustainable economic growth. It conducted stringent regulation policies in 2010, and the real estate industry crashed with a sharp fall in housing transactions. In the same year, the government strengthened financial, taxation, and land supports for public housing (low- and medium-income) residents, and some purchasing power originally in the private housing market was diverted. Moreover, as described in Section 6.2, the net profit margin of the industry as a whole decreased year by year after 2009. Real estate enterprises had less money in technological transformation and innovation under these circumstances. Therefore, all the above factors hindered the improvement of the industry's ability to innovate.

In addition, many other factors have led to a lack of innovation ability in the technology and management of the real estate companies. These include the following particularities of Chinese real estate industry: (1) The low market concentration degree of real estate market in China is much lower than that of developed countries, and thousands of small real estate companies hindered the innovation of the industry as a whole. (2) There is an imbalance between supply and demand. Due to the strong demand in the housing market, real estate companies can quickly sell out their stock without much innovation, which weakens the enthusiasm of innovation. Hence, the above factors helped lead to a deterioration trend in the capability of technological innovation of real estate companies.

6.4 Discussion

Listed real estate companies are representative of the industry overall: this means that the healthy and rapid development of listed real estate companies has a great significance for the Chinese real estate industry and plays an important role in the maturing industrial structure. Therefore, based on research results, the listed real estate companies should improve their efficiency in the following ways.

First, the overall TE of Chinese listed real estate companies is low, mainly due to low PTE. Enterprises should strengthen internal organization and management, and improve the level of resource utilization, including the integration of existing resources and technologies. Furthermore, scale inefficiency is a factor that leads to low TE; most enterprises show decreasing returns to scale. It is unwise for real estate enterprises to recklessly expand the scale of investment; a company should control the scale at a reasonable size according to its own condition and optimize allocation efficiency of production factors in order to take full advantage of scale.

Second, the slow growth of TFP of real estate companies mainly result from a declining capability for technological innovation. Enterprises should actively increase their investment in technological innovation products and promote independent innovation ability through the introduction and assimilation of new products. Large state-owned real estate enterprises should take responsibility for original innovation, while small- and medium-sized enterprises could learn from these companies through re-innovating, which could improve innovation capacity of the entire industry.

Third, the results of efficiency analysis show that developing the local market is a common practice of real estate companies with high TE; thus, companies should consolidate the local market and extend market share by local advantage. Moreover, the high employee turnover rate creates extra training costs, corporate culture building difficulties, and some management inconvenience, which affect the companies' efficiency. Therefore, enterprises should improve human resource management to attract and keep more excellent employees and promote participation of employees in enterprise development and improvement of efficiency through offering incentives to managers and general staff.

6.5   Conclusion

This chapter first described the current development of Chinese listed real estate companies with regard to market concentration, acquisition of land, sales performance, and sales revenue and financing channels. It is found that most listed real estate companies have inefficient operations, with weak market competitiveness and low management levels. DEA was used to compute efficiency through panel data of 33 listed real estate companies from 2004 to 2011. The results show that the overall TE of listed real estate companies was relatively low and that most of the real estate companies had decreasing returns to scale. Scale inefficiency and low resource utilization were responsible for the low TE. TFP of the listed real estate companies was measured and found that the average growth of TFP of listed real estate companies was only 1.6% and was hindered by a decline in the capability for technical innovation. Reasons for low efficiency and weak innovation aptitude are analyzed in terms of market environment and policies as well as the characteristics of the real estate industry in China. Some recommendations are given.

The Chinese real estate industry is gradually stepping into a way of specialization and branding. Competition between companies improved under stringent regulations, so real estate companies developed high efficiency to survive fierce industry competition. Real estate companies are supposed to pay more attention to enhancing soft power, such as qualities in professional management, property services, and brand influence, which improve the efficiency of the industry overall while bringing differentiated competitive advantages to the enterprises. The results also showed that the technological innovation capability of real estate companies is in a declining trend. Since innovation is the driving force of technological progress, Chinese real estate enterprises should actively learn from leading companies' re-innovations, which enhance the productivity of the entire industry. Finally, the factors affecting the efficiency gap between listed real estate companies have not been analyzed in this chapter due to space restrictions. This is an issue for future research.

Appendix Scale efficiency of 33 listed real estate companies (2004–2011)

Company	2004	2005	2006	2007	2008	2009	2010	2011
China Vanke	0.910	0.939	0.902	0.855	0.895	0.867	0.864	0.930
Shenzhen Zhenye	0.923	0.980	0.975	0.997	1.000	0.889	0.974	1.000
Shahe Industry	0.998	0.999	0.993	0.875	0.996	1.000	1.000	1.000
China Merchants	0.927	1.000	0.978	0.878	0.704	0.932	0.999	1.000
COFCO Property	1.000	0.990	1.000	1.000	0.998	0.887	0.773	0.985
Shenzhen Centralcon	0.906	0.976	0.989	0.994	0.995	0.948	0.914	0.995
AVIC Real Estate	0.958	1.000	0.999	0.943	0.990	0.928	1.000	0.996
Oceanwide Construction	0.997	0.993	0.994	0.989	0.998	0.999	0.924	0.994
Overseas Chinese Town	1.000	1.000	1.000	1.000	0.934	0.936	1.000	1.000
Financial Street	0.990	0.880	0.939	1.000	0.932	0.785	0.859	0.934
Shenyang Ingenious	0.989	0.934	0.998	0.993	0.988	0.989	1.000	0.990
Hainan Haide	1.000	1.000	0.976	1.000	1.000	0.760	1.000	1.000
Yicheng Real Estate	1.000	1.000	0.999	0.938	0.985	1.000	1.000	0.995
Myhome Group	1.000	1.000	0.970	1.000	0.999	0.983	0.943	0.998
Rongfeng Holding	1.000	1.000	1.000	1.000	1.000	1.000	1.000	1.000
COSMOS Group	1.000	0.952	0.948	0.986	0.992	0.846	0.996	0.991
Rise Sun	1.000	1.000	1.000	0.958	0.994	0.963	0.948	1.000
Hefei Urban Construction	0.909	1.000	1.000	1.000	0.936	0.933	0.993	0.968
Poly Real Estate	0.965	0.904	0.955	0.816	1.000	0.914	1.000	0.941

Continued

Company	2004	2005	2006	2007	2008	2009	2010	2011
Vantone Real Estate	0.981	0.985	0.969	0.942	1.000	0.877	0.998	1.000
Beijing Urban Construction	0.963	0.977	1.000	1.000	0.999	0.844	1.000	1.000
Tianjin Reality Development	0.992	0.997	0.998	0.962	0.997	0.958	0.922	0.994
Beijing Capital Development	0.995	0.985	0.634	0.871	0.932	0.874	0.836	1.000
Gemdale	0.911	0.958	0.958	0.879	0.921	0.703	0.923	0.936
Guangzhou Donghua	0.890	1.000	0.929	1.000	0.956	1.000	0.999	0.986
Nanjing Chixia	0.987	0.919	0.980	0.978	0.998	0.859	1.000	0.997
Shanghai Wanye	0.948	0.999	0.985	1.000	1.000	0.843	0.926	0.980
Lujiazui Properties	1.000	1.000	1.000	1.000	1.000	1.000	1.000	1.000
Tande	0.999	0.959	0.998	0.997	0.982	0.929	0.999	0.999
Shanghai Shinmay	1.000	1.000	0.902	0.671	0.910	0.700	0.545	0.975
Shanghai Industrial Development	0.998	1.000	0.989	0.966	1.000	0.856	0.972	0.999
Beih-Property	0.984	1.000	0.994	0.999	0.997	0.720	0.981	1.000
Shanghai Shimao	0.991	0.966	1.000	0.999	0.982	0.951	0.879	1.000
Mean	0.973	0.979	0.968	0.954	0.970	0.899	0.945	0.987

Acknowledgements

The authors wish to appreciate the support from Research Project of Shaanxi Provincial Education Department (No.2013JK0147).

References

Aigner, D., Lovell, C. A., & Schmidt, P. (1977). Formulation and estimation of stochastic frontier production functions models. *Journal of Econometrics*, 6(1), 21–37.

Banker, R. D., Charnes, A., & Cooper, W. W. (1984). Some models for estimating technical and scale inefficiencies in data envelopment analysis. *Management Science*, 30(9), 1078–1092.

Charnes, A., Cooper, W. W., & Rhodes, E. (1978). Measuring the efficiency of decision making units. *European Journal of Operational Research*, 2(6), 429–444.

Dong, M. S. (2012). The empirical research of efficiency of competitive state-owned and private enterprises. *Soft Science*, 1, 98–103 (in Chinese).

Färe, R., Grosskopf, S., Norris, M., & Zhang, Z. (1994). Productivity growth, technical progress, and efficiency change in industrialized countries. *The American Economic Review*, 84(1), 66–83.

Farrell, M. J. (1957). The measurement of productive efficiency. *Journal of the Royal Statistical Society, 120*(3), 253–290.

Horta, I. S., Camanho, A. S., & Costa, J. M. D. (2010). Performance assessment of construction companies integrating key performance indicators and data envelopment analysis. *Journal of Construction Engineering and Management, 136*(5), 581–594.

Hui, E. C. M., Wong, F. K. W., & Chiang, Y. H. (2005). The impact of capital offering on real estate developers and construction sector stock return in Hong Kong. *Property Management, 23*(3), 204–216.

Lee, B. L. (2013). Productivity, technical and efficiency change in Singapore's services sector, 2005 to 2008. *Applied Economics, 45*(15), 2023–2029.

Liu, Y. L., & Sun, Z. M. (2006). Evaluation of the efficiency of listed real estate companies by DEA. *Statistics & Information Forum, 21*(1), 74–78 (in Chinese).

Lu, J. C., & Zuo, X. F. (2010). Analyze the efficiency and its influencing factors of China's listed real estate companies based on super-efficiency DEA-Tobit model. *Luojia Management Review, 2*, 156–162 (in Chinese).

Meeusen, W., & van den Broeck, J. (1977). Efficiency estimation from Cobb–Douglas production functions with composed error. *International Economic Review, 18*(2), 435–444.

Meng, C. J., Xing, F., & Chen, Y. (2008). A DEA-based evaluation of real estate enterprises' efficiency. *Management Review, 7*, 57–62 (in Chinese).

Mostafa, M. M. (2009). Modeling the efficiency of top Arab banks: A DEA—Neural network approach. *Expert Systems with Application, 36*(1), 309–320.

Ran, M. S., & Xu, B. (2013). Using a DEA-PNN approach to model the efficiency of real estate public company. *Journal of Chongqing University (Social Science Edition), 19*(3), 59–64 (in Chinese).

Ren, F., & Qian, Z. (2009). Empirical research on efficiency measurement of real estate companies. *Construction Economy, 2*, 110–114 (in Chinese).

Resende, M. (2008). Efficiency measurement and regulation in US telecommunications: A robustness analysis. *International Journal of Production Economics, 114*(1), 205–218.

Sarica, K., & Or, I. (2007). Efficiency assessment of Turkish power plants using data envelopment analysis. *Energy, 32*(8), 1484–1499.

Wang, G., Lin, Y., & Han, Y. F. (2009). Research on the efficiency of Chinese real estate companies (2000–2006). *Modern Economics, 8*, 95–99 (in Chinese).

Wang, J. Q., & Yang, J. J. (2010). Analysis on dynamic investment efficiency in real-estate enterprises: Based on the Malmquist index approach. *Contemporary Economy and Management, 32*(1), 84–88 (in Chinese).

Yuan, F., & Gao, Y. (2009). Evaluation and optimization analysis of the efficiency of real estate industry in China-based on 20 Chinese listed real estate companies from 2000 to 2007. *Modern Business, 14*, 60–62 (in Chinese).

Zhang, B. (2006). To evaluate on the efficiency of listed real estate companies. *Statistics and Decision, 4*, 55–57 (in Chinese).

Zhao, N. X., & Li, C. (2011). Efficiency research of real estate in China. *Modern Economy Information, 16*, 274–275 (in Chinese).

Zheng, J. J., Han, X., & Pan, Z. Y. (2013). Analysis on TFP growth and convergence in real estate development companies based on Malmquist index method. *China Soft Science, 3*, 141–151 (in Chinese).

An appraisal of Xi'an real estate developers core competence

7

Y. Wang, P. Bai, E. Wang
Xi'an University of Architecture and Technology, Xi'an, China

7.1 Introduction

The competition among Xi'an real estate developers is increasingly fierce because of stringent government regulations, increasing industry concentration and rising external operation costs. Accordingly, the real estate developers must cultivate their core competence so as to gain sustainable competitive advantage. Many developers have tried to do this. However, above all, a company is supposed to identify its core competence first, thus the core competence evaluation of real estate developers is essential. With the growing marketization and increasingly stiff competition among Chinese real estate developers, the research on core competence appraisal has sprouted in China.

Xi'an is the capital of Shaanxi Province and the largest city in Northwest China. It is located on the Guanzhong basin, which lies in the middle of the Yellow River of China. The whole acreage is 9983 km^2; its completed urban area is 1066 km^2. By the end of 2012, four counties, including Zhouzhi, Lantian, Huxian, and Gaoling, and nine municipal districts, including Xincheng, Beilin, Lianhu, Yanta, Weiyang, Baqiao, Yanliang, Lintong, and Chang'an, are under its jurisdiction.

Since 1989, the Xi'an real estate market has gradually developed; however, after 2006, it began to experience a rapid growth featuring large-scale development and surging housing prices. In 2008, the U.S. financial crisis triggered a global financial crisis. The state adopted measures to rescue the market, and the real estate market began to rebound. But a lot of money flowing into the real estate market triggered a series of events: (1) Property prices rose sharply. (2) The speculative investment in the real estate market flooded. (3) Real estate market bubbles appeared. In order to regulate housing price, the central government has introduced relevant policies since 2010, including regulating the land market, curbing speculative investment demand, adjusting monetary policy, reducing the amount of loans to developers, implementing property tax, and adjusting the house supply structure. In short, it has upgraded the regulations on the real estate market.

In 2013, the annual GDP of Xi'an was 488.41 billion Chinese Renminbi. Local fiscal revenue exceeded 50 billion Chinese Renminbi with 11.1% of growth rate, which is twice the value of 2010. In 2013, Xi'an residential real estate transaction volume was 12.32 million m^2, with an increase of 19%. With the rapid economic development of Xi'an, the development of the real estate market developed fast. By 2013, Xi'an had 487 real estate developers, compared to 101 in 2005, and the number of firms is still in a consistent upward trend.

A high debt-to-asset ratio increases the operating risk of businesses. The debt-to-asset ratio of city real estate developers went up to over 70%, resulting in low anti-risk capability. The restriction on the speculative investment and the implementation of expecting property tax policy resulted in an increasing housing inventory, so destocking became the primary issue especially for small- and medium-sized enterprises. Besides, large developers originated in other major cities, such as Shenzhen and Shanghai, and dominated Xi'an's real estate development market. China Overseas Land & Investment, Ltd., one of the largest Chinese developers, developed residential housing in Xi'an tentatively, at first. Its first project lay to the south of the second ring road and was very successful. Subsequently, China Vanke Co. Ltd. and Greenland Group rushed into Xi'an market. By the end of 2005, Xi'an Gemdale had also established regional companies here. Hutchison Whampoa and Henderson from Hong Kong and Capitaland from Singapore also appeared.

These exotic real estate developers have strong capital and brand strength, an elaborate development philosophy and product lines, and advanced decision making and management capacity. They can rapidly respond to market changes and continually expand. In contrast, local developers were in a disadvantaged position, despite having advantages in acquiring land. With stronger government regulations, that advantage will be weakened.

7.2 Literature review

The research here fell into three categories.

First, the concept of core competence for real estate developers was identified. Wang and Xu (2008) discussed the characteristics, source, and specific forms of core competence for real estate developers and proposed that it involve the strategic planning capacity, the ability to integrate, the power of the brand, and the ability to control. They mentioned that importance should be attached to the management of core competence, particularly in its identification, cultivation, innovation, and enhancement, so as to bring sustainable competitive advantage for developers. Zhou and Xie (2005) analyzed the value creation process of the real estate developers in terms of the value chain theory and competitive advantage theory and refined the value creation strategic segments and source of competitive advantages. It concluded that the core competence for real estate developers included capability of strategic planning, resource integration, and innovation.

Secondly, much research is interested in how to build and enhance the core competence for real estate developers. Huang (2004) presented that information technology can enhance the core competence, and it can be realized by methods, such as a new marketing network, customer relationship management system, etc. Zhang (2004) deemed that a low-cost management mode can be implemented in real estate developers to improve its core competence. Xia and Zhan (2005), according to the basic meaning of the core competence theory and the characteristics of real estate industry, proposed some strategies to strengthen internal management so as to enhance the core competence for real estate developers. They also warned that in the process, developers need to emphasize underlying works, for instance, the establishment of a modern enterprise system, a rapid response mechanism to the enterprise, the improvement of the quality of corporate managers, and the clarification of the scope and task deadline of responsibilities. To some extent, the competition in Chinese real estate developers has changed from price competition to nonprice competition. In terms of it, operation in scale and unique core competence can help companies develop sustainably. Yan and Jing (2009) defined the core competence of China's real estate developers and proposed some measures to cultivate the core competence, for instance, differentiation management, technology innovation, establishing their own comparative advantages, strengthening corporate culture, and strengthening information application in the real estate developers. Zeng (2011) built the 4V marketing strategies (variation, versatility, value, and vibration) involving implementation of differentiated marketing, improvement of the flexibility of product features, increasing the value added of products, and promoting resonance between real estate developers and its customers.

Apart from that research into the core competence evaluation for real estate developers, studies in this field are inadequate. It is known that core competence theory got its start in the study of home appliances and other manufacturing sectors. However, real estate industry has its particularities, like locality, high value, differentiation, etc., so its core competence evaluation index system should be different from that of general business. Yan and Jiang (2006), combining the characteristics of core competence for real estate developers, established the core competence evaluation framework: the ability to obtain core resources; the ability to create value for customers, such as investment value, innovation capacity, and corporate culture. Mou, Liu, and Zhang (2012), according to the influencing factors analysis on the core competence for real estate developers, constructed the core competence evaluation model and conducted a case study with it. The indicators are about land resources conditions, human resources, innovation capacity, integration and development capabilities, financial situation, brand value, customer service, and management capabilities. The research evaluated three major listed real estate developers, including Vanke, Poly, and Hengda. The results suggested that the core competence of Vanke was the best, followed by Poly and Hengda. Vanke did not pursue the biggest land reserves volume but improved the quality of land, which avoided taking up a lot of money so as to ensure a reliable financial chain, and built a set of values and corporate culture attracting a large number of valuable white-collar workers.

Despite a number of related works on core competence for real estate developers, there are some deficiencies in this field. Further studies need to be improved upon in the indicators frame of the core competence and general appraisal models for all local enterprises. Most of the research focused on big, famous regional developers instead of local developers, who were always ignored but an important part of the local real estate industry. For example, in Xi'an, compared to major immigrant real estate developers, the development scale of every local company is smaller, but their total development quantity is responsible for a big share of Xi'an real estate market (about 70%); thus, they are good representatives of local market quality. Only the competence of these developers is improved, the competitiveness of local real estate developers can be largely enhanced. Hence, they deserve to be researched.

This chapter was organized as follows: Section 7.1 is the introduction, including the development of the Xi'an real estate industry. Section 7.2 is the literature review, which analyzes earlier research on the core competence for real estate developers. Section 7.3 identifies the core competence in terms of the value chain theory, then the study establishes an evaluation indicators model from both qualitative and quantitative perspectives. In Section 7.4, through an investigation of statistics and firms' questionnaires, the chapter collected data of 20 real estate developers in Xi'an on 20 key indicators; it selected the former 15 samples as training samples, the latter 5 samples as test samples, and conducted the support vector machine (SVM) intelligent evaluation model. Section 7.5 evaluates one real estate developer in Xi'an by the SVM intelligent evaluation model and analyzes the results. Section 7.6 presents the conclusion and the inadequacies of the study.

7.3   Methodology

The value chain analysis was put forward by the famous American Professor Michael Porter; he used a systematic approach to investigate the activities of enterprises and their mutual relations, and then determined the advantageous resources and capacity. The value chain analysis method can effectively pick up the activities of the enterprise exerted to competitive advantage and enable the company to achieve success. The method can also explain how to build competitive advantage by restructuring these activities. Developers' value chain means the sum of all the value-creating activities, the core competences of developers are from one or two certain activities of the value chain. Thus, the value chain is the basis of core competence of developers. By analyzing the importance of all parts of the value chain and their impacts on profit contribution, the chapter could find out the source of corporate competence (Li, 2009).

7.3.1   Appraisal index framework

Through the real estate development process analysis, this part extracted key segments of the value chain. Then, the relationship between the value chain and core competence was analyzed. At last, the chapter identified factors affecting real estate developer's core competence and established an evaluation index system.

7.3.1.1   Value chain analysis of real estate developers

In most of the research on the real estate project development business, the division of business process is almost similar. The value chain of real estate developers consists of five essential activities and four support activities (Wu, 2008). The basic activities are explained below:

(1) Preinvestment decision making
    Works in this stage include market research, feasibility studies, and assessment of the expected benefits and other activities, which aim to decide whether to develop the project.

(2) Construction preparation

This step provides resources and conditions for the subsequent construction activities, including land acquisition, project positioning, planning and design, materials and equipment, bidding, and relic exploration.

(3) Construction

This is the building phase of the project, which is key to the formation of the final product. During this stage, developers have to use a variety of knowledge, skills, information, methods, and tools to do "three controls and two managements and one coordination"—control of cost, schedule, and quality; contract management and information management; and coordination with the surrounding environment and the government.

(4) Marketing

This is the sales process, which realizes the value of building products and achieves profits through trading activities.

(5) After-sales service

This stage is mainly the daily management of the property company, which has a great impact on the image, reputation, and brand building. Many prestigious real estate companies have now begun to use satisfied property management services to enhance their core competence.

Further, the real estate developer's value chain's support activities include:

(1) Basic management

The basic management activities of real estate developers including strategic management, information management, financial management, cultural management, brand management, and other activities are the basis for all other activities. They generally run through the entire value chain activities in real estate development businesses.

(2) Human resource management

Real estate development is a complex system. It needs specialists with great psychological qualities and professional knowledge to support its efficient operations. The project development process requires lots of professionals in project management, architectural design, landscape design, cost management, financial management, marketing, and senior management personnel with better comprehensive capabilities. Developers should attach importance to personnel selecting, training, and developing, so that it can improve the core competitiveness of enterprises to maintain a competitive advantage (Jiang, 2006).

(3) Technology development and innovation

Real estate developers use technological innovation approaches to cope with the changing markets, which include management innovation, system innovation, new materials applications, and the implementation of new norms. Besides, planning and design innovation can build a distinguished community appearance and form. Accordingly, a new product line can enhance a product's value. Innovations play an important role in enhancing the core competence of developers (Wang, 2006).

(4) Procurement

Procurement in real estate developers is different from that of general business, which includes land acquisition by auction, bidding to select construction companies and supervision agents, raw material procurement, information acquisition, etc.

7.3.2 Evaluation index establishment

Based on the indicators of system establishment principles and the correlation analysis of the real estate developer's value chain and core competence, the chapter establishes the evaluation index system of the real estate developer's core competitive, as shown in Table 7.1.

Table 7.1 The evaluation system of real estate developer's core competence

First-level indicators	Second-level indicators
Personnel factors F_1	Proportion of technical staff F_{11}
	Technical staff work experience F_{12}
	Average education level of employees F_{13}
	Staff training mechanism F_{14}
	Employee's ability of value creating F_{15}
	Staff retention rate F_{16}
	Staff cohesion F_{17}
Organizational factors F_2	The level of corporate culture F_{21}
	Information management level F_{22}
	Corporate communications and resource sharing F_{23}
	Organization structure standardization F_{24}
	Regulations degree of perfection F_{25}
	Coordination between sections F_{26}
	Brand influence F_{27}
	Decision-making capacity F_{28}
	Risk management and control capacity F_{29}
Technical factors F_3	Investment decision-making capacity F_{31}
	Planning and design capacity F_{32}
	Cost controlling capacity F_{33}
	Management capacity F_{34}
	Innovation capacity F_{35}
	Fund operations capability F_{36}
Market factors F_4	Sales growth rate F_{41}
	Market share F_{42}
	Market preemption power F_{43}
	Customer satisfaction F_{44}
	Adaptability to the market F_{45}
Social factors F_5	Relationships with the bank F_{51}
	Relationships with the government F_{52}
	Relationships with suppliers F_{53}

7.3.2.1 Sample selection and data collection

Firstly, a five-score Likert questionnaire was designed into two parts. The first part explained its purpose and personal information of interviewees. The second part is the main part of the questionnaire, which included 33 choice questions and 7 open questions. All the questions are related to indicators system. For example, with regard to the proposed organizational factors, the question asks what you think of the perfection of your firm's rules; the choices include five levels.

The chapter collected data from Xi'an 20 real estate developers. These are Xi'an Tianlang, Xi'an Ziwei, Xi'an Gaoke, Xi'an Jingfa, Xi'an Qujiang Daming Palace, Xi'an Dongshang, etc. These companies are all local companies. Compared to major immigrant real estate developers, the development scale of every local company is smaller. For taking into account such factors as the level of qualification and scale, the study choose four qualified enterprises, eight second-qualification levels, and eight third-qualification level developers. One hundred fifty questionnaires were then distributed to the selected real estate developers, six to eight copies of each. One hundred forty-one copies were returned, with the return rate of 94%, which is relatively high. So the questionnaire could represent the real situation of Xi'an real estate business. Indicators F_{11}, F_{12}, F_{13}, F_{14}, F_{15}, F_{16}, F_{21}, F_{26}, F_{31}, F_{42}, and F_{45} were directly calculated by the data collected by the questionnaires.

Regarding the other 19 qualitative indicators, expert scoring method was used to obtain their values. First, basic data from the real estate developers were collected according to the survey questionnaire; then, 20 people who had a better understanding of these 20 real estate developers were invited to complete the work. Some were alumni who work in these enterprises; other participants were academic researchers in real estate economics and management who had rich professional knowledge because they were in constant contact with these companies and had a better understanding of the developers' basic situation. All guaranteed the accuracy of the results. Each participant gave a score within 0–9 points for each qualitative indicator; the average of scores rated by experts are regarded as the final score for each indicator.

7.3.2.2 Indicators data normalization

The different measurement dimensions of evaluation indicators will affect the evaluation results, thus the original data need to be normalized when applied to the model. Normalized data are all between [0, 1], achieved by scale transformation method. The study analyzed the normalized data sheet and comprehensively evaluated the core competence of these companies. The result would be graded into five levels:

Level I   Score at [0.8, 1], which means that the company has a strong core competence. It should continue to use the corporate culture and brand influence to strengthen its core competence.

Level II   Score at [0.6, 0.8], which means that the company has relatively strong core competence, and it need to consolidate the existing strengths and remedy weak production activities segments.

Level III Score at [0.4, 0.6], which means that the company's core competence is at an average level.

Level IV   Score at [0.2, 0.4], which means that the company's core competence is poor, and it needs to change the operation mode as soon as possible.

Level V   Score at [0, 0.2], which means that the company is of no core competence, and it needs to find and cultivate its core competencies.

Table 7.2 **Gray relational degree of indicators**

F_{42}	F_{43}	F_{32}	F_{31}	F_{51}	F_{11}	F_{19}	F_{21}	F_{53}	F_{41}
0.8127	0.7702	0.7679	0.7653	0.7613	0.7565	0.7557	0.7486	0.7425	0.7368
F_{44}	F_{35}	F_{34}	F_{36}	F_{17}	F_{28}	F_{29}	F_{23}	F_{26}	F_{25}
0.7321	0.7273	0.7241	0.7230	0.7082	0.7079	0.7077	0.7069	0.7051	0.6939
F_{24}	F_{16}	F_{52}	F_{12}	F_{22}	F_{27}	F_{45}	F_{33}	F_{13}	F_{14}
0.6900	0.6892	0.6577	0.6576	0.6519	0.6485	0.6477	0.6340	0.6136	0.6069

The study obtained grading standards through rating sample data so the users could compare the results calculated by the model with these grading standards and then put forward some discussions.

7.3.2.3 Indicator system reduction

The steps of indicator system reduction using the gray relevancy coefficient method were shown as follows: (1) To get referential sequence and compared sequence. Referential sequence is the core competence evaluation results of sample enterprise, while compared sequence is the value of each indicator. (2) To calculate sequence difference. (3) To obtain the difference values between maximum and minimum of each indicator. (4) To calculate the gray relational coefficient. (5) To calculate the gray relational degree. The result of gray relational degrees order is shown as in Table 7.2. (6) Indicator system reduction. According to the gray relational degrees order, the chapter extracted the first 20 indicators as the key evaluation indicators of real estate development enterprises core competence, which are the key factors affecting the real estate developers core competence.

7.4 Evaluation model based on support vector machine

SVM is proposed to solve the function regression problem after introducing the concept of loss function. The basic idea is that through nonlinear mapping, input space data x is mapped into a high-dimensional feature space and then the linear regression estimation is done in the high-dimensional space (Fang, 2007).

This chapter employed SVM to conduct the core competence evaluation, in which the real estate developer was treated as training samples, and evaluation indicator values of developers were input vector, thus the output value was the evaluation results of the core competence. That transformed the problem of forecasting the estimated output value into the core competence evaluation problem (Deng & Tian, 2009).

Through the survey questionnaires and expert scoring, the original data of real estate enterprises core competence index system were obtained. The model learning samples were obtained after adjustment. The samples are data of 20 Xi'an real estate developers on 20 key indicators. The chapter selected the first 15 samples as training samples and the latter 5 samples as test samples, then conducted a suitable analysis, and finally got the SVM intelligent evaluation model.

7.4.1   Kernel function and parameter selection

When the nonlinear regression model is built based on SVM, kernel function and three-parameter values (kernel parameter σ, penalty parameter C, and ε-insensitive loss function ε) selection should be done. The chapter used Gaussian radial basis function (RBF kernel) to be the kernel function and got the three parameters by cross-validation method.

First, ε-insensitive loss function and kernel parameters were fixed; $\varepsilon = 0.01$, $\sigma = 2$. The chapter made the penalty factor C change within the range of 0.5–300, with the stepsize of 0.5, testing for 600 times, and then calculated the root-mean-square (RMS) error of SVM predictive value. According to the results, it can be seen that RBF kernel parameter σ has an impact on the accuracy of SVM regression prediction significantly. Particularly, when the interval is in between [0.5, 10], the RMS error of model training decreased greatly, but in the interval [10, 100], the error did not change. Then, the parameters C and ε were fixed, $C = 90$, $\varepsilon = 0.01$. The chapter adjusted RBF kernel parameter σ, making it fluctuates in the range of 0.01–10, with the stepsize of 0.1. As shown in Figure 7.1, when $\sigma = 0.810$, the RMS error of model training is minimal.

Finally, the parameters σ and C were fixed, $\sigma = 0.81$, $C = 90$. The chapter made the model insensitive loss function ε change in the range of 0.0001–0.01 with the stepsize of 0.0001, testing for 100 times. According to results, when ε is between (0.0003), RMS error was small and did not change significantly. When $C = 90$, $\sigma = 0.81$,

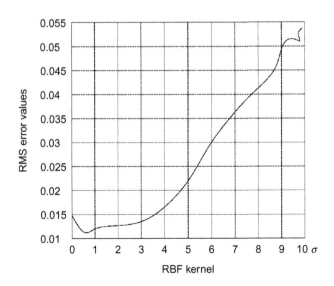

Figure 7.1 Error changes graph.

Table 7.3 RBF kernel SVM model actual value and prediction value error comparison

Corporate ID	Predictive value	Actual value	Relative error
1	0.9475	0.9573	0.0092
2	0.8528	0.8633	0.0103
3	0.3732	0.3961	0.0229
4	0.2593	0.2166	0.0427
5	0.0492	0.0264	0.0458

$\varepsilon = 0.0003$, the RMS error is a minimum of 0.0102, and the SVM training model is the best model.

SVM model actual value and predictive value were compared, as shown in Table 7.3. Thus, cross-validation method was used to choose the parameters, and relative error of actual and predicted values of the test sample was within 5%, which met the investment risk prediction accuracy requirement.

This study chose RBF kernel as the kernel function of SVM intelligent evaluation model of real estate developers' core competence. Based on the predicted values, the predictive evaluation level was identical with the actual evaluation level.

7.4.2 Core competence intelligent evaluation model

According to the RBF kernel function and three parameters selected before, the core competence evaluation intelligent model was built. The program algorithm was achieved by MATLAB7.0, $b^* = 0.53894$, and finally the chapter obtains the real estate developers' core competence evaluation model:

$$f(x) = \sum_{i=1}^{n} (a_i - a_i^*)(x \cdot x_i' + 1) + 0.53894$$

Where x_i' is support vector, the number of support vectors is $n = 8$. Support vector were the 1st, 3rd, 4th, 6th, 7th, 11th, 13th, 16th samples of the 20 real estate developers samples. x is index value vector of real estate developers' core competence to be evaluated.

$a_i - a_i^*$ is Lagrange multiplier, and suppose $a_i - a_i^* = d_i$, according to the results of the program running, respectively: $d_1 = 0.19805$, $d_3 = 0.23497$, $d_4 = 0.02212$, $d_6 = 0.26768$, $d_7 = 0.1873$, $d_{11} = 0.27431$, $d_{13} = 0.77398$, $d_{16} = 0.14569$.

This is the SVM evaluation model of the real estate developers' core competence. Based on testing results of training samples and predicting results of the prediction samples, its accuracy was within 5%, which basically met the forecast (evaluation) accuracy. This model can be applied to any early warning evaluation of core competence of real estate developers.

7.5   Case analysis and discussion

This chapter used the above-completed model to evaluate the core competence of a real estate developer: Xi'an Tiandi Ltd. This enterprise had the top-level development qualification, and ranked first place among the local enterprises. It has developed a number of real estate projects, and the market reputation was good. Its relationship with the local government and banks were close, so it had easy access to a variety of resources. However, the company had a low level of internal management and innovation comparatively. At first, indicator data were collected through questionnaires, the quantitative indicator values can be obtained directly from statistics data, and qualitative indicators are acquired by expert scoring. Original data sequence on key indicators are $x = (7, 21, 10.8, 5, 6, 8, 6, 6, 5, 468, 8, 7, 8, 0.37, 7, 0.9, 7, 6, 7)$. In order to meet the needs of SVM evaluation model, each indicator data should be normalized, the normalized data sequence was $x' = (0.8562, 0.5083, 0.7354, 0.3322, 0.4268, 0.375, 0.625, 0.7572, 0.4287, 0.8614, 0.875, 0.7668, 0.6731, 0.5992, 0.5, 0.2739, 0.5632, 0.6856, 0.375, 0.5669)$. When the above data were applied to the evaluation model, the calculated result was 0.7389. According to the evaluation grade standards, it was within the interval [0.6, 0.8), which meant that enterprise's core competence was in a relatively strong level.

On further analysis, the study found that the company was not concerned with fostering innovation capabilities in management innovation, technological innovation, or product innovation, which led to its setback from the original display. It is known that if a company ignores the change, it will be defeated at the market.

Moreover, the enterprise was weak in staff loyalty, brand influence, and information sharing, but it had advantages in social factors, including the relationship with the banks and the government. The company needed to correct the weakness. It can improve the overall quality of staff by cultivating corporate culture and improving the enterprise system. It could enhance its sense of belonging through the rational incentive and training mechanisms and achieve a sustainable competitive advantage in the fierce market competition.

Further, through corporate culture and market influence, the enterprise can gradually shape its corporate brand and enhance its brand value, because the competition in today's real estate market can be considered as a brand competition.

Actually, in 2013, the volume of housing trading set a historical record. The number of real estate developers was also increasing, but most of them were small- and medium-sized enterprises with weak strengths. So far, Xi'an has 16 qualified real estate developers, accounting for only 1.2%. There are 31 second-level enterprises, with a proportion of 6.4%; others are the third- or fourth-qualification class developers, accounting for more than 90%. Hence, most of real estate developers in Xi'an are small- and medium-sized enterprises with lower development capabilities. However, the small- and medium-sized Xi'an real estate developers are supposed to dig out their own core competence in order to not be squeezed out of the market. Therefore, recommendations were made to foster and promote the core competences for all the local developers.

(1) In terms of personnel factors, the enterprises can enhance their core competence by decision makers, administrators, or executives. They need to make quality decisions and guide the company. Managers must improve their risk management capabilities and find ways to enhance their staff's cohesion and sense of belonging. All in all, personnel are the guarantees of enterprise development and the foundation to cultivate core competence.

(2) In terms of organizational factors, the real estate developers first need to improve the organizational structure in order to ensure its efficient functioning. It must also improve the enterprise's rules and regulations, which can constrain the daily behaviors of employees and ensure the normalization of enterprise development. At the same time, the enterprise needs to establish a persistent and efficient internal communication and coordination mechanism that can strengthen the collaboration within and across sectors. Finally, the construction of corporate culture must be given greater importance so that employees can fully integrate into the corporate community.

(3) In terms of technical factors, developers need pay attention to innovation, which includes management innovation, technological innovation, and product innovation, because innovation can make enterprises consolidate and enhance their competitive advantage. Further, a good information-sharing mechanism within the enterprise is helpful in enabling every sector to obtain timely information that can improve operational efficiency so as to enhance the core competence of enterprises.

(4) In terms of market factors, companies should continue to strengthen their controlling ability in order to respond to market changes in a timely way and continue to explore new markets so as to enlarge their market share. Companies must improve sales, which is an important part of corporate profits and suggests that the products are recognized and accepted by the market (Liu, 2011; Xie & Zhang, 2009). All aspects of market positioning, product design, quality management, and property management contribute to market reputation. A product's design not only determines the cost of the building but also the acceptance of products and the return of project investment. In addition, since the project was not built by the real estate developer directly, and the whole project involves the delegate supervision, construction firms, decoration companies, equipment suppliers, and installation firms, real estate companies play an important role of coordination and quality control. After sales, many real estate developers often neglect property management. However, qualified property management is welcome to consumers and can easily influence consumers' satisfaction.

(5) In terms of social factors, by providing good products and services, the developers can acquire a good corporate image and establish a strong relationship with the government, banks, and other partners. These behaviors are conducive to enhance the core competitive of enterprises.

7.6 Conclusions

By analyzing the importance of all aspects of the value chain in the market competition and their impact on profit contribution, this chapter established a real estate developer's core competence evaluation system, including 5 first-level indicators (human factors, organizational factors, technical factors, market factors, and social factors) and 30 secondary indicators, including both qualitative and quantitative indicators. The study reduced indicators, excluding the ones only slightly impacting the core competence, so as to facilitate the collection of raw data and optimize the intelligent evaluation model. Using support vector regression, the intelligent evaluation model was established. The chapter verified the accuracy of the model when used in an evaluation of the real estate development enterprises core competence. Finally, the chapter conducted a case study of a Xi'an real estate development enterprise by the intelligent evaluation model. The results showed that the local real estate development companies in Xi'an neglected the fostering of their core competence and lacked innovation capability and brand awareness. Hence, the chapter presented specific measures about how to enhance the core competence of local enterprises.

However, there were some inadequacies of this chapter. First, most of the core competence evaluation indicators are qualitative indicators. The chapter quantified such indicators by an expert scoring method, so the results were affected by the subjectivity of experts. Therefore, the way to quantify qualitative indicators needs further studies. In terms of the parameters, most studies determine them empirically. The chapter used cross-validation methods to determine model parameters, which is relatively objective. So how to use the scientific method to select and optimize the parameters is a very important area of research based on the characteristics of the problem.

Acknowledgments

The authors wish to appreciate the support from Research Project of Shaanxi Provincial Education Department (No.2013JK0147).

References

Deng, N. Y., & Tian, Y. J. (2009). *Support vector machines—Theory, algorithms and expand.* Beijing: Science Press (in Chinese).

Fang, R. M. (2007). *Analysis of support vector machine theory and application.* Beijing: China Electric Power Press (in Chinese).

Huang, F. Y. (2004). Real estate enterprise informatization and its core competence. *Statistics and Decision, 6,* 127–128 (in Chinese).

Jiang, J. Z. (2006). *Analysis of human resource management based on value chain theory.* PhD dissertation. Tianjin: Tianjin University (in Chinese).

Li, Q. D. (2009). Method for comprehensive evaluation of enterprise core competence and its application. *Canadian Social Science, 5*(1), 53.

Liu, H. (2011). *Evaluation and promotion strategies to the competence of real estate enterprises.* PhD dissertation. Zhejiang University (in Chinese).

Mou, L. L., Liu, P., & Zhang, J. M. (2012). Comprehensive assessment on Chinese real estate development enterprise core competence. *Hebei University of Technology, 4,* 98–103 (in Chinese).

Wang, Y. (2006). *Analysis of real estate enterprises core competence based the value chain theory.* PhD dissertation. East China Normal University (in Chinese).

Wang, Y., & Xu, W. K. (2008). Approaches on improving core competences for real estate developers at present stage. *Journal of Socialist Theory Guide, 7,* 104–106 (in Chinese).

Wu, P. (2008). *Analysis of real estate enterprises core competence based on value chain theory.* PhD dissertation. Chongqing University (in Chinese).

Xia, H. P., & Zhan, Q. F. (2005). How to enhance the core competence of real estate enterprises. *Quest, 3,* 46–50 (in Chinese).

Xie, N., & Zhang, H. (2009). Estate enterprise core competence cultivation. *Chinese Real Estate, 8,* 43–45 (in Chinese).

Yan, A. M., & Jiang, X. H. (2006). Research on estate enterprises core competence characteristics and evaluation system. *Zhuzhou Institute of Technology, 6,* 105–108 (in Chinese).

Yan, H. (2013). Shaanxi real estate business core competence. *Xi' an University of Architecture and Technology, 45,* 105–118 (in Chinese).

Yan, Z. M., & Jing, Y. Y. (2009). Discussion of enhancing the core competence of real estate enterprises. *Gansu Science and Technology, 22,* 101–102 (in Chinese).

Zeng, C. S. (2011). 4V marketing strategy to enhance the core competence of the real estate business. *Enterprise Economy, 4,* 159–161 (in Chinese).

Zhang, H. (2004). Implementation of project management to enhance the core competence of the real estate business. *Urban Development, 16,* 50–54 (in Chinese).

Zhou, S. F., & Xie, Y. L. (2005). Analysis of real estate enterprises core competence based on the value chain theory. *Business Research, 14,* 135–138 (in Chinese).

Empirical study of eWOM's influence on consumers' purchase decisions

L. Yang[a], Q. Cheng[a], S. Tong[b]
[a]Xi'an Jiaotong University, Xi'an, China; [b]University of Maryland, College Park, MD, USA

8.1 Introduction

Word of mouth (WOM) is an important source of information for customers and could affect their purchase decision. A good reputation could bring sustainable profit to entities. Nowadays, the Internet provides a great convenience for customers to search for product information. The research by Henning-Thurau (2003) pointed out that people relied more on the information from other customers in making decisions. Julian Villanueva and Hanssens (2008) believed that what customers gained from traditional marketing could bring more short-term value to the company, while what customers gained from WOM could bring a long-term value that is double that of traditional marketing.

The rapid development of China's Internet in the past decade has provided a convenient platform for the spread of WOM regarding products or services. The development of the Internet on one hand allowed customers to search for reviews from other customers; on the other hand, it makes one more willing to share his or her rating or user experience about a specific product or service. Word of mouth could break through the traditional forms of oral communication.

A research on Chinese online shopping in 2011 from CNNIC showed that 43.3% of people believed that buyers' comments are the most important factor in their purchase decision. The second important factor is advice from friends or relatives, accounting for 34.7%. People relying on advice from experts or famous website only 18.6% of the time. Based on Nielsen's survey of Taiwan consumers, 41% of respondents trust online WOM when making purchase decision; 31% rely on information in several online forums. Only 14% of respondents referred to information on influential blogs. All the above information indicate that comments from online users surpass friends' advice and have become the key factor affecting purchase decision and the most important external information.

Online comments about a product or service reduce the information asymmetry and uncertainty during shopping, which helps consumers choose the proper product or service. A statistical report in 2013 from CNNIC showed that the number of China's online shopping users reached 242 million, and that online shopping increased to 42.9% by December 2012. The sales volume of Taobao reached 19.1 billion on

November 11, 2012. I-research pointed out that the transaction of online shopping market has exceeded 1.3 trillion in 2012. "Internet will involve from the era of internet users to internet business," said Ma Yun. Therefore, online WOM will be more and more influential on consumers' purchase decision.

The current study on online WOM mainly adopts experimental method, multiple regression, structural equation modeling, content analysis, structured interviews, and social network analysis with some results achieved. But in general, the study on online WOM in China is still in the primary stage, with imperfect modeling and great controversy and gaps in theory.

8.2 Relevant theoretical foundations

8.2.1 The content of online WOM

Currently, researchers on WOM generally consider that negative WOM has a greater impact on potential consumers than positive WOM (Arndt, 1967; Mizersk, 1982) and support this conclusion through a survey. In the absence of information, the percentage that a consumer decides to buy a new product is 42%. When there is positive WOM, the proportion only increases to 54%; the portion drops to 18% when there is negative WOM. So what is the reason for the result?

First of all, negative information is clearer than positive information, which reduces the uncertainty for consumers' assessment of a product (Wyer, 1974).

In addition, Chatterjee (2001) found out that when a consumer felt satisfied about a product, he may share his experience with others. However, when a consumer felt unsatisfied, he would probably tell everyone he met about it. As the saying goes, "Bad news has wings." This is an important reason why negative WOM has a greater effect than positive WOM.

8.2.2 Participants of online WOM

The study by Dichter (1966) shows that the communication process of WOM involves two participants: senders and receivers. Thus, the factors affecting the communication of WOM come from sender and receivers.

8.2.2.1 The characteristic of WOM senders

The senders of WOM are the main source of information for online WOM. It has also been the main part of online WOM communication. Their willingness and ability are the most important factors that determine the influence of WOM. This study mainly concluded the variables of the senders' credibility and strength of relationship.

(1) The credibility of the reviewer

Zhou (2011) points out in his article that the credibility of a reviewer includes his professional competence and reliability. This indicates the ability to provide correct information and professional performance as well as the degree of trust and acceptance from the receivers about reviewers' comments.

(2) Strength of relationship

Strength of relationship means the relationship between senders and receivers of WOM (Cheng & Zhou, 2011).

8.2.2.2 Characteristic of WOM receivers

(1) Involvement

Zaichkowsky (1985) defines the degree of importance and relevance perceived by consumers about a certain product based on his own desires, values, and concerns.

(2) Professionalism

Professionalism is the sign of a receiver's confidence toward a product or service, which reflects the level of consumers' self-assessment on a product (Zheng, 2011).

(3) Trust propensity

Trust propensity is the individual characteristic of a consumer, which means the willingness to rely on others after long-term socialism. This is an individual's propensity for confidence in human nature and trust in others (Mcknight, Choudhury, & Kacmar, 2002).

8.3   Modeling and hypothesis

From the above analysis, it is easy to figure out that the sender and receiver jointly affect consumers' decision during the transmission of online WOM. Therefore, we define them as the arguments in the model. What is more, as consumers will face different WOM content before purchase, the searching and need for online WOM is different for consumers under different contents of WOM. We subdivide WOM into positive and negative. The influence of arguments on dependent variables may differ depending on the content of WOM. Thus, we believe that the content of WOM may play a role in the relationship between arguments on dependent variables. It should be noted that with the widespread and strict supervision of online shopping, there are seldom problems on the operational level. Furthermore, consumers have the ability to verify the authenticity of online products. In conclusion, we establish the following model, as shown in Figure 8.1.

In this chapter, we will first verify the conclusions of previous scholars.

(1) The study of Mizersk (1982) concludes that the influence of consumers' perception and belief in a product by negative WOM will be much greater than that by positive WOM. We brought up the following hypotheses based on the above statement.

H1: Negative WOM will have a greater influence on the consumer's perception of a product.

H2: The content of WOM has an effect on the senders of WOM and the purchase decision.

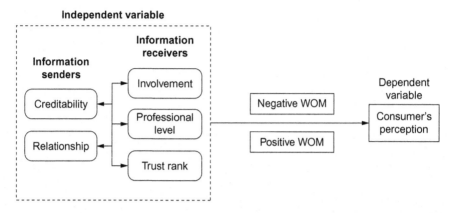

Figure 8.1 Model.

H3: The content of WOM has an effect on the receivers of WOM and the purchase decision.

(2) According to the analysis of this chapter, the credibility of the senders and the strength of relationship are the two main factors that affect the receivers' decision. Therefore, we made the following two hypotheses based on this and the content of the WOM.

H4: The higher the credibility of the senders, the greater the influence of WOM on consumers' purchase decision.

H5: The stronger the relationship, the greater the influence of WOM on consumers' purchase decision.

(3) The factors of the receivers themselves that will affect the purchase decision are the degree of involvement, the level of professionalism, and the propensity to trust WOM. We brought up the following hypotheses by choosing these three factors as arguments.

H6: The higher the degree of involvement of the receivers, the greater the influence of WOM on consumers' purchase decision.

H7: The higher the professional level of the receivers, the greater the influence of WOM on consumers' purchase decision.

H8: The higher the propensity to trust receivers, the greater the influence of WOM on consumers' purchase decision.

Considering that there are interactions between the senders and receivers, we propose the expanded hypothesis for the study of the interactions.

H9: There are relationships between the two factors of senders and the three factors of receivers.

8.4 Questionnaire and empirical analysis

8.4.1 The design of the questionnaire and measurement

There are 23 variables in 6 classifications in the basic study. We adopted the seven Likert scale to measure each variable. The options range from 1, which stands for totally disagrees with that, to 7. The reliability and validity of the questionnaire is analyzed. As shown in Table 8.1, for all variables, the KMO values are above 0.7 and the

Table 8.1 Reliability and validity analysis of WOM

Reference	Variables	Questions	Cronbach's α	Factor loadings
Li (2007)	The content of WOM	Which aspect of WOM do you think is more reliable?	0.766	0.703
		Which aspect of WOM do you pay more attention to?		0.645
		What content of WOM will influence more of your purchase decision?		0.695
	Cumulative variance explanation rate			68.108%
	Credibility	The comments of experts are useful for you		0.578
		You trust the comments of experts		0.647
Zhou (2011)		The comments of experts will affect your purchase decision	0.809	0.729
		You pay attention to the comments of experts		0.601
	Cumulative variance explanation rate			63.883%
	Strength of relationship	The degree of usefulness of friends' comments		0.670
		You trust the comments of friends		0.707
Cheng and Zhou (2011)		The comments of friends have a great influence on you	0.851	0.721
		You pay attention to the comments of friends		0.673
	Cumulative variance explanation rate			69.289%
	Degree of involvement	You think the comments about a product are useful		0.719
		You trust the online comments about the product		0.663
Zaichkowsky (1985)		The comment about the product will affect your purchase decision	0.834	0.689
		You will pay attention to the comments about the products		0.616

Continued

Table 8.1 Continued

Reference	Variables	Questions	Cronbach's α	Factor loadings
		Cumulative variance explanation rate		67.013%
	Professionalism	The degree of usefulness of this product		0.675
		The level of trust about the comments on the product		0.616
Zheng (2011)		The influence of this product on you	0.829	0.746
		The level you are concerned about the comments for the product		0.614
		Cumulative variance explanation rate		66.260%
	Propensity to trust	Online comments will provide guidance for my online shopping		0.669
		You trust online comments during online shopping		0.709
Xu (2007)		Online comments will affect your purchase decision during online shopping	0.770	0.759
		The level you are concerned about the online comments for the product during online shopping		0.551
		Cumulative variance explanation rate		54.591%
	The influence of WOM	Comments of experts will affect your purchase decision		0.526
		Comments of friends will affect your purchase decision		0.531
		The level of influence on your purchase decision by products (expensive or cheap)		0.645
		The level of influence on your purchase decision by products (familiar or unfamiliar)	0.818	0.651
		The level of influence on your purchase decision by online comments		0.658
		Cumulative variance explanation rate		58.205%

Table 8.2 **Demographic information of respondents**

Variables	Options	Frequencies	Percentage	Cumulative percentage
Gender	Male	178	47.1	47.1
	Female	200	52.9	100.0
Education level	Bachelor	312	82.5	82.5
	Master or above	66	17.5	100.0
Frequency of online shopping	Never	8	2.1	2.1
	Sometimes	117	31	33.2
	Often	253	66.9	100.0
The products	Expensive	249	65.9	65.9
	Cheap	129	34.1	100.0
Products	Familiar	266	70.4	70.4
	Unfamiliar	112	29.6	100.0

significant levels of Chi-square test are below 0.05. This indicates that the variables reach the generally acceptable level. The Cologne Bach reliability coefficients of the variables are above the acceptable level of 0.7 and the factor loadings for each question are above 0.5. Therefore, the design of the questionnaire is reasonable and qualifies the requirements of study.

This study is conducted by random distribution among individuals and the online questionnaire. We collected 405 questionnaires in the research. There are 378 valid questionnaires with the collection rate of 93.33%. As shown in Table 8.2, 47.09% of the respondents are male and 52.91% female. The numbers of male and female are nearly equal. We focus on young people from the ages of 18 to 25 when distributing the questionnaire. This group frequently receives online WOM, which is appropriate in terms of being our research participants.

8.4.2 Correlation analysis

This study adopted the Pearson's simple correlation to test the relationship among variables. As shown in Table 8.3, the two characteristics of senders (credibility and strength of relationship) and the three characteristics of receivers (involvement, professionalism, and propensity to trust) have a correlation relationship under the significant level of 0.01. Accordingly, H9 stands.

The studies conducted previously by scholars usually retain variables based on the interests of researchers. Most of them believe that a correlation coefficient above 0.8 will indicate severe multi-co-linearity. No correlation coefficient between variables in his chapter is above 0.8. Therefore, the effect on regression is relatively low.

Table 8.3 The correlation relationship between different variables

		Credibility	Strength of relationship	Involvement	Professionalism	Propensity to trust	The influence of WOM
Credibility	Pearson's correlation	1					
Strength of relationship	Pearson's correlation	0.238*	1				
Involvement	Pearson's correlation	0.201*	0.119	1			
Professionalism	Pearson's correlation	0.196*	0.000	−0.185	1		
Propensity to trust	Pearson's correlation	−0.275	0.000	0.000	0.000	1	
The influence of WOM	Pearson's correlation	0.478*	0.391*	0.368*	0.289*	0.300*	1

*Significant correlation under the level of 0.01 (two-tailed).

8.4.3   Regression analysis of the model

We adopted stepwise regression to study in this chapter. The results are listed in Table 8.4.

The result of the regression for the model shows that the tolerance of all variables is significantly greater than 0.1. There is no multi-co-linearity. We adopted a DW value to figure out whether there is serial correlation. The DW value of the model is 2.131, which indicates that there is no serial correlation. What is more, the significant level of the whole model reaches 0.01, and thus the model is established. This indicates that the senders and receivers of WOM significantly affect the influence of WOM. Therefore, H4–H8 stand.

8.4.4   The adjustment effect of the content of WOM

We use the regression model with product term to verify the adjusted variables. The results are shown in Table 8.5.

The results indicate that the equation to WOM content is significant as a whole, while the content of WOM itself is not regression. This means that the content of WOM will not significantly affect the influence of WOM on consumers' purchase decision. When we put the interaction of WOM content and arguments, the equation becomes significant, R^2 increases to 0.659 and ΔR^2 becomes 0.035. At this time, the standardized correlation regression coefficient of interaction between WOM content and credibility is 0.379. The standardized correlation regression coefficient of interaction between WOM content and strength of relationship is 0.17. The standardized correlation regression coefficient of interaction between WOM content and involvement is 0.293. All of them are significant under the level of 0.01. Therefore, we prove H2 and overthrow H3.

Based on the above analysis, we can conclude the verification of our hypotheses in Table 8.6.

8.5   Conclusion and outlook

8.5.1   Conclusion

Based on the above empirical study, we come to the following conclusions:

(1) The characteristics of participants and the influence of WOM

The characteristics of online WOM senders will have a positive influence on consumers' purchase decision. As the credibility and strength of relationship of the senders mean a lot to consumers, more attention will be paid to these two factors. The higher the credibility and the stronger the relationship is, the stronger the influence is on consumers' purchase decision.

As for the receivers, some hypotheses have been supported. The professionalism and trust propensity will promote purchase positively. The involvement shows positive effect on WOM, but the relationship is not significant. This indicates that the effect of

Table 8.4 The stepwise regression of the model

Model		Nonstandardized regression coefficient	Standard error	Standardized regression coefficient			Multi-co linearity
				Beta	t-Value	Sig.	Tolerance
1	(Constant term)	1.426	0.161		8.846	0.000	
	Trust propensity	0.752	0.029	0.800	25.858	0.000	1.000
2	(Constant term)	0.461	0.148		3.109	0.002	
	Trust propensity	0.568	0.027	0.604	20.911	0.000	0.760
	Strength of relationship	0.338	0.024	0.401	13.886	0.000	0.760
3	(Constant term)	0.167	0.141		1.189	0.235	
	Trust propensity	0.387	0.033	0.411	11.767	0.000	0.437
	Strength of relationship	0.278	0.023	0.331	11.908	0.000	0.692
	Professionalism	0.294	0.035	0.306	8.459	0.000	0.408
4	(Constant term)	0.106	0.137		0.774	0.440	
	Trust propensity	0.353	0.033	0.376	10.832	0.000	0.418
	Strength of relationship	0.244	0.024	0.290	10.285	0.000	0.632
	Professionalism	0.256	0.035	0.266	7.391	0.000	0.388
	Credibility	0.124	0.025	0.147	4.889	0.000	0.553
5	(Constant term)	0.113	0.135		0.832	0.406	
	Trust propensity	0.322	0.034	0.343	9.542	0.000	0.381
	Strength of relationship	0.234	0.024	0.278	9.849	0.000	0.619
	Professionalism	0.202	0.038	0.210	5.262	0.000	0.308
	Credibility	0.112	0.025	0.133	4.418	0.000	0.541
	Involvement	0.107	0.035	0.122	3.083	0.002	0.316

Notes: The dependent variables is the influence of WOM, $DW_{value} = 2.131$.
$F = 332.513$; $R^2 = 0.817$; $P < 0.001$.

Table 8.5 Hierarchical regression analysis

Variables	Influence of WOM		
	Step 1 model	Step 2 model	Step 3 model
Step 1: The main effect of the arguments	Correlation coefficient		
Credibility	0.141**	0.142**	0.131**
Strength of relationship	0.211**	0.212**	0.144**
Involvement	0.313**	0.316**	0.437**
Professionalism	0.281**	0.271**	0.342**
Trust propensity	0.119**	0.116**	0.127**
Step 2: Adjusted variables added			
Content of WOM		0.034	0.322*
Step 3: Interactions added			
Content of WOM* credibility			0.379**
Content of WOM* strength of relationship			0.170**
Content of WOM* involvement			0.103
Content of WOM* professionalism			0.211
Content of WOM* trust propensity			0.293**
F-value	31.598**	29.334**	17.484**
R^2	0.624	0.624	0.659
ΔR^2	0.624	0	0.035

*$P < 0.05$.
**$P < 0.01$.

involvement is not significant in China's Internet environment. This is because there are certain loopholes for the supervision of the Internet in China. Most consumers do not prefer to buy expensive products online, which reduces the influence of involvement on WOM.

(2) The interaction between the characteristics of WOM senders and receivers

We proved that there are interactions between the two factors of WOM senders and the three factors of WOM receivers based on the analysis of regression and correlation. This fully demonstrates the significance of the study of interaction effects. In China's Internet environment, we should pay attention to both the characteristics of senders and receivers. Only with the simultaneous interaction of two participants, can WOM drive consumers' behavior better.

(3) The adjusting effect of WOM content

The adjusting effects of WOM content on the five arguments have been partially verified. The relationships among credibility, strength of relationship, trust propensity, and the influence of WOM have been adjusted by the content of WOM. This fully demonstrates that the proportion of positive and negative online WOM could affect the purchase decision of consumers. Therefore, when companies establish online WOM strategies focusing on senders, they should pay attention to the adjustment effect of the content. Good control of the proportion of positive and negative WOM will better drive consumers' purchase behavior.

Table **8.6** **Hypotheses conclusion**

Study content	Hypothesis	Result
Content of WOM	H1: Negative WOM will have a greater influence in consumers' perception of a product	Support
Credibility	H2: The content of WOM has an effect on the senders of WOM and the purchase decision	Support
	H3: The content of WOM has an effect on receivers of WOM and the purchase decision	Not Support
	H4: The higher the credibility of the senders, the greater the influence of WOM on consumers' purchase decision	Support
Strength of relationship	H5: The stronger the relationship, the greater the influence of WOM on consumers' purchase decision	Support
Degree of involvement	H6: The higher the degree of involvement of receivers, the greater the influence of WOM on consumers' purchase decision	Not support
Professionalism	H7: The greater the professional level of the receivers, the greater the influence of WOM on consumers' purchase decision	Support
Trust propensity	H8: The higher the propensity to trust receivers, the greater the influence of WOM on consumers' purchase decision	Support
Interaction	H9: There are relationships between the two factors of senders and the three factors of receivers	Support

8.5.2 *Marketing strategies*

The conclusions reached in this chapter about the senders and receivers of WOM will serve as guidance for entities to create WOM marketing online.

First of all, for websites that provide WOM information, enhancing the professional image of the website will increase consumer confidence. The website should provide valuable service by better managing user-generated content, retaining high-quality posts, and increasing the credibility of the website.

Second, entities should collect and filter comments from the group that used or intended to use the product to ensure the reliability and relevance of the information. The company could even invite consumers to review the products, using their real names so that people could communicate with people they know. This can guarantee the strength of relationship between the senders and receivers, which could positively affect the purchase decision. What is more, the company could spread more positive comments under the supervision of online WOM in order to expand its influence.

Third, companies could introduce the product to consumers in more detail. The introduction should not be limited to just pictures and literal descriptions. The company can provide more information about the product, like the certification of quality and actual store locations. Consumers will be more willingly to pay attention to online WOM information and buy the products if they are more familiar with them.

Finally, the company should treat negative WOM in the right way. As different consumers show different attitudes toward and trust in online WOM, the levels of influence of WOM on consumers are different. It is not proper to totally delete all the negative comments. The existence of negative WOM could prove the veracity of online WOM about the product. On the other hand, some negative WOMs are based on consumers' personal habits but not on the product itself. Such WOM could help consumers better understand the product. Accordingly, companies should establish WOM marketing strategies based on different type of products and consumers.

References

Arndt, J. (1967). Role of product-related conversations in the diffusion of a new product. *Journal of Marketing Research, 8*(6), 291–295.

Chatterjee, P. (2001). Online review: Do consumers use them? *Advance in Consumer Research, 28*, 129–131.

Cheng, X., & Zhou, M. H. (2011). *Internet word of mouth for consumer decision-making behavior influence research.* Jiangsu Commercial Forum, Jiangsu, China, November 2011.

Dichter, E. (1966). How word-of-mouth advertising works. *Harvard Business Review, 44*, 147–166.

Henning-Thurau, W. G. (2003). Electronic word of mouth: Motives for and consequences of reading customer articulations on the Internet. *International Journal of Electronic Commerce, 8*(2), 51–74.

Julian Villanueva, S. Y., & Hanssens, D. M. (2008). The impact of marketing-induced versus word-of-mouth customer acquisition on customer equity growth. *Journal of Marketing Research, 45*(1), 48–59.

Li, X. (2007). The effect of negative word-of-mouth on consumer purchase intention. *Macro Information, 11*, 325–326.

Mcknight, D., Choudhury, V., & Kacmar, C. (2002). The impact of initial consumer trust on intentions to transact with a web site: A trust building model. *Journal of Strategic Information Systems, 11*(3–4), 297–323.

Mizersk, R. W. (1982). An attribution explanation of the disproportionate influence of unfavorable information. *Journal of Consumer Research, 9*(3), 301–310.

Wyer, R. S. (1974). Category ratings as "Subjective Expected Values": Implications for attitude formation and change *Psychology Review, 80*(November), 446–467.

Xu, L. (2007). An empirical study on the factors influencing the credibility of online word-of-mouth. *Finance and Trade Research, 5*, 113–117.

Zaichkowsky, J. (1985). Measuring the involvement construct. *Journal of Consumer Research, 12*, 341–352.

Zheng, Y. (2011). EWOM's type impact on consumer decision-making mechanism. Master thesis, *Shanghai Jiaotong University.*

Zhou, H. (2011). *A study of the impact of commodity recommendation and customer review of shopping website on the impulse buying intention.* Master thesis, South China University of Technology.

Research on online shopping problems behind the "Double Eleven" shopping festival

9

L. Yang[a], R. Gao[a], S. Tong[b]
[a]Xi'an Jiaotong University, Xi'an, China; [b]University of Maryland, College Park, MD, USA

9.1 Introduction

With the growth in the number and the transformation in the concept of Chinese Internet users and consumers, online shopping market has shown great potential. The number of businesses joining the e-commerce industry has grown rapidly in this context; in order to carry out online shopping business, the number of shops has mushroomed. From the "large" online mall to the "tiny but excellent" Taobao shop, customers have more choices as the online shopping industry intensifies with the growth of the style and species of products in online shops. However, competing companies need to do more than just meet consumer demand for basic products, they must also use a combination of various marketing strategies, to provide low prices or exceptional service to ensure their competitive advantage, attract customers, and earn profits. In this context, the "Double Eleven" online shopping festival has emerged in a clever combination of holiday consumer psychology and consumer price promotion marketing.

The "Double Eleven" online shopping festival was launched in 2009 by Taobao. On "Singles' Day," which is November 11 of each year, the electricity supplier website holds a massive discount promotion, with prices often cut in half. Due to the large and wide range of discounts, plus its catering to young consumers, the "Double Eleven" online shopping festival has become the largest commercial activity and the most popular event with regard to the Chinese Internet market.

As of early 2014, the event has been successfully held for five times. This promotional model has brought huge economic benefits, which have increased year by year, and annually refresh the record single-day net purchase transaction amount (Table 9.1).

However, managers should also note that on the one hand, the "Double Eleven" competitive environment has undergone great changes, whether it is the number of participating "Double Eleven" activities or that the electricity supplier website has become more complex and offers a diverse product range compared with the number of promotions 5 years ago. On the other hand, more and more "Double Eleven" problems have been exposed and urgently resolved. For example, during "Double Eleven" festival, there are media reports about logistics' warehouse explosion, as well as complained customers for receiving fake products.

Based on the above, with the "Double Eleven" online shopping festival as the research object, this chapter sets out to understand the "Double Eleven" status quo

The Strategies of China's Firms.

Table 9.1 **2009–2013 Alipay "Double Eleven" day trading volume (unit: 100 million yuan)**

Year	2009	2010	2011	2012	2013
Turnover	0.50	2.50	53.00	181.00	350.19

Source: Taobao official website.

through empirical research and finds problems that must be solved in order to propose appropriate measures to promote the long-term development of the model.

9.2 Literature review

In the emerging marketing model of "Double Eleven," many scholars have studied the causes, evolving marketing strategies, the advantages and disadvantages of the model, along with other aspects.

Many scholars have studied the reasons for the "Double Eleven" produced. Although they did not draw consistent conclusions, studies were analyzed based on the macro-environment, industry environment, and business strategy. Shi Yajun believes that "Double Eleven" is the result of the combination of right time and right generation of customers. And from the perspective of macro-environment and industry's background, Li Pingxiu pointed out: The success of the model of "Double Eleven" online shopping festival was all because of the change of customers' shopping habit, China's remaining high CPI, poor operations of traditional retail business, and heightened propaganda by related websites.

The literature on the "Double Eleven" marketing strategy summarizes and analyzes the strengths and weaknesses of businesses in the "Double Eleven" event. Lu Ying analyzes the marketing strategy from the perspective of discounts during the "Double Eleven" period, including traditional discount form, super-low discount forms (such as Suning Tesco's 0 yuan purchase activity), presented in the form of class discounts (e.g., coupons, double points, red envelopes, gifts, etc.), and buy discount form (e.g., poly cost-effective). Li and Hou (2013) studied the business marketing strategy by time sequence for 5 years during the "Double Eleven" period for a longitudinal comparison summary; since the founding of the festival, marketing efforts have increased. Huang (2012) analyzed the marketing strategy from the show price discounts strategy of the businesses, including changes in the price of narrative formed illusion discount (e.g., spend 100 yuan, 130 yuan redemption value of goods; audience Qizhe, 99 yuan optional, etc.), nine mantissa pricing strategy, ladder price (the price fluctuates over time), and other ways to make consumers experience greater discount efforts.

Many scholars analyzed the "Double Eleven" model merits or success from different angles. Siyang Yu believes that the activities make clever use of consumer herd mentality. Liu (2013) believes that the model can effectively motivate consumers to generate impulse buying behavior (buying behavior that goes beyond what has been planned). Yu and Xiao (2013) think the "Double Eleven" event uses psychological tactics to mobilize consumer desire to buy by using the curiosity of people in a "single culture." Jie and Fu (2014) found that "Double Eleven" puts a single group as the center of its marketing activities creating an "eyeball economy" that attracts the public's attention in order to create wealth. But in the model itself there are problems, such as Ming (2013) pointed out: "Double Eleven" led to unsustainable overdraft consumer spending, and business enterprises will fall into a homogenization of prices. Li Pingxiu pointed out that this pattern will lead "Taobao Brands," those online brands which became popular on taobao.com, to a disadvantage position.

9.3 Research methods and research program

The main purpose of this study is to find the current problems of the "Double Eleven": how they appeared, how wide and severe their influence is, if they will affect customers who participate in "Double Eleven" again, and so on. By reading the "Double Eleven" relevant literature, we found that current "Double Eleven" problems in a wide range of performance forms. Moreover, these problems are mainly related to the five main characters: consumers, merchants, online shopping platform, logistic providers, and payment providers. In order to fully understand the "Double Eleven" situation and make recommendations on related subjects, we use questionnaires and interviews to study the problems. We study "breadth" perspective to understand the "Double Eleven" and the problems within it through a survey questionnaire. Our study includes in-depth interviews of different aspects of the "depth" of the "Double Eleven" issue to explore manifestations of problems and their causes and solutions.

9.3.1 Questionnaire

Since this study focused on the "Double Eleven" problems, the survey of this study is mainly of consumers with online shopping experience. This chapter's object is not limited to those consumers who have participated in the "Double Eleven" event. An analysis of the reasons those consumers did not participate offers new ideas.

The questionnaire contents of this study is divided into three parts: the basic situation, the reason or reasons for participation, and the "Double Eleven" satisfaction problem. The first part is used to understand the respondents, including gender, age, employment status, network age, online shopping frequency, and holiday shopping tendencies. The second part aims to explore the reasons for consumers to participate or not participate in the "Double Eleven" activities. The third part of the analysis considers five issues of satisfaction in the consumer experience: the 2013 "Double Eleven" business satisfaction, online shopping platform, logistics providers, and payment providers satisfaction, universality evaluation problems, and the problems and issues that affected consumer's participation in the campaign again. Last three issues mentioned some problems about "Double Eleven," which came from existing literatures and an interview hosted by the author with 20 experienced online shoppers.

The survey was conducted in early May 2014 via paper questionnaires and two forms of electronic questionnaires. The paper questionnaire distributed in the streets of Xi'an took the form of random interviews, questionnaires, and an electronic version of the questionnaire on the Star website.

9.3.2 Interview

This study selected two experienced customers who had participated "Double Eleven" shopping festival. One was the campus courier who worked during "Double Eleven" for two years. Another was a Taobao shopkeeper during the shopping festival.

Interviews were conducted through two forms: face-to-face and video. Interview questions are mainly semi-structured problems. The structural questions are similar to questionnaire questions, and the nonstructural questions were designed for further study of answers to those structural questions.

9.4 Survey results

In this study, 59 copies of paper-based questionnaires and 128 copies of online questionnaires were collected, 181 of them were valid.

The age of the samples were mainly 21–25 years of age, accounting for 56.4% of the total sample. Second, the age of the samples are mainly 26–30 years old and 15–20 years old, respectively, accounting for 20.4% and 9.9%. A total of 86.7% of the age distribution of the sample were between 15 and 30 years of age. People in this age group are the subject of online shopping, which makes the findings of this study more convincing.

From an employment situation, students and on-duty people in a sample of primary employment, respectively, accounted for 63.5% and 34.3%. The study took into account the fact that contemporary college students are receptive to new things and more accustomed to online shopping but that workers have a stable source of income, so these two groups are a major force in online shopping.

From the network point of view of age and online shopping frequency, around 60% of the respondents network for more than 3 years, and more than the respondents in the frequency of online shopping once a month or more, which is before the actual set of questionnaires target survey group, that is, the online shopping experience of consumers is consistent.

Regarding the festival propensity to consume, 58.6% of the respondents selected "Needs to purchase immediately, will not consider holiday promotional activities"; 23.2% chose "Needs can wait until holidays and promotions arrive," which means this part of customer will postpone their purchase behaviors, and centralize all their purchasing needs until holiday discounts come. While only 18.2% of people choose "No demand they buy something because of holiday promotions," which some people's needs are created by promotional activities. This propensity to consume will cause some problems: in the "Double Eleven" buying spree, people purchased unnecessary goods, which meant they had to return them or they were unsatisfied with the "Double Eleven." Such consumers' shopping is not a rational is worthy of our attention in order to consider the long-term development of this model.

According to the cause analysis results of the reasons, 126 consumers participate in the "Double Eleven," 70.6% of respondents shopped online because there is indeed a need, and there are discounts to be involved in the price activity. The proportion selected to participate several other reasons less often, for example, 13.5% completely buying for the cheap prices and do not consider demand; a very small number of consumers join in the fun by participating in the activities of others. These results suggest that the vast majority of consumers are participating in the "Double Eleven" campaign for rational reasons.

Further investigating those 55 consumers who had never participated in the "Double Eleven" campaign, we found that 65.5% of consumers did not participate because they had no shopping needs, and 25.2% of consumers believed that there is no time and effort involved in buying. In addition, 7% gave as reasons a fear that logistics were too slow, a product or brand was not involved in the campaign, they would not achieve the expected benefits, they worry that product quality cannot be guaranteed, and several other reasons.

For consumers in the 2013 "Double Eleven" survey, results show that they had an above-average level of satisfaction: 88% of people chose the "3 General 'and' 4–6 is better"; the average is 3.34 (out of 5). For the evaluation of the four subjects, the logistics provider took the lowest level of satisfaction, an average score of 2.81.

Regarding universal problems for "Double Eleven," the survey results show that the most common problem is slow merchant shipping, the average score given here was 3.65 (1 is the least common, 5 is the most common); false promotions (3.56), which was significantly higher than the prevalence of other issues, in the first echelon. False evaluations included businesses create a gimmick to attract customers and payment difficulties: the average for false propaganda was between 3.28 and 3.36, in the second echelon.

Regarding the investigation of the issue of universality, the most serious problems perceived by consumers as well as consumers participating in the "Double Eleven" had tremendous impact. According to the survey results, the current severity of the top five issues were false promotions (19.0%), slow merchant shipping (15.9%), slow logistics (13.5%), false propaganda (11.9%), and businesses creating a gimmick to attract customers (10.3%). The percentage of those who selected the remaining issues was lower than 8%. The problem most affecting consumer participation in the event again was false promotion (27%), which was significantly higher than the other problems. False propaganda (12.7%) is ranked second. Slow logistics ranked third (9.5%). This shows that the current consumer participates in the "Double Eleven" again mainly due to their marketing efforts.

9.5   "Double Eleven" main problems and solutions

In this chapter, we will focus on the issues of "Double Eleven" as defined as the presence of online shopping's effect on the consumer online shopping experience; they are ubiquitous, more serious, and result in a greater impact on consumer participation in "Double Eleven" campaign issue one more time.

Through questionnaires and interviews, this chapter studies the widespread extent of the problem of the "Double Eleven" online shopping event, the most serious problem for consumers who once again participate in the "Double Eleven" activities, and the biggest problem affecting the performance of the four forms of problem levels. To help us better identify the main issues, we will choose different angles as a result of these issues summarized in Table 9.2.

Table 9.2 **"Double Eleven" sort results during the existence of the problem**

Involving body	Question number and description	"Double Eleven" widespread problem ranking	"Double Eleven" in the most serious problem ranking	Have most affect consumers again participate in the "Double Eleven" ranking
Shop keeper	(A) Deceptive description	6	4	2
	(B) Deceptive promotion	2	1	1
	(C) Product of poor quality	10	10	5
	(D) False and deceptive comments	5	6	9
	(E) Businesses create a gimmick to attract customers and shortage supply	3	5	4
	(G) Slow delivery	1	2	6
	(H) Wrong, less products	11	11	11
	(K) Poor attitude of service staff	14	12	13
	(L) Returns, refunds difficulties	8	9	10

Table 9.2 **Continued**

Involving body	Question number and description	"Double Eleven" widespread problem ranking	"Double Eleven" in the most serious problem ranking	Have most affect consumers again participate in the "Double Eleven" ranking
Pay service providers	(F) Payment difficulties	4	8	8
Logistic service providers	(I) Slow logistics	7	3	3
	(J) Parcels lost in transit or others impersonator	15	15	15
Online shopping platform	(M) Activist difficult	12	13	14
	(N) Complaints were not taken seriously, long acceptance period	9	14	12
Shopkeepers and logistics providers	(O) Privacy disclosure	13	7	7

Notes: Sort description: No. 1 indicates that the problem is most common and most serious or most influential. No. 15 means that the problem is the rarest, the least serious or has minimal impact.

Integrating the three sorting results, we found that the current "Double Eleven" is more general but also for consumers once again participating in the "Double Eleven," greater impacts include false promotions, false propaganda, businesses creating a gimmick to attract customers and insufficient supply, payment difficulties, slow delivery of businesses, and slow logistics. The first three violated the interests of consumers, and the last three issues affected consumers' shopping experience. Now we combine the results of the above survey and interviews of each subject in Table 9.2.

Identify the problems and present conditions, analyze the causes, and bring out countermeasures.

9.5.1   The problem about violation of consumers' rights

This kind of problem includes three issues: false promotions, false propaganda gimmick to attract customers, and businesses manufacture and supply shortage.

False promotion is the most common problem at present that "Double Eleven" faces; this is also a noteworthy issue for consumers who are once again participating in the "Double Eleven" event. False promotion is inconsistent with promotional discounts that consumers actually. False promotion takes many forms, but is difficult for consumers to identify in its high degree of concealment. For example, consumers say the most common problem is that the virtual business raises is original price and then cuts it in half, creating a huge discount illusion for consumers. In addition, the "Double Eleven" slogan is displayed in many shops—"half of the audience"—but when consumers come into the store to buy the product, they found that only a part of the product is half-price, half the audience is not propaganda. More subtly, some businesses in the back half of the audience add the little word "from" and playing a word game with consumers. In addition, businesses are still offering "full one hundred to send one hundred," "one hundred flowers as two" and coupon redemption activity moves from the mind. While consumers reached Fanquan standards after the publicity they will get the amount of coupons, but these coupons are have extremely poor conditions for use.

These are just a few of the most common forms of false promotion; in practice, there are many other ways. It is difficult to investigate its causes because of a lack of rules and regulations and scarce supervision. Although Lynx introduced virtual price increases specifically for "Double Eleven" in the rules in 2012, this clearly defines the benchmark price on discounted goods under the counter price of the product line, commodity prices, or bureau approved the prices, but that still cannot completely solve the problem. On the one hand, there are loopholes in the rules that give businesses a way out. For example, businesses can modify the price on the product label, which can improve the original price of goods without being detected. There are very strict rules for gift vouchers, as mentioned in this issue; the site still has no corresponding management system. On the other hand, the burden of proof under the existing system is difficult for consumers; the complicated complaints process causes many consumers against the legitimate rights and interests received, when complaints about claims are prohibitive.

The most important manifestation of false propaganda issue in the "Double Eleven" is that physical and picture text descriptions do not match or there is no in-kind match. In order to attract more consumers, businesses will exaggerate the advantages of commodities (such as using flashing characters, large fonts, etc., to demonstrate merits) and avoid shortcomings by not mentioning the product. This results in consumers not fully comprehending the true product situation. Regarding the current status of Taobao, we found the main reason for problems is that online shopping platform has a false evaluation of supervision and lacks effective punitive measures. Although Taobao put "consistent description" as one of the indicators evaluating its business reputation and service levels, and the score comes mainly from consumers, it shows a lack of unified objective evaluation. And it is difficult to determine the punishment for this issue, with false propaganda determining the lack of standards, leading Taobao to various provisions against false propaganda that just stay at the institutional level and are difficult to be effectively implemented.

Similar to false propaganda, when businesses create a gimmick to attract customers but there is a supply shortage, the problem is mainly about the businesses' purposeful lack of supply. This issue in the "Double Eleven" is very common. For example, in order to attract customers, "Double Eleven" launched many shops, such as mobile phones for 10 yuan; huge discounts; and other discount promotions. Many involved in buying activity reflect that a lot of low discount merchandise on sale often sold out within 1 min, right off the shelf. In the end, customers started to wonder the real reason that lead to a 1-min-sold-out. Is it because of the product's popularity, or just because the seller intentionally had a supply shortage? In addition, consumers reflect, even after having completed payment, that the merchant may notify them that the product cannot be shipped due to a lack of inventory. This is against the interests of consumers. The problem with the current generation of online shopping platform is that there is a lack of rules and regulations related to such issues. Further, it is difficult to identify such problems and define the characteristics of this problem. In the end, for super-cheap goods, is it illegal that businesses were not prepared with enough inventory? What should the punishment be for this kind of illegal business? When they oversell commodity, not, how should consumers be compensated for their time and effort? These questions are worthy of consideration by the relevant departments.

As for the issue of consumer rights violations, combined with empirical results, we found that solving this problem starts with the following aspects. First, businesses should have an established and consumer-centric sense of integrity, provide incentives for consumers, and resolutely put an end to consumer fraud. Second, online shopping platforms such as Taobao should accelerate the construction of merchant credit evaluation system to solve the problem of asymmetric information shopping. For low credibility, false promotion, or false propaganda, outlets can publish notices criticizing the entire site or even set up a special logo to warn consumers to be cautious of shopping with these merchants. Third, governance should be improved and false propaganda and false promotional issues related to systems made explicit for consumer fraud judgment standards, methods of supervision, punishment, and compensation methods. The existing supervision and punishment for violations of a "zero tolerance" attitude should be increased. Emphasis should be placed on the enforceability of the relevant provisions to effectively address such issues as the focus and the ultimate goal.

9.5.2 The impact of consumers' problems with "Double Eleven" shopping experience

Such problems will seriously affect consumers "Double Eleven" impression and satisfaction, including payment of a total of three questions related to difficult, slow merchant shipping, and slow logistics.

Payment difficulties refer to the need to continue payments after consumers in the "Double Eleven" wait for a long time, recurring payments situation fails, or the page cannot be opened. Alipay, the main payment method on Taobao.com, experienced a lot of challenges from the midnight of "Double Eleven." According to NetEase Finance data, the total number of transactions in the "Double Eleven" period amounted to 188 million, which included 45.18 million wireless payment, were 1.77 times last year and 5 times the day of the event. Faced with a surge in payment orders, the server

Alipay was added. While limited were measures taken, payment difficulties were still a serious problem.

Analyzing the causes of the problems, we found that in addition to the payment processing provider itself limiting payment levels, relevant agencies paid suppliers for a lower degree of attention to the problems related to the lack of response measures. While Taobao and Tmall used Alipay to complete transactions in the "Double Eleven" event, consumers still need to be paid through port into the net banking system treasure provided the money is transferred to Alipay, which relates to the capacity of the online banking system itself. This is not a huge amount to pay, the existing level of hardware can satisfy payment demand on weekdays, so banks must upgrade their system, and perform a low technical capacity expansion initiative. When the resulting "Double Eleven" peak when paying online banking system is paralyzed, consumers cannot successfully complete payment.

Slow delivery means that a single complete payment from the consumer to the merchant to the parcel delivery company takes a long time. The problem mentioned plus the issue of logistics behind the slow delivery of goods will increase the time for consumers and the impact of the actual net consumer's shopping experience. The problem in the "Double Eleven" is more common and deserves some attention.

Through interviews, we learned that delivery businesses need to go through the steps of the print order, sorting products, verification packing, carrying out extra details for express orders, delivering packages, and so on. However, due to the surge in "Double Eleven" orders, the workload of businesses grows exponentially, resulting in prolonged delivery time. In the interview, the number of businesses that have a small sorting staff, cannot automatically print delivery orders (such as the need for a single shop staff member to fill orders by hand, one by one), couriers pick up slowly, leading to slower business delivery problems.

Slow delivery in "Double Eleven" is prevalent, and related issues such as "warehouse explosion," etc., in the annual period will be subject to much media's attention. According to the survey, many consumers worry about the slow logistics because they will not participate again in "Double Eleven" activities. Specifically, the problem is from the merchant shipping to the customer, who waits a long time to receive the goods.

According to interviews with the courier, we found that the main cause of the problems is that the parcel courier company has a capacity shortage. The amount of parcels during the "Double Eleven" surge causes limited storage capacity, packaging staff shortages, insufficient number of couriers, and express delivery vehicles limited in capacity and in number. While the courier company has taken certain measures, such as increasing the storage capacity, hire temporary couriers, etc., the problem is still very serious. Urgent solutions have been proposed.

To solve the above problems affecting consumers in the "Double Eleven" shopping experience, first, logistics providers, payment providers, and businesses should improve their ability to cope with the surge of orders processed during the "Double Eleven" trading volume, by, for example, increasing personnel and accelerating information systems and hardware updates. Second, Taobao and other sites should introduce appropriate assessment and incentives. On the one hand, the rules and regulations limit the latest delivery time; however, on the other hand awards result in good business (e.g., businesses with fast delivery are granted a special logo, and so on). Third, businesses should effectively establish service awareness, and put the interests of consumers first. Satisfaction with the "Double Eleven" long-term development is closely linked to the customer.

9.6 Conclusion

For 5 years, the promotional activities of "Double Eleven" online shopping festival have become one of the most popular festivals in online shopping. Also, the transaction amounts on this one day have rapidly grown and keep setting new records.

Through questionnaires and interviews to dig into the current problems of the "Double Eleven" event, the problem of universality and influence were found to be in violation of consumer rights; the impact of two major categories of consumer experience result in a total of six concerns. On this basis and combining the results of an analysis of empirical research on the causes of the problem, and management implications proposed accordingly.

"Double Eleven" online shopping problems exist in a wide variety and in many forms and are closely related to the future development of this festival. Collaborative efforts from different entities in this festival are needed to improve the current situation, improve customer satisfaction, and ultimately promote the long-term development of this festival.

References

Huang, Q. D. (2012). Reviews double eleven electricity supplier marketing warfare. *Computers and Telecommunications, 11*, 5–7.

Jie, C. M., & Fu, Z. F. (2014). Marketing based on the economic effect of a single network—To Taobao example. *Inner Mongolia Radio & TV University, 1*, 5–8.

Li, G. Y., & Hou, K. (2013). Taobao "Double Eleven" e-commerce marketing strategy. *Technology Vision, 31*, 159.

Liu, Y. (2013). E-commerce impact on consumer impulse buying behaviour research. *Promotional Market Weekly, 2*, 46–47.

Ming, Z. (2013). "Double eleven" promotion thinking. *Foreign Trade Practices, 4*, 47–50.

Yu, G., & Xiao, B. (2013). Network analysis of consumer psychology and marketing strategy—To Taobao "double 11" shopping festival example. *Providers, 31*, 217.

The way to globalized transformation of the photovoltaic industry: inspiration from the Suntech bankruptcy reorganization

J. Zhu[a], Y. Wu[a], F. Henderson[b]
[a]Jiangnan University, Wuxi, China; [b]Victoria University, Melbourne, VIC, Australia

10.1 Introduction

Since the beginning of the twenty-first century, the Chinese photovoltaic (PV) industry has sprung up and commanded worldwide attention. The Suntech Power Holdings Co. Ltd. (Suntech) was the leading star of the Chinese PV industry. Founded in 2001, Suntech listed on the New York Stock Exchange in 2005 and became the world's biggest PV producer in 2010, having supplied more than 8 GW PV panels to more than a 1000 customers in more than 80 countries (Suntech Power Holdings Co. Ltd., 2012). The business, however, faced a large financial loss in 2011, ran into great trouble with the low ebb of the whole PV industry in 2012, and was finally declared bankrupt and requiring reorganization by the District Court of Wuxi City, China, in March 2013 for failing in maturing debt obligations (Xinhua Newspaper, 2013). During the period of bankruptcy reorganization, the company has encountered a great restructuring of duties.

The course of development of Suntech, on one hand, demonstrates how a global business faces circumstances of high uncertainty, difficulties, and high risks. On the other hand, the cataclysm of Suntech provides researchers and analysts with possibly a typical case for exploration of a business's waterloo. The research answers the following questions: Why was Suntech so successful in the past? Why did Suntech decline so quickly? Why are there still companies willing to merge with it even at this point of bankruptcy reorganization? What is the inspiration to Chinese PV industries?

The research group has been maintaining regular contact with Suntech executives since 2003. Written permission to conduct research was obtained from Suntech in December 2010, and systematic surveying occurred from 2010 to 2011. Data for the four questions were collected by analyzing Suntech's Annual Reports from 2002 to 2013; the Suntech weekly newspaper; industry journals; stock exchange documents from 2005 to 2013; and a variety of books, reports, and comments on Suntech. There have been formal and informal group interviews and workshops with more than 20 Suntech top and middle managers, and many employees from its Departments of Research and Development, Human Resources, Legal and Marketing. Notes of main

The Strategies of China's Firms.

ideas were kept and cross-checked through subsequent follow-up questions. Qualitative data were entered into Microsoft Excel for a thematic analysis.

Findings have been grouped under the two key themes of "Successful experiences of the early Suntech" and "Causes and lessons from the failures of Suntech."

10.2 Successful experiences of the early Suntech

Looking back upon the developmental process of Suntech, despite the ups and downs, the researchers could easily find some striking characteristics that contributed much to the early success of Suntech.

10.2.1 Accurate positioning

Suntech management explained what they believed to be accurate positioning in entering the market at the right time, choosing the factory location at the right place, and developing with the help of the right people. The right time means the factory was set up in 2001 when the PV industry was an emerging market in China; it profitably caught sudden European market demands due to a policy change in Europe; and next dived smoothly into the Internet market in 2004. The right place points to the Suntech factory being located in well-supported Wuxi City, which lies in the rapidly developing Yangtze Delta, where at the same time Suntech took advantage of the low-cost Chinese labor. The right people included the helpful and well-serviced council officials who undertook creating an encouraging policy with the local government and excellent technical personnel, management, and skilled workers.

10.2.2 Internationalized management

Compared with other Chinese PV companies, one of the most striking characteristics of Suntech was the ability to adapt to globalization, global vision, and global management. From an identity view, the founder of Suntech, Zhengrong Shi, had an overseas study and work background and was familiar with both Chinese and Western cultures. In terms of constituents of the team, most of the technicians had studied or worked in Australia. From the angle of the industrial chain, the original materials and markets of Suntech were mainly overseas. All of the above contributed to the original genes of Suntech's globalization. The features of globalization were particularly important since the firm was listed on the New York Stock Exchange in 2005, which entailed absorbing a large percentage of overseas investing funds as well as foreign or overseas experienced executives. To sum up, the business took full advantage of Australian technology, the German market, and Chinese low-cost manufacturing to build itself successfully as an international firm with a great global perspective (Suntech Power Holdings Co. Ltd., 2010).

10.2.3 Emphasis on technological innovation and brand building

Suntech was insistent on the advocacy of simple and high efficiency technology. It devoted itself to promoting the exchange rate from sunshine to electricity, fulfilling the standard ratio by improving the production processes, controlling the product quality, and prolonging the life cycle by management system building. Suntech paid much attention to research and was seemingly good at translating the experimental research to commercial products, which enabled the business to quickly build its intangible assets. According to Suntech Power Holdings Co. Ltd. (2006), Suntech possessed 201 issued patents and 294 patents pending by the end of 2011. In order to protect its intangible assets, Suntech registered the brand mark in the United States, Canada, EU, Australia, New Zealand, India, Japan, South Korea, Israel, South Africa, and elsewhere. By 2013, Suntech possessed nearly 400 registered brands and more than 100 domain names (Suntech Power Holdings Co. Ltd., 2012).

10.2.4 Stressing on speed and scale

At the very beginning of its establishment, according to the high-demand situation of the European market, Suntech decided to improve manufacturing capacity as its breakthrough at that time (Li, 2007; Shi, 2008). Suntech built a 10 MW manufacturing line in 2002 and a 15 MW one in 2003; it built another new one in 2004, whose capacity was the sum of all the lines built in the past two years (CPC Jiangsu Provincial Research Center, 2006; Deng & Jiang, 2007). During the process of preparation for the listing in 2005, the firm constructed three lines with a manufacturing capacity of 30 MW, respectively. That is to say, the total manufacturing capacity of Suntech was up to 145 MW within only 4 years (Li, 2010; Zhao, 2009).

After being listed on the New York Stock Exchange, Suntech developed stably into the world's number one in terms of production capacity. The firm proudly possessed 2400 MW solar battery production capacity and 1600 MW silicon chip production capacity in 2011, which was 240 times the production capacity of the original factory set-up (Suntech Power Holdings Co. Ltd., 2012). The rapid production increase was appropriate to cater for the world's PV market expansion. There was no doubt that, facing the rapid expansion of the emerging PV industry, Suntech acquired great success in its beginning stage by enlarging its production scale.

10.3 Causes and lessons from the failure of Suntech

From a tiny factory established by a returnee, Suntech turned into a builder of the latest technology, then developed into a solar pioneer, and quickly became an industry leader paving the way for the commercialization of advanced solar PV products. Falling down like a flashing meteor, Suntech declined rapidly, attracting its fellow competitors' attention worldwide. At the point of its bankruptcy, researchers can now see that it was not only wrong business decisions but also environmental circumstances—both domestic and abroad—that led to such tragic consequences.

10.3.1   Rapid scale-expansion

The early success of Suntech was mainly due to its rapid expansion to meet the market requirements. At that time, investment streamed to the PV industry, which led to price disorder and competition in the market (China Energy Network, 2013). Taking the example of original silicon materials, the industry saw a critical shortage of silicon in 2005, which yielded a jump in the price of silicon. High-profit margins, which attracted a great deal of Chinese investment, poured into the field of producing silicon materials (Li & Wang, 2007). From 2005 to 2010, the Chinese total polycrystalline silicon construction scale was over 1 billion tons; the total investment outstripped 100 billion RMB. The Chinese polycrystalline silicon production rose from below 1% of the total in 2006 to 8% in 2007, and rocketed to 37% in 2008, and subsequently to more than 40% (Yang, Liang, Zhang, & Li, 2009). Being similar to polycrystalline silicon, many PV battery factories and manufacturing lines were set up. Take the example of Suntech, the production capacity of 10 MW in 2002 extended to 2400 MW in 2011, an increase of 83.9% annually. In other words, Suntech enlarged the capacity from 1.8 to 2.4 GW within 2011 only; the amount (0.6 GW) added was equal to the Chinese total grid-connected PV capacity in 2010. The speed of production expansion was much faster than the expansion of the market; the oversupply resulted in a difficulty in recovering the financial outlays. Large scale suddenly became a burden (Chen, 2009).

10.3.2   Unstable executives involving fraud, debts, and legal action

The executives of Suntech could generally be divided into three kinds. The first were hired through head-hunting companies or known by Suntech through their business contacts; the second pointed to the group of managers who were cultivated from the forefront production line of Suntech and were very familiar with the factory and manufacturing process. The third group was minor; some of them had local government backgrounds. In general, those overseas background paratroops were the overall majority among senior executives, and some of them were not Chinese.

There were three relatively intensive adjustments during the history of Suntech, shocking the firm greatly. These points of adjustment corresponded with the following three main business crises of Suntech in 2008, 2010, and 2011, respectively. The first adjustment: the chief operating officer (non-Chinese) deserted his job in 2008. The second adjustment occurred when several executives left their jobs when facing the PV industry winter: for example, the chief operating officer of Suntech (non-Chinese) quit his job in 2010; several other important people quit, including Suntech's president of America (American Chinese), the former chief financial officer (Chinese) who served at Suntech for nearly 6 years, and vice Presidents (both Chinese), who joined Suntech at the very beginning.

The third readjustment came with a restructuring process that started in 2012. With the crisis deepening, undercurrents surged within the management team and the senior executive teams changed frequently. Sectarian strife began to appear. Unfortunately, Suntech was involved in a 4.3 billion Euro counter-guarantee fraud on July 30, 2012

(Li & Ou, 2012) which led directly to the stock price falling to below US$1 (NYSE: STP, 2012); Suntech therefore faced gigantic pressure and risked being suspended from the stock market listing. At that point, the former CFO (non-Chinese) of Suntech took the place of the founder of Suntech, becoming CEO of Suntech on August 15, 2012. The new, non-Chinese CEO gradually took complete charge of the executives and finance by being responsible for purchasing, marketing, and producing, which led to contradictions between Suntech's Chinese founder and the investigators' non-Chinese CEO delegate.

The urgent financial crisis of a 4 billion dollar debt due in March 2013 caused further dramatic action. The board of directors of Suntech declared that Susan Wang would replace Zhengrong Shi as the president. Soon afterwards, according to the Bankruptcy Law, the intermediate People's Court of Wuxi City ruled for a bankruptcy reorganization on March 20, 2013 (Wang, S., 2013; Wang, Y., 2013). Recently, Shunfeng Photovoltaic International Limited successfully won the bid for acquisition and reorganization of the new entity, Wuxi Suntech, with an aggregated consideration of RMB 3,000,000,000 and announced the full acquisition of the Wuxi Suntech Group on April 7, 2014.

10.3.3 Strategic decision-making neglecting technical progress

Making reasonable strategic decisions in a market full of unpredictable fluctuations is a very important management skill. This skill was only partially evident in relation to the purchasing of certain components.

Silicon wafers are the most important raw material for making PV products. Starting from 2003, due to the rapid growth of the PV industry, the availability and price of silicon wafers have increasingly been affected by the demand of the PV industry. Silicon suppliers have been raising their prices and adding manufacturing capacity in response to the growing demand in recent years. From 2006 to 2007, the silicon market showed a rising price trend with $300 per kg in 2006, and $400 per kg by the end of 2007, which topped at a spot market price of $500 per kg (The New Materials Industry, 2009). The business who obtained sufficient quantities of silicon and silicon wafers, who can convert its manufacturing capacity to production, therefore takes over the sun-battery market. Suntech was successful in winning a series of multi-year supply agreements with some globally known silicon suppliers (Suntech Power Holdings Co. Ltd., 2006). At that time, in order to secure adequate and timely supply of silicon wafers, such decisions seemed very reasonable, even a victory over the competition, since almost all the solar battery businesses were suffering from a severe shortage of production materials.

Suntech signed with one of the ten biggest global suppliers, Deutsche Solar AG, a subsidiary of Solar Word AG, for a 10-year, 6-billion dollar supply agreement in July 2006, then entered into another 10-year cooperation agreement with LDK Hi-Tech Co. Ltd. (Suntech Power Holdings Co. Ltd., 2006). The high profit margin attracted a lot of investors. The new silicon factories had already gone into mass production from the last quarter of 2008 (Chen, 2010). At the same time, production costs fell off remarkably with a technical breakthrough (Science and Technology Daily, 2014). The price of

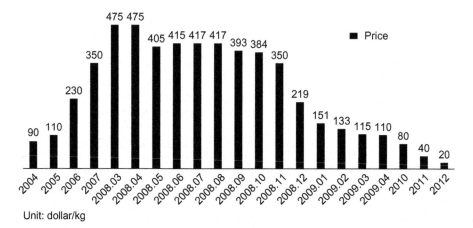

Unit: dollar/kg

Figure 10.1 The trend of the spot price of polysilicon.
Source: Ruijiang Hong, 2011 Wuxi New Energy Conference (with amendments).

the silicon material began to drop considerably with the great development of silicon producers, such as GCL-Poly Energy, and LDK Solar Co. Ltd. As shown in Figure 10.1, from the $428 per kg at the beginning of 2008, the price fell sharply to $151 at the end of the year, then went on declining to $80 in 2010, $40 in 2011, and plunged to $20 per kg in 2012 (Wang et al., 2010). Unfortunately Suntech was encumbered by those long-term contracts signed during 2006–2007.

10.3.4   Like sheep others entered the domestic industrial environment

When Suntech commenced its business operation in May 2002, the overall level of Chinese PV industry lagged far behind developed countries. Owing to the success of Suntech, large amounts of capital invaded the PV field, which led to cut-throat and disordered competition. Chinese productivity of PV panels ran up to 1088 MW, which exceeded the 1062.8 MW of Europe and the 920 MW of Japan, and became the largest PV panel-producing country in 2007 (The Electronic Information Industry Network, 2011). China became the PV industrial agglomeration in 2010: multicrystalline productivity made up 60% of the world's supply; silicon chip production capacity accounted for 70%; PV panels covered nearly 70%; and PV hybrid solution occupied 70% of the world's supply (Ministry of Industry and Information Technology Saidi Research Institttue, 2012).

Several businesses competed with Suntech domestically, each with a distinct identity. The expansion speed of Jiangxi Solar Hi-Tech Co. Ltd. was outstanding, and Yingli Solar gained cost advantages with a complete PV industrial chain and orders at a low price. The gross margin percentage of Suntech was relatively lower than that of other corporates, such as Changzhou Trina Solar Energy Co. Ltd. However, the production capacity of JA SOLAR Co. Ltd. was probably greater than Suntech's

(Xiang, 2009). Besides all those existing PV corporations, some new potential competitors appeared; for example, Foxconn International Holdings Limited, well known as an original equipment manufacturer, openly allocated 100 billion RMB to the production of solar panels (Liang, 2011).

10.3.5 Complicated international trade environment

The overseas market has been the most important market for the Chinese PV industry. Therefore, the subsidy policies of applicable foreign governments, the changes surrounding international politics and their economies, the floating of exchange rates, and the integration of the PV industry all brought many uncertainties to Suntech.

Europe is the largest market for Suntech, among which Germany, Spain, France, Czechoslovakia, and Italy were the most important markets, especially Germany, which accounted for about half of the global installed capacity (Zhao, 2010). However, the German government dramatically decreased the subsidies in 2010. Compared with 41.4% of the net sales of Suntech in 2009 (Suntech Power Holdings Co. Ltd., 2010) from the German market, the number fell to 28% in 2010 and 20% in 2011 (Suntech Power Holdings Co. Ltd., 2012). The French seemed to copy Germany with their subsidy restrictions. The demands of the Spanish market dropped to one-third because of economic problems and overinvestment from 2009 to 2011 (Suntech Power Holdings Co. Ltd., 2012). On the positive side, the PV industry investment of the Czech Republic took up 0.4% GDP, and the PV power capacity was about 3.3% of the total power generating capacity, which is relatively high in Europe (Consultation Network of China Investment, 2011). Some Italians expressed disagreement with the rapid development policy of the PV industry and called for a capacity ceiling, which cast a cloud over PV development (Suntech Power Holdings Co. Ltd., 2012). The significant decline in demand of the European market in general was a sign of market supply exceeding demand; overcapacity then haunted Suntech (see Figure 10.2).

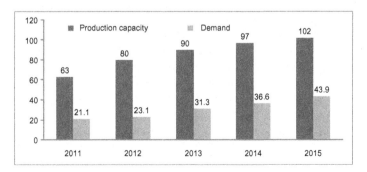

Figure 10.2 2010–2015 Global solar cell production capacity and installed capacity situation and forecast.
Source: Production data from the Energy Research Centre of the European Union (JRC, 2012, p. 9); Demand data from the European Photovoltaic Industry Association (EPIA, 2012, p. 6).

Besides the traditional overseas market shrinkage, Suntech was facing increasingly complex global business risks. With over 90% of its business overseas, Suntech established a marketing network, customer service focus, production line, logistics center, and R&D system; it dealt with changing foreign politics, multiple governing institutions, labor laws, tax laws, overseas branches, and exchange-rate flexibility; Suntech developed strategies to maintain the marketing network, to respond to the legal requirements and to cope with trade protection (Suntech Power Holdings Co. Ltd., 2011).

In the case of trade friction, in October 2011, the U.S. branch of the German company Solar World, in conjunction with six other manufacturers, formally proposed to the U.S. Department of Commerce a "dual" (anti-dumping, anti-subsidy) investigation into Chinese PV products, which was formally opened in November 2011. Suntech was represented by 14 domestic enterprises who argued against the U.S. "double reverse" survey (The Global PV Network, 2011). On October 10, 2012, the U.S. Department of Commerce made a final determination of China's PV anti-dumping, countervailing duty rate. Suntech and Trina's dumping margins were, respectively, 31.73% and 18.32%, the other 59 major exporters were identified with dumping margins of 25.96%, and the other Chinese companies with a dumping margin of 249.96% (First Financial Daily, 2012). This incident shows the complexity of multinational operations. At the same time, the world's largest PV market, the European Union, also adopted trade protection measures, which had a huge impact on Suntech and the entire solar industry.

10.4 Suggestions for the PV industry and domestic enterprise development environment

Currently, the Chinese government has launched a series of policies to stimulate the domestic PV market (Chinese Enterprises Cooperation Association, 2012), the EU-China trade dispute of PV has reached a "price guarantee" agreement (Xinhua Internet, 2013a), the EU sanctions have eased from the initial proposal (Xinhua Internet, 2013b), the orders of some battery manufacturers are increasing (The People's Daily, 2013), new development opportunities are beginning to appear (Ye & Han, 2013), and many companies and investors are itching for a new round of PV development (Zhang, L. 2014; Zhang, Y. F., 2014). It should also be noted, however, that while the policy supports of European countries have weakened, the background to the rise of trade protectionism among countries has not changed; uncertainties still exist in the international market. The case of Suntech has brought both positive and negative thinking; the whole Chinese PV industry should take lessons from Suntech, as each business expands into new markets, attempts to regulate the industry environment, enhances core competitiveness, and takes a route of sustainable development.

10.4.1 Expansion based on innovating technology systems

Technological innovation was considered before other forms of innovation. Not only Suntech but also all Chinese PV enterprises that are dedicated to surviving this round of industry reshuffling should increase R&D investment to accelerate the pace of technological innovation. Suntech has shown that blind expansion led to a lose–lose price competition within the industry. It is wise for Chinese PV industry to ensure the quality of products, to seek breakthroughs in key technologies to improve the photoelectric conversion efficiency, to improve production processes and reduce production costs, to diminish the gap with the traditional energy prices, and to achieve competitive advantages with the product. Another innovation embodies standardized products that enable enterprises to jump from production competition to brand competition to standards competition. A trade standard is the entry into the international market. If the company's technical superiority rises to national or international standards, not only the strength of the enterprise will be widely recognized within the industry, but they are also able to gain huge market and economic interests. To participate in making the standards of raw materials, for example, polysilicon, Suntech could promote its raw material requirement as the industry standard, therefore making more raw material production upstream to meet this standard, and then expand the range of sources of raw materials, thus reducing its procurement costs. Being involved in cell components and other product standards allows a business to tailor industry access thresholds according to their own level of technology and eliminate backward production. Involvement in the standards construction of PV power plants and PV downstream industries can contribute to the development of downstream industries and expand the scope of application of their products.

Enterprises should strengthen the supply chain management, lower raw material costs and ensure high-quality, low price and stable supply of raw materials; make full use of existing production equipment to carry out lean production, enhance on-site management, reduce process loss, shorten order lead times, reduce inventory, and reduce the cost of the manufacturing process. In a word, enterprises should improve profitability by reducing the consumption per unit of product.

10.4.2 Cultivating the world-class brand with stable executives

Business operations play an essential role in a thriving business. Suntech expected to realize a quick transformation to modern management by hiring excellent managers who had worked in famous global businesses. Though some of these "paratroops" played an important role in the development of Suntech, most of them soon quit because of difficulties in adapting themselves to the Chinese business culture and local environment. Today's complicated economic environment demands that modern managers not only should have abundant experience and global perspectives but also agree with the corporate culture and devote themselves to the business at hand.

At the same time, developing broad brand recognition is more and more important for a company. It is interesting that there are still some companies willing to buy Suntech Power on the occasion of its suffering and bankruptcy reorganization. One important reason is the brand value of Suntech in the international arena. Although its many practices needed to be examined and adjusted in its growth process, Suntech focused on brand building, which indeed won for it a second chance. Other solar companies should also cultivate brand image to develop sustainable competitive advantage from culture, talent, technology, management, and some other aspects along with changing internal and external environments.

In terms of corporate culture, staff should foster a strong sense of social responsibility; sincerity; innovation; dare to reform, especially in the face of difficulties; and never give up, never say die spirit. The managers of the enterprises should focus on the development of corporate culture, act in response to cultural conflicts, and promote the integration of the original corporate culture with other cultures.

In terms of improving brand image, the enterprises should dedicate themselves to brand image promotion and increase visibility and reputation both internationally and domestically. There should be a management goal to improve relationships with the end customers, to enhance social visibility especially at the time of opening up the domestic market, and to establish a good brand image on the client terminal.

In terms of personnel structure, the enterprises should pay attention to the establishment of senior executives, middle-level leaders, and junior staff. The senior executive leadership team should not only understand both international business and trade practices but also be well versed in the Chinese situation. The middle-level cadres should be engaged in technology, marketing, sales, production, logistics, and so on. As for the junior staff, communication is important to ensure their engagement and the relative stability of the line staff in case of regional or periodic labor shortage.

The cultural integration should be especially noted between those "foreign executives" with overseas backgrounds and localized recruitment. It is important for enterprises to train all executives to be culturally sensitive and culturally aware. Due to the lack of talent in the PV industry, the Chinese rival PV businesses often poach professionals from each other, so enhancing staff management, improving the quality of staff, increasing the attractiveness of payment, reducing the ratio of employees to management, may make the workforce more stable. It may also be appropriate to collaborate with institutions to set up PV professional groups and cultivate high-level professionals who contribute to help the enterprises build human capital and provide personnel to achieve strategic objectives.

Technology is the support behind the brand. The enterprises should establish a technology development roadmap and schedule, strengthen and enhance research and development capabilities, continue with technological innovation, introduce new products regularly, and provide better products at the same price. Compared with European, Japanese, and U.S. counterparts, Chinese businesses must maintain the advantage of lower costs; compared with domestic enterprises, they must maintain the advantage of higher quality and brand image. In a phrase, enterprises should establish their own market positions in both the international and domestic markets through highlighting their quality and value for money. When it comes to multinational operations, the enterprises should pursue both global thinking and local operations; accumulate the experiences of overseas management; build an R&D base, production base, and sales center; establish a global marketing network; and keep long-term and stable relations upstream and downstream.

10.4.3 Establishing scientific decision-making and operational systems

A definite requirement is the innovation of corporate management, improving the mutual cooperation and efficiency of the corporate sectors and employees, focusing on R&D institutions and external collaborative innovation, and making strategic decisions based on technological innovations. To grow into a giant industry and to achieve sustained, everlasting growth, an enterprise must establish a scientific decision-making and operational system. Faced with the rapidly changing market, companies should be on the alert for preventing "big business" shortcomings, to keep the decision making speedy and market responsive characteristics. At the same time, the enterprises should keep an eye on the outside political, economic, social, and technical events to strengthen research on future trends of the industry, to predict future industrial patterns, be ahead of industry competition, establish effective corporate vision, and plan business strategy and long-term goals. With the adjustment of the strategic environment and strategic objectives, according to the principles of the "structure follows strategy" (Chandler, 1962), the enterprises should carry on organizational innovation, adjust the distributed organizational functions, optimize management processes, overcome bureaucratic inefficiencies, manage with flat structures, strengthen horizontal communication between departments, take the customer-oriented principle, and make the organization operation more efficient.

The Chinese PV enterprises should draw lessons from Suntech on the silicon material procurement "long-term contract" decisions such as making thin film battery production lines in Shanghai, looking for deep-seated causes of the decision-making mechanism. Meanwhile, in the operation of the process, they should not only strengthen management on the production of plants, subsidiaries, and affiliates, but also strengthen supervision to strategic partners to avoid the events with big social and economic impacts, such as the "hoax donation case" and "counter-guarantee fraud" case.

In short, the Chinese PV firms should perfect scientific decision-making mechanisms, handle centralization and decentralization, democratic and autocratic, vertically and integrated decision-making, leadership and expert staff decision making, and establish effective internal coordination operation mechanisms. Multinational enterprises should adopt culturally acceptable ways to properly handle the relationship between localized decisions and global integration decisions, strengthen coordination and cooperation between departments, improve information-sharing systems, and finally establish an effective communication mechanism between sales, production, research, and development services.

10.4.4 Standardizing the market competition, improving the industrial coordination mechanism

Competition is essential for the healthy development of the China PV industry. Over the past few years, a large number of PV companies have not been suitable for high-tech industries, whether in terms of capital, scale, or technology. Taking advantage of the new energy boom by producing inferior products and earning a vicious reputation for competitive prices, companies in the solar market seeking to fish in troubled waters undermine the overall industry as well as the reputation of Chinese enterprises. On the occasion of starting a new round of development, the Chinese PV market competition should be regulated (Zhang, L. 2014; Zhang, Y. F., 2014). Strengthening the leadership of the industry, authorities may prevent unhelpful competition among enterprises, enhance the effective guidance of the industry, and avoid risk-taking in the industry.

Specifically speaking, the industry authority should strengthen the PV business approvals and regulations and set the threshold strictly in terms of technology and scale to avoid overcapacity, which causes damage to the entire industry. The authority should formulate appropriate regulations and policies, make a critical review of PV business licenses, and eliminate unethical businesses.

Perhaps brand can be built by cultivating a number of internationally known companies through participating in discussions regarding amendments to international PV standards, national PV standards, PV industry standards, and PV local standards and promoting the improvement and development of enterprise technology. Governments should encourage enterprises to import, digest, absorb, and re-innovate advanced PV technology. The government should give incentives to support business technological innovation. For example, providing financial subsidies to enterprises for introducing advanced equipment from abroad and to firms for bringing in needed personnel. Technological innovation contributes to forming technology and products with independent intellectual property rights, which is conducive to the development of new products and beneficial to process improvements, helping to reducing costs.

The Chinese PV industry associations and alliances should fulfill their roles in the development of the Chinese PV industry. The PV industry association and alliances should help the Chinese PV industry keep abreast of industry trends and international marketing information. Information changes in the market are threats as well as opportunities for businesses. They should build an efficient solar PV industry information service platform that concerns the market and focuses on both international and domestic counterparts by collecting all related information about technology, standards, marketing, policy and personnel, industry trend, and so on. As with other professional and industry bodies, the PV industry association and alliances should coordinate the relationship among enterprises, help Chinese enterprises gain an overall advantage, and give a timely and effective response—for instance, when an antidumping crisis of PV products in international trade occurs.

10.4.5 Start the domestic PV market and expand into new markets overseas

First, according to several opinions (State Council, 2013), the Chinese PV industry should start reviewing the domestic market as soon as possible. Chinese domestic market share was less than 3% of the global PV market before 2010, yet in 2013 shared 2.8 GW of the global total of 16 GW (Wang, S., 2013; Wang, Y., 2013). The rise of the Chinese PV market should be able to absorb excess PV product capacities of Chinese companies to a large degree. As for policy, Chinese businesses should earnestly implement the "Renewable Energy Law" (Standing Committee of National People's Congress, 2009), in particular the implementation of an Internet price subsidy policy, which can effectively avoid abusing investment subsidies and ensure project quality as well as the actual utilization of the system. The government should expand the scope of the "Roof Plan," which involves using the building roof-mounted PV installations. By means of government procurement, the government could encourage a priority use of PV products in urban construction and public buildings, and launch solar lighting demonstration projects. It is vital to exclude the impact of institutional factors, such as monopoly power, that is strangling the development of the PV industry. China should take the experience of developed countries to create favorable industry patterns of accessing rooftop PV power and PV power plants online. China should foster diversified and open markets to attract state-owned, private, and even multinational companies (Miao, 2011).

Second, China should develop new overseas markets. Europe is the traditional market of PV products; Chinese PV companies can improve product quality, reduce production costs, and enhance service to further enhance the market competitiveness in these areas. In addition, enterprises should also aim at the U.S. and Japanese markets and look for the next strong growth point by monitoring market demands, overcoming the trade barriers and the difficulties caused by market practices by taking a localized production and sales strategy. Some emerging economies in Asia and Africa also have a huge market potential. It would be strategic for Chinese PV companies to explore and speed up entering those emerging markets, strengthening ties with them and searching for new market opportunities.

10.5   Conclusions: The future of Chinese PV industry

The photovoltaic industry is still in critical situation, with 38.7 GW of PV installations in 2014, the global PV market continued to expand, especially in Asia and the Americas, but with a limited growth compared to the past years. With 177 GW of PV installations, 1% of the world PV electricity demand were covered by PV (IEA, 2014). Therefore, seen from the perspective of the industry cycle, the PV industry is still a long sunrise industry (Liu, 2012).

The cost of a PV power generation system, however, is much higher than the current mainstream power generation; the PV applications are still government-driven. The last round of large-scale development of the global PV industry came to an end due to the financial support policy shift of Germany, Japan, the United States, and other European countries. Nevertheless, Japan's Fukushima Daiichi nuclear accident on March 12, 2011, allowed people to re-examine the applicability of nuclear power, especially those countries such as Germany and Japan, who have many nuclear power plants. Based on the awareness of the dangers of nuclear power plants, people have begun to hope again for the development of new energy for the PV industry. It is foreseeable that more countries will increase again their efforts to support the PV industry.

Emerging markets in the Asia-Pacific area developed rapidly. India, Australia, Thailand, Malaysia, and the Philippines have carried out Feed-in-Tariff subsidy policies (Martin, 2009). Among them, Thailand has also built the largest PV power station of the region, and India has released a massive development of PV power plant projects. Especially in recent years, the Chinese government has actively supported and promoted the PV industry in the application of PV products; related unhelpful policies have also been removed, and there are strengthening signs that a huge domestic market is slowly starting (National Energy Administration, 2012).

Generally speaking, policy and technology are the key points leading the future development of the PV industry. Government encouragement and support policies will greatly promote the development of the PV industry, and the PV industry has to embrace continuing technological breakthroughs during the future development process. It is possible that once the new disruptive technologies emerge, there will be further changes to the existing competitive landscape.

The extension of the industrial chain upstream and downstream should lead to the expansion of PV production equipment, installation, and associated ancillary markets. The advances in technology should make the PV products more economical and closer to a market price that is open to all. Critically, in terms of the developmental process, the industry must avoid the herd investment and blind expansion mentality.

References

Chandler, A. D. (1962). *Strategy and structure: Chapters in the history of the American industrial enterprise.* Chicago: Massachusetts Institute of Technology.

Chen, J. (2009). Wuxi Suntech: Life-or-death policy. *Commentary of Commercial World, 7,* 69–73.

Chen, X. (2010). *Study on international competitiveness of photovoltaic industry.* University doctoral thesis. Nankai.

China Energy Network. (2013). *Special topic discussion: Review and development of photovoltaic industry.* Available at: http://www.china5e.com/subject/show_697.html.

Chinese Enterprises Cooperation Association. (2012). Intensive introduction of supportive policies from many ministries, the domestic PV market heating up. *The Economic Information Daily.* Retrieved on October 23, 2012, from http://www.qyhz.org/shownews.asp?id=3087.

Consultation Network of China Investment. (2011). *Deep observation on 2011 China PV market (2011).* Retrieved on June 16, 2011, from http://www.ocn.com.cn/book/chapter_10893_24752.html.

CPC Jiangsu Provincial Research Center. (2006). Stand on the forefront of the world's photovoltaic industry. *Xinhua Daily,* August 6, 2014. Retrieved on March 28, http://530.wnd.gov.cn/news_info.aspx?__id=20090907042107687500&__key=2009082411622484307&__list=false.

Deng, B., & Jiang, S. M. (2007). Overseas returnees turned into China's richest man. *Overseas Students, 3,* 38–41.

The Electronic Information Industry Network. (2011). PV entering the era of 1 RMB, with high-quality as well as low-cost [electronic version]. *China Electronics News.* Retrieved on June 29, 2011, from www.cena.com.cn, http://xny.cena.com.cn/2011-06/29/content_151433.htm.

EPIA. (2012). Outlook and analysis of photovoltaic industry in China in 2012. Retrieved on March 19, 2012, from http://guangfu.bjx.com.cn/news/20120319/348710.shtml.

First Financial Daily (November 9, 2012). U.S. photovoltaic products to China "double reverse" the final ruling landed [electronic version].

The Global PV Network. (2011). SolarWorld accused Chinese manufacturers of dumping solar panels in the United States. Retrieved on October 24, 2011, from http://www.pvall.com/news/content-46209.aspx.

IEA. (2014). A snapshot of global PV Markets 2014, the website of "international energy agency photovoltaic power systems programme," http://www.iea-pvps.org.

JRC. (2012). Outlook and analysis of photovoltaic industry in China in 2012. Retrieved on March 19, 2012, from http://guangfu.bjx.com.cn/news/20120319/348710.shtml.

Li, F. (2007). From scientist to entrepreneur—Zhengrong Shi, chairman of Suntech Power Holdings Co., Ltd. *Economic Perspective*, 5, 25.

Li, F. (2010). Make money from the Sun—Interview with the Chairman of the Suntech Power Zhengrong Shi. *Economic Perspective*, 6, 26–28.

Li, Y., & Ou, C. (2012). Suntech: Involved in a 4.3 billion Euro counter-guarantee fraud. *Oriental Morning Daily*, July 31, from http://www.dfdaily.com/html/113/2012/7/31/ 833515.shtml.

Li, J., & Wang, S. (2007). *China solar PV report 2007.* Beijing: China Environmental Science Press.

Liang, Z. (2011). Taiming Guo invested RMB one hundred billion in photovoltaic industry layout in Shanxi and Jiangsu Provinces. *Century Business.* Retrieved on September 21, 2011, from http://tech.qq.com/a/20110921/000245.htm.

Liu, F. (2012). Correctly grasp the characteristics and trends of the solar power industry development [electronic version]. *China Energy*, A, 24, 25 June.

Martin, D. (2009). *Feed-in tariff (FIT) serve several purposes, drive PV industry growth.* Available at: http://www.semi.org/ch/MarketInfo/ctr_031895.

Miao, L. (2011). Emphasis on fostering domestic market [electronic version]. *Economic Observation*, 27, Feb. 14.

Ministry of Industry and Information Technology Saidi Research Institute. (2012). The development strategy for China's photovoltaic industry. *Electronic Information Industry Research*, 45, 7.

National Energy Administration. (2012). *National Energy Administration on the issuance of solar power development, "Twelfth Five-Year Plan"* National Energy Administration New Energy No. 194 [electronic version]. Retrieved on July 7, 2012, from http:// zfxxgk.nea.gov.cn/auto87/201209/t20120912_1510.htm.

The New Materials Industry (2009). Polysilicon prices return pressing domestic PV market development. *The New Materials Industry, 1*, 14–15.

NYSE:STP (2012). Available at: http://xueqiu.com/S/STP.

The People's Daily (August 7, 2013). Around seventy percent of the photovoltaic business were of profitable during first half year, industry out of the downturn [electronic version].

PV Industry. (2012). The development strategy for China's photovoltaic industry, electronic information industry research, electronic version of the August 15, 2012, 7, total 45.

Science and Technology Daily. (2014). Polysilicon strikes back: From enslaved to striking— Focus on China Materials Science and Technology Development (2) [electronic version]. Retrieved on July 23, from http://digitalpaper.stdaily.com/http_www.kjrb.com/kjrb/html/ 2014-07/23/content_270676.htm?div=-1.

Shi, Z. (2008). Being a person chasing light. *China High-Tech Zone*, 7, 112–114.

Standing Committee of National People's Congress. (2009). Standing Committee of National People's Congress on amending decision "People's Republic of China Renewable Energy Law" 2009, December 26, 2009 [electronic version]. From the website of the Central People's Government of the People's Republic of China, http://www.gov.cn/flfg/2009-12/26/ content_1497462.htm.

State Council. (2013). Several opinions of the state council on promoting the healthy development of China PV Industry No. 24, July 15, 2013 China. From the website of the Central People's Government of the People's Republic of China, http://www.gov.cn/zwgk/2013- 07/15/content_2447814.htm.

Suntech Power Holdings Co. Ltd. (2006). *STP annual report 37* (p. 46).

Suntech Power Holdings Co. Ltd. (2010). *Suntech annual sustainability report good green great*. Beijing: Suntech.

Suntech Power Holdings Co. Ltd. (2011). *STP annual report*. Period: December 31, 2011, filed: April 27, 2012.

Suntech Power Holdings Co. Ltd. (2012). *STP, Form 20-F*. Filed: April 27, 2012, Period: December 31, 2011 (p. 38).

Wang, S. (2013). The PV industry development trend in the first half of 2013 and policy recommendations. *Solar Energy, 16*, 24–26.

Wang, Y. (2013). Zhengrong Shi Mortgage stock to resize chairman place. *North Young Internet*. Retrieved on March 8, 2013, from http://dycj.ynet.com/3.1/1303/08/7872970.html.

Wang, Y. D., Shao, Y. B., Xu, D. M., Wang, X. X., Zhao, C. C., Hao, L., et al. (2010). Industry technology roadmap and solar photovoltaic industry development research—The case of Baoding City. *Science of Science and Management, 1*, 17–22.

Xiang, B. (2009). Wuxi Suntech V.S. LDK Solar, comparing with patterns of resource integration. *Chinese Technology Investment, 12*, 47–50.

Xinhua Internet. (2013a). PV-EU dispute reached a price undertaking. *Xinhua Internet Series Reports*. Retrieved in August 2013 from http://www.xinhuanet.com/energy/zt/gc/09.htm.

Xinhua Internet. (2013b). EU: EU-China PV trade negotiations reached a "friendly" solution, Brussels. Retrieved July 27, 2013, from http://news.xinhuanet.com/fortune/2013-07/27/c_116710226.htm.

Xinhua Newspaper. (2013). Suntech bankruptcy reorganization. Why the industry "Excellence" is the first "knock out". Retrieved on March 21, 2013, from http://www.xinhuanet.com/energy/zt/xzt/08.htm.

Yang, X. W., Liang, P., Zhang, H. H., & Li, X. W. (2009). Excitement polysilicon [electronic version]. *"Outlook" Newsweekly, 36*. Retrieved from http://www.outlookweekly.cn/htm/content_5069.htm.

Ye, C., & Han, Y. (2013). Market uncertainties eliminate end "PV power" blueprint emerging (2014). *Xinhua Internet*, Shanghai. Retrieved August 6, 2014, from http://www.chinanews.com/gn/2013/08-06/5130607.shtml.

Zhang, L. (2014). PV: Winter dawn—2013 PV market review [electronic version]. *Southern Weekend*, January 28.

Zhang, Y. F. (2014). Standardized management photovoltaic manufacturing industry "long way to go" Photovoltaic industry observation. From the China Photovoltaic Industry Alliance website: http://www.chinapv.org.cn/html/view/market/2014/0425/2808.html.

Zhao, X. J. (2009). The success of Suntech international growth factor analysis. *Shanghai Enterprises, 3*, 74.

Zhao, Y. W. (2010). PV industry strategic outlook and policy thinking. *Nonferrous Metallurgy Energy-Saving, 12*(6), 1–5.

Index

Note: Page numbers followed by *f* indicate figures and *t* indicate tables.

Printed in the United States
By Bookmasters